Anonymous

A Woman's Philosophy

Anonymous

A Woman's Philosophy

ISBN/EAN: 9783337350963

Printed in Europe, USA, Canada, Australia, Japan

Cover: Foto ©Thomas Meinert / pixelio.de

More available books at **www.hansebooks.com**

A WOMAN'S PHILOSOPHY OF WOMAN;

OR

WOMAN AFFRANCHISED.

AN ANSWER TO MICHELET, PROUDHON, GIRARDIN, LEGOUVÉ,
COMTE, AND OTHER MODERN INNOVATORS.

By MADAME D'HÉRICOURT.

Translated from the last Paris Edition

NEW YORK:
CARLETON, PUBLISHER, 413 BROADWAY.
M DCCC LXIV.

CONTENTS

PART II.

INTRODUCTION

TO THE AMERICAN EDITION.

The general interest evinced in the theories of Michelet and other philosophers concerning the functions and province of woman, and the lively opposition to these theories manifested in many quarters, have called forth an American translation of the present work. This remarkable book of Madame d'Héricourt on woman is conceded to be the best reply to these philosophers extant. The work, intended by the author as " a refutation of, the coarse indecency of Proudhon, and of the perfumed pruriency of Michelet, and the other false friends and would-be champions of woman," has had a remarkable history. Published first at Brussels, it was interdicted in France, and notice was given that all copies found would be seized. Madame d'Héricourt appealed to the censorship to know the reason of this interdiction, and was informed in reply that the reason for such proceedings never was given. Not content with this, she wrote to Napoleon III, enclosing a copy of the work, and called his attention to the fact that a book by a French author could be suppressed in France without any reason being given for it, and without any chance being offered to the author to clear herself of the implied charge of immorality. Immediately upon the reception of the letter, the Emperor withdrew the interdiction.

Madame d'Héricourt is well known in France as an able contributor to various philosophic journals, and also as a member of the medical profession, in which she holds a high and respected position. Her opinions are entitled to great weight, and will be welcomed as throwing much light on the practical question of the sphere of woman, which is becoming one of increasing interest. The better to adapt the book to the American public, it has been slightly abbreviated in portions of local interest, referring chiefly to French legislation. It has been well received in England, as is testified by the following extract from the *London Critic*, one of the ablest of the English critical journals :

" The work is calculated to do an immense service to French society at the present time — just when the literature of the country is on the verge of decay from the rottenness which is eating to its very core. ' La Femme Affranchie ' points out the remedy to the social cancer which gnawed away the vital principle of domestic life in France, and caused that antagonism between the sexes which foreigners behold with the most profound amazement. Madame d'Hericourt's bold and nervous arguments completely destroy the brutal commonplaces of Proudhon as regards the moral and intellectual capacity of women. She takes him on his own ground, and to his medical propositions returns medical objections of far greater weight and power, being more competent to judge the question, as she has passed examinations as ' Maitresse sage femme ' of ' La Clinique,' and received her diploma as medical practitioner many years ago."

AUTHOR'S PREFACE.

Readers, male and female, I am about to tell you the end of this book, and the motives which caused me to undertake it, that you may not waste your time in reading it, if its contents are not suited to your intellectual and moral temperament.

My end is to prove that woman has the same rights as man.

To claim, in consequence, her emancipation ;

Lastly, to point out to the women who share my views, the principal measures that they must take to obtain justice.

The word emancipation giving room for equivocation, let us in the first place establish its meaning.

To emancipate woman is not to acknowledge her right to use and abuse love ; such an emancipation is only the slavery of the passions ; the use of the beauty and youth of woman by man ; the use of man by woman for his fortune or credit.

To emancipate woman is to acknowledge and declare her free, the equal of man in the social and the moral law, and in labor.

At present, over the whole surface of the globe, woman, in certain respects, is not subjected to the same moral law as man ; her chastity is given over almost without restriction to the brutal passions of the other sex, and she often endures alone the consequences of a fault committed by both.

In marriage, woman is a serf.

In public instruction, she is sacrificed.

In labor, she is made inferior.

Civilly, she is *a* minor.

Politically, she has no existence

She is the equal of man only when punishment and the payment of taxes are in question.

I claim the rights of woman, because it is time to make the nineteenth century ashamed of its culpable denial of justice to half the human species;

Because the state of inferiority in which we are held corrupts morals, dissolves society, deteriorates and enfeebles the race;

Because the progress of enlightenment, in which woman participates, has transformed her in social power, and because this new power produces evil in default of the good which it is not permitted to do;

Because the time for according reforms has come, since women are protesting against the order which oppresses them; some by disdain of laws and prejudices; others by taking possession of contested positions, and by organizing themselves into societies to claim their share of human rights, as is done in America;

Lastly, because it seems to me useful to reply, *no longer with sentimentality*, but with vigor, to those men who, terrified by the emancipating movement, call to their aid false science to prove that woman is outside the pale of right; and carry indecorum and the opposite of courage, even to insult, even to the most revolting outrages.

Readers, male and female, several of the adversaries of the cause which I defend, have carried the discussion into the domain of science, and have not shrunk before the nudity of biological laws and anatomical details. I praise them for it; the body being respectable, there is no indecency in speaking of the laws which govern it; but as it would be an inconsistency on my part to believe that blamable in myself which I approve in them, you will not be surprised that I follow them on the ground which they have chosen, persuaded that Science, the chaste daughter of Thought, can no more lose her chastity under the pen of a pure woman than under that of a pure man.

Readers, male and female, I have but one request to make ; namely, that you will pardon my simplicity of style. It would have cost me too much pains to write in the approved fashion ; it is probable, besides, that I should not have succeeded. My work is one of conscience. If I enlighten some, if I make others reflect; if I awaken in the heart of men the sentiment of justice, in that of women the sentiment of their dignity ; if I am clear to all, fully comprehended by all, useful to all, even to my adversaries, it will satisfy me and will console me for displeasing those who love ideas only as they love women : in full dress.

TO MY ADVERSARIES.

Many among you, gentlemen, adversaries of the great and holy cause which I defend, have cited me, evidently without having read me, without even knowing how to write my name. To such as these I have nothing to say, unless that their opinion matters little to me. Others, who have taken the trouble to read my preceding works in the *Revue Philosophique* and the *Ragione,* accuse me of *not writing like a woman,* of being harsh, unsparing to my adversaries, nothing but a *reasoning machine, lacking heart.*

Gentlemen, I cannot write otherwise than as a woman, since I have the honor to be a woman.

If am I harsh and unsparing to my adversaries, it is because they appear to me to be those of reason and of justice ; it is because they, the strong and well armed, attack harshly and unsparingly a sex which they have taken care to render timid and to disarm ; it is, in short, because I believe it perfectly lawful to defend weakness against tyranny which has the audacity and insolence to erect itself into right.

If I appear to you in the unattractive aspect of a *reasoning*

machine, is, in the first place, because Nature has made me
so, and I see no good reason for modifying her work; secondly,
because it is not amiss for a woman that has attained majority
to prove to you that her sex, when not fearing your judgment,
reasons as well, and, often, better than you.

I have no heart, you say. I am lacking in it, perhaps, towards tyrants, but the conflict that I undertake proves that I
am not lacking in it towards their victims; I have therefore
a sufficient quantity of it, the more, inasmuch as I neither desire to please you, nor care to be loved by any among you.

Be advised by me, gentlemen; break yourselves of the habit
of confounding heart with nerves; cease to create an imaginary
type of woman to make it the standard of your judgment of
real women; it is thus that you pervert your reason and become, without wishing it, the thing of all others the most hateful and least estimable — tyrants.

TO MY FRIENDS.

Now to you, my friends, known and unknown, a few lines
of thanks.

You all comprehend that woman, as a human being, has the
right to develop herself, and to manifest, like man, her sponta-
neity;

That she has the right, like man, to employ her activity;
that she has the right, like man, to be respected in her dignity
and in the use which she sees fit to make of her free will.

That as half in the social order, a producer, a tax-payer,
amenable to the laws, she has the right to count as half in
society.

You all comprehend that it is in the enjoyment of these various rights that her emancipation consists; not in the faculty of
making use of love outside a moral law based on justice and
self respect.

Thanks first to you, Ausonio Franchi, the representative of

Critical Philosophy in Italy, a man as eminent for the profundity of your ideas as for the impartiality and elevation of your character; and who so generously and so long lent the columns of your *Ragione* to my first labors.

Thanks to you, my beloved co-laborers of the *Revue Philosophique* of Paris, Charles Lemonnier, Massol, Guepin, Brothier, etc., who have not hesitated to bring to light the question of the emancipation of my sex; who have welcomed the works of a woman to your columns with so much impartiality, and have on all occasions expressed for me interest and sympathy.

Thanks to you, in particular, my oldest friend, Charles Fauvety, the indefatigable searcher after truth, whose elegant, refined and limpid style is solely and constantly at the service of progressive ideas and generous aspirations, as your rich library and your counsels are at the service of those who are seeking to enlighten humanity. Why, alas! do you join to so many talents and noble qualities the fault of always remaining in the background to give place to others!

Thanks to you, Charles Renouvier, the most learned representative of Critical Philosophy in France, who join to such profound doctrine, such acute perception and such sureness of judgment; I would add, such modesty and unpretending virtue, did I not know that it displeases you to bring you before the public.

It is from your encouragement and approbation, my friends and former co-laborers, that I have drawn the strength necessary to the work I am undertaking; it is just, therefore, that I should thank you in the presence of all.

It is equally just that I should publicly express my gratitude to the Italian, English, Dutch, American and German journals that have translated many of my articles; and to the men and women of these different countries as well as of France, who have kindly expressed sympathy for me, and encouraged me in the struggle which I have undertaken against the adversaries of the rights of my sex.

To you all, my friends, both Frenchmen and foreigners, I dedicate this work. May it be useful *everywhere* in the triumph of the liberty of woman, and of the equality of all before the law; this is the sole wish that a Frenchwoman can make who believes in the unity of the human family, as well as in the legitimacy of national autonomies, and who loves all nations, since all are the organs of a single great body, — Humanity.

CHAPTER I.

MICHELET.

Several women have sharply criticised Michelet's "Love."

Why are intelligent womeh thus dissatisfied with so upright a man as Michelet?

Because to him woman is a perpetual invalid, who should be shut up in a gynœceum in company with a dairy maid, as fit company only for chickens and turkeys.

Now we, women of the west, have the audacity to contend that we are not invalids, and that we have a holy horror of the harem and the gynœceum.

Woman, *according to Michelet*, is a being of a nature opposite to that of man; a creature weak, *always wounded, exceedingly barometrical*, and, consequently, unfit for labor.

She is incapable of abstracting, of generalizing, of comprehending conscientious labors. She does not like to occupy herself with business, and she is destitute, in part, of judicial sense. But, in return, she is revealed all gentleness, all love, all grace, all devotion.

Created for man, she is the altar of his heart, his refreshment, his consolation. In her presence he gains new vigor, becomes inspirited, draws the strength necessary to the accomplishment of his high mission as worker, creator, organizer.

He should love her, watch over her, maintain her; be at once her father, her lover, her instructor, her priest, her physician, her nurse, and her waiting-maid.

When, at eighteen, a virgin in reason, heart and body, she is given to this husband, who should be twenty-eight, neither more nor less, he confines her in the country in a charming cottage, at a distance from her parents and friends, with the rustic maid that we just mentioned.

Why this sequestration in the midst of the nineteenth century, do you ask?

Because the husband can have no power over his wife in society, and can have full power over her in solitude. Now, it is necessary that he should have this full power over her, since it belongs to him to form her heart, to give her ideas, to sketch within her the incarnation of himself. For know, readers, that woman is destined to reflect her husband, more and more, until the last shade of difference, namely, that which is maintained by the separation of the sexes, shall be at last effaced by death, and unity in love be thus effected.

At the end of half a score years of housekeeping, the wife is permitted to cross the threshold of the gynœ-ceum, and to enter the world, or *the great Battle of Life*. Here she will meet more than one danger; but she will escape them all if she keeps the oath she has taken *to make her husband her confessor*. . . . It is evident that Michelet respects the rights of the soul. The husband, who at this epoch has become absorbed in his profession, has necessarily degenerated, hence there is danger that the wife may love another; may become enamored, for instance, of her young nephew.

In the book, she does not succumb, because she confesses
everything to her husband; still it may happen that she
succumbs, then repents, and solicits correction from her
lord and master. The latter should at first refuse, but,
if she insists, rather than drive her to despair, Michelet
— who would on no account drive a woman to despair
— counsels the husband to administer to his wife *the
chastisement that mothers infliction their darlings.*

There must be no separation between the husband
and wife; when the latter has given herself away, she
is no longer her own property. She becomes more and
more the incarnation of the man who has espoused her;
fecundation transforms her into him, so that the children
of the lover or of the second husband resemble the first
impregnator. The husband, being ten years older than
the wife, dies first; the woman must preserve her widowhood; her rôle henceforth until death is to fructify within
her and about her the ideas which her husband has be-
queathed, to remain the center of his friendships, to
raise up to him posthumous disciples, and thus remain
his property until she rejoins him in death.

In case the husband survives, which may happen, the
author does not tell us whether he should re-marry.
Probably not, since love exists only between two; unless
Michelet, who reproves polygamy in this world, admits
it as morality in the life to come.

You see, my readers, that in Michelet's book, woman
is created for man; without him she would be nothing;
he it is who pronounces the *fiat lux* in her intellect; he
it is who makes her in his image, as God made man in
his own.

Accepting the Biblical Genesis, we women can appeal
from Adam to God; for it was not Adam, but God,

who created Eve. Admitting the Genesis of Michelet, there is no pretext, no excuse for disobedience; woman must be subordinate to man and must yield to him, for she belongs to him as the work to the workman, as the vessel to the potter.

The book of Michelet and the two studies of Proudhon on woman, are but two forms of the same thought. The sole difference that exists between these gentlemen is, that the first is as sweet as honey, and the second as bitter as wormwood.

Nevertheless, I prefer the rude assailant to the poet; for insults and blows rouse us to rebel and to clamor for liberty, while compliments lull us to sleep and make us weakly endure our chains.

It would be somewhat cruel to be harsh to Michelet, who piques himself on love and poetry, and, consequenly, is thin skinned; we will therefore castigate him only over the shoulders of M. Proudhon, who may be cannonaded with red-hot shot; and we will content ourselves with criticising in his book what is not found in that of Proudhon.

The two chief pillars of the book on Love are,

First, that woman is a wounded, weak, barometrical, constantly diseased being;

Second, that the woman belongs to the man who has fructified and incarnated himself in her; a proposition proved by the resemblance of the children of the wife to the husband, whoever may be the father.

Michelet and his admirers and disciples do not dispute that the only good method of proving the truth of a principle, or the legitimateness of a generalization, is *verification by facts;* neither do they dispute that to make general rules of exceptions, to create imaginary laws, and to take these pretended laws for the basis of argument, belongs only to the aberrations of the Middle Age, profoundly disdained by men of earnest thought and severe reason. Let us apply these data unsparingly to the two principal affirmations of M. Michelet.

It is a principle in biology that *no physiological condition is a morbid condition;* consequently, the monthly crisis peculiar to woman is not a disease, but a normal phenomenon, the derangement of which causes disturbance in the general health. Woman, therefore, is not an invalid because her‾ sex is subject to a peculiar law. Can it be said that woman is wounded because she is subjected to a periodical fracture, the cicatrice of which is almost imperceptible? By no means. It would be absurd to call a man perpetually wounded who should take a fancy to scratch the end of his finger every month.

Michelet is too well informed to render it necessary for me to tell him that the normal hemorrhage does not proceed from this wound of the ovary, about which he makes so much ado, but from a congestion of the gestative organ.

Are women ill on the recurrence of the law peculiar to their sex?

Very exceptionally, yes; but in the indolent classes, in which transgressions in diet, the lack of an intelligent physical education, and a thousand causes which I need not point out here, render women valetudinarians.

Generally, no. All our vigorous peasant women, our robust laundresses, who stand the whole time with their feet in water, our workwomen, our tradeswomen, our teachers, our servant-maids, who attend with alacrity to their business and pleasures, experience no uncomfortableness, or at most, very little.

Michelet, therefore, has not only erred in erecting a physiological law into a morbid condition, but he has also sinned against rational method by making general rules of a few exceptions, and by proceeding from this generalization, contradicted by the great majority of facts, to construct a system of subjection.

If it is of the faculty of abstracting and generalizing that Michelet, as he employs it, robs woman, we can only congratulate her on the deprivation.

Not only is woman diseased, says Michelet, in consequence of a biological law, but she is always diseased; she has uterine affections, hereditary tendencies, which may assume a terrible form in her sex, etc.

We would ask Michelet whether he considers his own sex as always diseased because it is corroded by cancer, disfigured by eruptions, tortured as much as ours by hereditary tendencies; for hereditary tendencies torture it as much as ours, and it is decimated and enfeebled far more fearfully by shameful diseases, the fruits of its excesses.

Of what, then, is Michelet thinking, in laying such stress on the diseases of women in the face of the quite as numerous diseases of men?

The wife should never be divorced or re-marry, because she has become the property of the husband. This is proved by the fact that the children of the lover or of the second husband resemble the first husband.

If this is true, there are no children that resemble their mother.

There are no children that resemble the progenitors or collateral relatives of their parents.

Every child resembles the first that knew his mother.

Can you explain, then, why it is that so often he does *not* resemble him?

Why he resembles a grandfather, an uncle, an aunt, a brother, a sister of one of the parents?

Why, in certain cities in the south of France, the inhabitants have preserved the Greek type, ascribed to the women, instead of that of their barbaric fathers?

Why negresses who conceive from a white, bring into the world a mulatto, oftenest with thick lips, a flat nose, and woolly hair?

Why many children resemble portraits which had attracted the attention of the mother?

Why, in fine, physiologists, impressed by numerous facts, have thought themselves justified in declaring woman *the preserver of the type?*

In the face of these undeniable facts, I ask you, yourself, what becomes of your theory?

It returns to the domain of chimeras.

Some think that woman possesses a plastic force, which makes her mould her fruit after the model which love, hate, or fear has impressed within her brain; so that the child thus becomes merely a sort of photograph of a cerebral image of the mother.

By the aid of this theory, we might explain the resemblance of the child to the father, to the first husband, to beloved relatives or to friends, either living or dead; but it would be impossible, thereby, to explain how a woman can reproduce in her child the features of a progenitor of her husband or of herself, whose portrait, even, she has never seen; or how, in spite of her wishes, the child resembles no one that she loves, etc. Let us keep a discreet silence; the laws of generation and of resemblance are unknown. If we succeed in discovering them, it will be only by long and patient observation, with the aid of judicious criticism, and an honorable determination to be impartial. Laws are not created, but discovered; ignorance is more healthful for the mind than error; to make general rules of *a few* facts, without taking into account facts more numerous by thousands which contradict them, is not to form a science, but a system of poetical metaphysics; and these metaphysics, however gracefully draped they may be, are opposed to reason, to science, and to truth.

Michelet will pardon me this short lesson in method. I should not presume to give it to him, were not men repeating, like well-trained parrots, after him and Proudhon, that woman is destitute of high intellectual faculties, that she is unsuited to science, that she has no comprehension of method, and other absurdities of like weight.

Allegations such as these place women in a wholly exceptional position, with respect to courtesy and reserve: they owe no consideration to those who deny them these; their most important business at the present time is to prove to men that they deceive themselves, and that they are deceived; that a woman is fully capable of teaching the chief among them how a law is discovered, how its reality is verified, how, and on what conditions we have a right to believe, and to style ourselves, rational, and rationalists.

Before concluding, let us dwell on a few passages of the book on Love. I am curious to know what woman Michelet addresses when he says:

" Spare me your elaborate discussions on the equality of the sexes. Woman is not only our equal, but in many points our superior. Sooner or later she will know everything. The question to decide here is, whether she should know all in her first season of love.

Oh, how much she would lose by it! Youth, freshness, poetry — does she wish, at the first blow, to abandon all these? Is she in such haste to grow old?'

Pardon me, sir; you have already decreed that *there are no longer any old women;* nothing, therefore, can make woman grow old.

" There is knowledge of all kinds," you say; "likewise, at all ages, the knowledge of woman should be different from that of man. It is less science that she needs, than the essence of science, and its living elixir."

What is this *essence,* and this *living elixir* of science? Poetry aside, can you, in exact and definite terms, explain to me what they mean?

Can you prove to me, a woman, that I desire to possess knowledge differently from you?

Take care! disciple of liberty, you have not the right to think and to wish in my place. I have, like you, an intellect and a free will, to which you are bound, by your principles, to pay sovereign respect. Now I forbid you to speak for any woman; I forbid you in the name of what you call *the rights of the soul.*

" You by no means deny," you say, " that, strictly speaking, a young woman can read everything, and inform herself of everything; can pass through all the ordeals to which the mind of man is subjected, and still remain pure. You only maintain," you add, " that her soul, withered by reading, palled by novels, living habitually on the stimulus of play-houses, on the aquafortis of criminal courts, will become, not corrupted, perhaps, but vulgar, common, trivial, like the curb-stone in the street. This curb-stone is a good stone; you have only to break it to see that it is white within. This does not hinder it from being sadly soiled outside, in

2

every respect as dirty as the street gutter from which it has been splashed.

" Is this, madam, the ideal to which you lay claim for her who should remain the temple of man, the altar of his heart, whence he daily rekindles the flame of pure love ? "

A truce to imagery and oratorical outbursts ; none of us deman l for woman any degradation whatever. There would be no need for us to demand what you censure, since it is thoroughly authorized and practised. I by no means wish to accuse you of bad faith, of want of reflection, and of too much moral tolerance ; yet let us strip off your poetic mantle, and translate your thought into prose ; the drapery will no longer make us forget the idea.

When instruction has been demanded for the people, has any one ever taken it into his head to fancy that tho point in question was to make them read novels, to swell the attendance on criminal courts, and to multiply theatres ?

No, you will say.

What authorizes you, then, to believe that those who demand a solid education for woman, are seeking that of of which you, on your part, do not dream for the people ?

On the other hand, do you cultivate the intellect of man by novels, theatres, and spectacles of criminal courts ? Is it in these things that his knowledge consists ? No, you will say. What is there, then, in common between that which you censure, and the knowledge that we desire for woman ; and why attribute to us absurd ideas, that you may have the pleasure of wrangling with phantoms ?

All your fine ladies are nurtured on novels, plays, and

judicial excitements ; yet they are neither vulgar, nor trivial, nor comparable to curb-stones sullied by the mud of the streets; what you tell them, therefore, is no more true than kind.

But if you pay them doubtful compliments, which they do not deserve, you absolve them too easily, in turn. Listen to our principles, that you may not run the risk of appearing unjust with respect to us.

Corruption in our eyes, is not merely the want of chastity, or the shameful suit of gallantry, but all habitual improper sentiment, all weakening of the moral sense, and we absolutely condemn everything which has power to lessen the sensibility of the soul, and to turn it aside from the practice of justice, of virtue, and of self-respect.

In consequence, we profess that the spectacles of criminal courts habituate the heart to insensibility, and should be avoided as much as executions.

We profess that the modern drama is generally evil, because it excites interest for adulterers, robbers, seducers and prostitutes; that the intellect is subjected in theatres to an unhealthy and enervating atmosphere.

We profess, lastly, that novels should be read with great moderation, because, in general, when they do not corrupt the morals, they pervert the judgment and waste precious time.

Though we love and esteem Art, we are indignant at the bad use which is made of it, and we have little esteem for those who avail themselves of it to lead the heart astray, and to pervert the moral sense.

We say to woman : Educate yourselves, be worthy and chaste ; life is earnest, employ it earnestly.

You see that *woman in the image of the stained curbstone*, is by no means the ideal of which we dream.

Can you, a man of heart, can you treat women as wretched and corrupt because they are willing no longer to be slaves ?

And besides, do you think that liberty, which in man engenders individuality and virtue, would produce in woman moral degradation ?

Ah ! leave these calumnies to those who have no heart ; they ill befit you, who may deceive yourself through the lofty poetry of your soul, but who can wish for evil only because you believe it to be good.

The women who ask to be free, great, mistaken poet, are those who are conscious of their dignity, of the true rôle of their sex in humanity ; those who desire that the women who follow them in the career of labor should no longer be obliged *to live by man*, because to live by him is at least to prostitute their dignity, and almost always, their whole person. They wish that woman should be the equal of man, in order to love him holily, to devote herself without calculation, to cease to deceive him or to rule him by artifice, and to become to him a useful auxiliary, instead of a servant or a toy. They know our influence over you ; slaves, we can only debase you ; at present, we render you cowardly, selfish, and dishonest ; we send you out every morning, like vultures, upon society, to provide for our foolish expenses or to endow our children ; we, women of emancipation, are unwilling that our sex should longer play this odious rôle, and be, through its slavery, an instrument of demoralization and of social degradation,—and this you impute to us as a crime !

Ah ! I do not believe it ; you yourself will say that I ought not to believe it.

Looking from a deplorably narrow stand point, you

fancied that you saw all woman-kind in a few valetudinarians, your kind heart was moved for them, and you sought to protect them. Had you looked far and high, you would have seen the workers of thought and muscle; you would have comprehended that inequality is to them a source of corruption and suffering.

Then, in your lofty and glowing style, you would have written, not this book of Love which repels all intelligent and reflective women, but a great and beautiful work to demand the right of half the human race.

The misfortune, the irreparable misfortune, is that instead of climbing to the mountain top to look at every moving thing under the vast horizon, you have shut yourself up in a narrow valley, where, seeing nothing but pale violets, you have concluded that every flower must be also a pale violet; whilst Nature has created a thousand other species, on the contrary, strong and vigorous, with a right, like you, to earth, air, water and sunshine.

Whatever may be your love, your kindness and your good intentions towards woman, your book would be immensely dangerous to the cause of her liberty, if men were in a mood to relish your ethics : but they will remain as they are ; and the dignity of woman, kept waking by their brutality, their despotism, their desertion, their foul morals, will not be lulled to sleep under the fresh, verdant, alluring and treacherously perfumed foliage of this manchineel tree, called the book of *Love*.

In Michelet's later work, " Woman," by the side of many beautiful pages full of heart and poetry are found things that we regret to point out, for the sake of the author.

M. Michelet has evidently amended, as we shall preson him ; but as a spice of vengeance, he pretends that their language has been dictated by directors, *philosophers and others.* We know some of these ladies personally, and can assure him that they have had no director of any kind — quite the contrary.

Is it also in consequence of rancor that the author pretends that woman loves man, not for his real worth, but because he pleases her, and that she makes God in her own image, " a God of partiality and caprice, who saves those who please him ? " " In feminine theology," adds Michelet, " God would say : I love thee because thou art a sinner, because thou hast no merit ; I have no reason to love thee, but it is sweet to me to forgive."

Very well, your sex loves woman *for her real worth ;* we never hear a man, enamored of some unworthy creature, say :" What matters it, I love her ! " Your love is always wise, and given reasonably ; none but deserving women can please you. I ask why so many honest women are abandoned and unhappy, while so many that are impure and vicious, yet sought and adored, are in possession of the art of charming, of ruining and of perverting men ?

Michelet deplores the state of divorce which is established between the sexes ; we deplore it likewise ; but our complaints do not remedy it. Men shun marriage from motives that do them no credit : they have at their pleasure the poor girls whom want places at their mercy ; they shun marriage because they do not wish a real, that is, an autonomous wife at their side ; for themselves, they wish liberty, for their wife, slavery.

On their side, women tend to enfranchisement, which is well for them as it is for men : they should not suffer themselves to be turned aside from their pursuit; on the other hand, as men are attracted by a costly toilette, and neglect plainly dressed women, if the latter, in the wish to please and retain them, imitate public women, whose is the fault? Is it ours, who desire to please you and to be loved by you, or yours, who can only be attracted by dress? If you loved us *for our real worth*, and not because our dresses and jewels please your eye, we would not ruin you.

Let us point out in a few lines the contradictions and differences that are found between Michelet's first and second works.

In both, woman is the flame of love and of the fireside, religion, harmony, poetry, the guardian of the domestic hearth, a housewife whose cares are ennobled by love: civilization is due to her grace, she should be the representative of grace if not of beauty.

In both books, the household must be isolated; the wife must have no intimate friendship; mother, brothers and sisters prevent her from becoming absorbed as she ought to be in her husband. What we think of this absorption is already known; we will only say here that if the friends and relatives of the wife should be expelled, those of the husband should be none the less so; the mother and friends of the husband have more power to injure the wife than those of the wife to injure the husband; numerous sad facts prove this.

In "Love," woman is a receptive power, incapable of comprehending conscientious works; she must receive everything from her husband in the intellectual and moral point of view.

In "Woman," she is half of the couple, in the same ratio as man is capable of the most lofty speculations,

and thoroughly understands administration. She gives
the child the education that before all else will influence
the rest of his life. "So long as woman is not the
partner of labor and of *action*," says the author, "we
are serfs, we can do nothing — she may even be the
equal of man in medical science; she is a school, she
- is sole educatress, etc."

Very well, thus far; and doubtless Michelet would
have been consistent, had he not got into his head a
masculine and a feminine ideal which spoils everything;
he reasoned to himself: "Man is a creator, woman a
harmony whose end and destination is love;" and, consequently, he marks out for the latter a plan of education
different from that by which man should be developed;
the natural sciences are suited to woman, history should
only be taught her to form in her a firm moral and religious faith. As love is her vocation, to each season of
the life of woman should correspond an object of love;
flowers, the doll, poor children, next the lover, then the
husband and children, then the care of young orphans,
prisoners, etc.

In "Love," the wife alone seems bound to confess to
the husband. In "Woman," the obligation is mutual.

The widow, in "Love," should not marry again, in
"Woman," she may espouse a friend of the husband, or
still better, the one whom he may choose on his death-
bed; if she is too old, she may watch over a young
man; but she will do better to protect young girls, to
make peace in families, to facilitate marriages, to superintend prisons, etc.

We will carry the analysis no further; our objections
to the author's doctrine will be found in the article on
Proudhon, and in the sequel of the work.

CHAPTER II.

PROUDHON.

The tenth and eleventh studies of the last work of M. Proudhon, " Justice in the Revolution and in the Church," comprise the author's whole doctrine concerning Woman, Love, and Marriage.

Before analyzing it and criticising its chief points, I must acquaint my readers with the polemical commencement which *appears* to have given rise to the publication of the strange doctrines of our great critic. In the *Revue Philosophique* of December, 1856, the following article by me was published under the title, *Proudhon and the Woman Question :* —

" Women have a weakness for soldiers, it is said. It is true, but they should not be reproached for it ; they love even the show of courage, which is a glorious and holy thing. I am a woman, Proudhon is a great soldier of thought. I cannot therefore prevent myself from re. garding him with esteem and sympathy ; sentiments to which he will owe the moderation of my attack on his opinions concerning the rôle of woman in humanity. In his first " Memoir on Property," note on page 265, edition of 1841, we read the following paradox in the style of the Koran :

2*

"Between man and woman may exist love, passion, the bond of habit, whatever you like; there is not *true society. Man and woman are not companions.* The difference of sex gives rise between them to a separation *of the same nature as that which the difference of races places between animals.* Thus, far from applauding what is now called the emancipation of woman, I should be much more inclined, were it necessary to go to this extremity, *to put woman in seclusion.*"

In the third "Memoir on Property," we read:

"This signifies that woman, *by nature and by destination,* is neither *associate, nor citizen, nor public functionary.*"

I open the "Creation of Order in Humanity," and read there:

"It is in treating of education that we must determine the part of woman in society. Woman, until she becomes a wife, is *apprentice,* at most *under-superintendent,* in the work-shop, as in the family, she *remains a minor, and does not form a part of the commonwealth.* Woman is not, as is commonly affirmed, *the half nor the equal of man,* but the living and sympathetic *complement* that is lacking to make him an individual."

In the "Economical Contradictions," we read:

"For my part, the more I reflect on the destiny of woman outside of the family and the household, the less I can account for it: *courtesan or housewife,* (housewife, I say, not servant,) I see no medium."

I had always laughed at these paradoxes; they had no more doctrinal value in my eyes than the thousand other freaks so common to this celebrated critic. A short time since, an obscure journal pretended that Proudhon, in private conversations, had drawn up a formula of an entire system based on masculine omnipotence, and published this system in its columns. One of two things is certain, said I to myself; either the journalist speaks falsely, or he tells the truth; if he speaks falsely, his evident aim is to destroy Proudhon in the confidence of the friends of progress, and to make him lose his lawful share of influence, in which case, he must be warned of it; if he tells the truth, Proudhon must still be warned of the fact, since it is impossible that, being the father of *several daughters*, paternal feeling should not have set him on the road to reason. At all events, I must know about it. I wrote to Proudhon, who, the next day, returned me an answer which I transcribe *verbatim* :

" MADAM :

" I know nothing of the article published by M. Charles Robin in the *Telegraphe* of yesterday. In order to inform myself with regard to this paraphrase, as you entitle the article of M. Robin, I examined my first " Memoir on Property," page 265, Garnier edition, (I have no other,) and found no note there. I examined the same page in my other pamphlet, and discovered no note anywhere. It is therefore impossible for me to reply to your first question.

" I do not exactly know what you call *my opinions* on woman, marriage and the family ; for I believe I have given no one a right to speak of my opinions on these subjects, any more than on that of property.

" I have written economical and social criticisms ; in making these criticisms (I take the word in its highest signification), I may have indeed expressed judgments to a greater or less degree relative, concerning a truth.

I have no where that I know of, framed a dogma, a theory, a collection of principles; in a word, a system. All that I can tell you is, in the first place, as far as concerns myself, that my opinions have been formed progressively and in an unvarying direction; that, at the time at which I write, I have not deviated from this direction; and that, with this reserve, my existing opinions accord perfectly with what they were seventeen years ago when I published my first memoirs.

"In the second place, with regard to you, Madam, who, in interrogating me do not leave me in ignorance of your sentiments, I will tell you with all the frankness which your letter exacts, and which you expect from a compatriot, that I do not regard the question of marriage, of woman, and of the family in the same light as yourself, or any of the innovating authors whose ideas have come to my knowledge; that I do not admit, for instance, that woman has the right at the present time to separate her cause from that of man, and to demand for herself special legislation, as though her chief tyrant and enemy were man; that further, I do not admit that, whatever reparation may be due to woman, of joint thirds with her husband (or father) and her children, the most rigorous justice can ever make her the EQUAL of man; that neither do I admit that this inferiority of the female sex constitutes for it either servitude, or humiliation, or a diminution of dignity, liberty, or happiness. I maintain that the contrary is true.

"I consider, therefore, the sort of crusade that is being carried on at this time by a few estimable ladies in both hemispheres in behalf of the prerogatives of their sex, as a symptom of the general renovation that is being wrought; but nevertheless, as an exaggerated symptom, *an infatuation that proceeds precisely from the infirmity of the sex and its incapacity to understand and to govern itself.*

" I have read, Madam, a few of your articles. I find that your wit, capacity and knowledge place you certainly above an infinity of males who have nothing of their sex but the proletary faculty. In this respect, were it necessary to decide on your thesis by comparisons of this kind, you would doubtless gain the cause.

" But you have too much good sense not to comprehend that the question here is by no means to compare individual with individual, but the whole feminine sex in its aggregate with the whole masculine sex, in order to know whether these two halves, the complements of each other, are or are not equals in the human androgynus.

" In accordance with this principle, I do not believe that your system, which is, I think, that of equality or equivalence, can be sustained, and I regard it as a weakness of our epoch.

" You have interrogated me, Madam, with Franche-Comtois abruptness. I wish you to take my words in good part, and, since I doubtless do not agree at all with you, not to see in me an enemy of woman, a detractor of your sex, worthy of the animadversions of maidens, wives and mothers. The rules of fair discussion oblige you to admit at least that you may be deceived, that I may be right, that in such case it is I who am truly the defender and friend of woman; I ask nothing more.

" You and your companions have raised a very great question, which I think that you have hitherto treated quite superficially. But the indifferent manner in which

this subject has been treated should not be considered as
conclusive reason for not receiving it; on the contrary,
I regard it as another reason for the advocates of the
equality of the two sexes to make greater efforts. In
this respect, Madam, I doubt not that you will signalize
yourself anew, and await with impatience the volume
that you announce, which I promise to read with all the
attention of which I am capable."

On reading this letter, I transcribed the note which
M. Proudhon had not succeeded in finding, and sent it
to him, with the article of M. Charles Robin. As he
did not reply, his silence authorizes me to believe the
journalist.

Ah! you persist in maintaining that woman is inferior, minor! you believe that women will bow devoutly
before the high decree of your autocracy! No, no; it
will not, it cannot be so. To battle, M. Proudhon!
But let us first dispose of the question of my personality.

You consider me as an exception, by telling me that,
if it were necessary to decide on my thesis by comparison
between a host of men and myself, the decision would
be, doubtless, in favor of my opinions. Mark my reply:

" *Every true law is absolute.* The ignorance or folly
of grammarians, moralists, jurisconsults, and other philosophers, alone invented the proverb: There is no rule
without an exception. *The mania of imposing laws on
Nature, instead of studying Nature's own laws, afterwards confirmed this aphorism of ignorance.*" Who
said this? You, in the " Creation of Order in Humanity." Why is your letter in contradiction with this
doctrine?

Have you changed your opinion? Then I entreat

you to tell me whether men of worth are not quite as exceptional in their sex, as women of merit in theirs. You have said : " Whatever may be the differences existing between men, they are equal, because they are human beings." Under penalty of inconsistency, you must add : Whatever may be the differences existing between the sexes, they are equal, because they form a part of the human species — unless you prove that women are not a part of humanity. Individual worth, not being the basis of right between men, cannot become so between the sexes. Your compliment is, therefore, a contradiction.

I add, lastly, that I feel myself linked with my sex by too close a solidarity ever to be content to see myself abstracted from it by an illogical process. I am a woman — I glory in it ; I rejoice if any value is set upon me, not for myself, indeed, but because this contributes to modify the opinion of men with respect to my sex. A woman who is happy in hearing it said : " *You are a man*," is, in my eyes, a simpleton, an unworthy creature, avowing the superiority of the masculine sex ; and the men who think that they compliment her in this manner, are vainglorious and impertinent boasters. If I acquire any desert, I thus pay honor to women, I reveal their aptitudes, I do not pass into the other sex any more than Proudhon abandons his own, because he is elevated by his intellect above the level of foolish and ignorant men ; and if the ignorance of the mass of men prejudges nothing against their right, no more does the ignorance of the mass of women prejudge anything against theirs.

You affirm that man and woman do not form *true society*.

Tell us, then, what is marriage, what is society.

You affirm that the difference of sex places between man and woman a separation of the same nature *as that which the difference of races places between animals.* Then prove:

That the race is not essentially formed of two sexes;

That man and woman can be reproduced separately;

That their common product is a mixed breed, or a mule;

That their characteristics are dissimilar, apart from sexuality.

And if you come off with honor from this great feat of strength, you will still have to prove:

That to difference of race corresponds difference *of right;*

That the black, the yellow, the copper-colored persons belonging to races inferior to the Caucasian cannot truly associate with the latter; that they are minors.

Come, sir, study anthropology, physiology, and phrenology, and employ your serial dialectics to prove all this to us.

You are inclined to seclude woman, instead of emancipating her?

Prove to men that they have the right to do so; to women, that it is their duty to suffer themselves to be placed under lock and key. I declare, for my part, that I would not submit to it. Does Proudhon remember how he threatens the priest who shall lay his hand on his children? Well, the majority of women would not confine themselves to threats against those who might have the Mussulmanic inclination of Proudhon.

You affirm that by *nature*, and by *destination*, woman is neither *associate*, nor *citizen*, nor *functionary*. Tell us, in the first place, *what nature* it is necessary to have to be all these.

Reveal to us the *nature* of woman, since you claim to know it better than she does herself.

Reveal to us her *destination*, which apparently is not that which we see, nor which she believes to be such.

You affirm that woman, until her marriage, is nothing more than *apprentice,* at most, under-superintendent in the social workshop ; that she is *minor* in the family, and *does not form a part of the commonwealth.*

Prove, then, that she does not execute in the social workshop and in the family works *equivalent,* or equal, to those of man.

Prove that she is less useful than man.

Prove that the qualities that give to man the right of citizenship, do not exist in woman.

I shall be severe with you on this head. To subordinate woman in a social order in which she must *work in order to live* is to *desire prostitution ;* for disdain of the producer extends to the value of the product ; and when such a doctrine is contrary to science, good sense, and progress, to sustain it is *cruelty,* is *moral monstrosity.* The woman who cannot live by working, can only do so by prostituting herself; the equal of man or a courtesan, such is the alternative. He is blind who does not see it.

You see no other fate for woman than to be courtesan or housewife. Open your eyes wider, and dream less, and tell me whether all those useful and courageous women are only housewives or courtesans, who support themselves honorably by arts, literature, instruction ;

Who found numerous and prosperous manufactures ;

Who superintend commercial establishments ;

Who are such good managers, that many among them conceal or repair the faults resulting from the careless-ness or dissipation of their husbands.

Prove to us, therefore, that all this is wrong;

Prove to us that it is not the result of human progress ;

Prove to us that labor, the stamp of the human spe. cies — that labor, which you consider as the great eman-cipator — that labor, which makes men equal and free, has not virtue to make women equal and free. If you prove this to us, we shall have to register one contradic-tion more.

You do not admit that woman should have the right of claiming for herself special legislation, as though man were her chief enemy and tyrant.

You, sir, are the one that legislates specially for wo-man ; she herself desires nothing but the common law.

Yes ; until now, man, in subordinating woman, has been her tyrant and enemy. I am of your opinion when, in your first " Memoir on Property," you say that, so long as the strong and the weak are not *equals*, they are *strangers*, they cannot form an alliance, *they are enemies*. Yes, thrice yes, so long as man and wo-man are not equals, woman is in the right in considering man as her *tyrant* and *enemy*.

" The most rigorous justice cannot make woman the EQUAL of man." And it is to a woman whom you set in your opinion above a host of men, that you affirm such a thing! What a contradiction!

" It is *an infatuation* for women to demand their right !" *An infatuation* like that of slaves, pretending that they were created freemen ; of the citizens of '89, proving that men are equal before the law. Do you know who were, who are the infatuated ? The masters, the nobles, the whites, the men who have denied, who do deny, and who will deny, that slaves, citizens, blacks, and women, are born for liberty and equality.

" The sex to which I belong is incapable of understanding and governing itself," say you !

Prove that it is destitute of intellect;

Prove that great empresses and great queens have not governed as well as great emperors and great kings ;

Prove against all the facts patent that women are not in general good observers and good managers ;

Then prove that all men understand themselves perfectly and govern themselves admirably, and that progress moves as if on wheels.

" Woman is neither the *half* nor the *equal* of man ; she is *the complement that finally makes him an individual;* the two sexes form *the human androgynus.*" Come ; seriously, what means this jingle of empty words ? They are metaphors, unworthy to figure in scientific language, when our own and the other higher zoölogical species are in question. The lioness, the she-wolf and the tigress are no more the halves or the complement of their species than woman is the complement of man. Or Nature has established two *exteriorities*, two wills, she affirms two unities, two entireties not one, or *two halves;* the arithmetic of Nature cannot be destroyed by the freaks of the imagination.

Is equality before the law based upon *individual* qualities ? Proudhon replies in the " Creation of Order in Humanity " :

" Neither birth, nor figure, *nor faculties*, nor fortune, nor rank, nor profession, nor talent, nor anything that distinguishes individuals establishes between them a difference of species; all being men, and *the law regula-*

ing only human relations, it is the same for all; so that
to establish exceptions, it would be necessary to prove
that the individuals excepted are *above* or *beneath* the
human species."

Prove to us that women are *above* or *beneath* the human species, that they do not form a part of it, or, *under
penalty of contradiction,* submit to the consequences of
your doctrine.

You say in the " Social Revolution ; "

" Neither conscience, nor reason, nor liberty, nor labor, pure forces, *primary and creative faculties,* can be
made mechanical without being destroyed. Their reason of existence is in themselves ; in their works they
should find their reason of action. In this consists the
human person, a sacred person, etc."

Prove that women have neither conscience, nor reason,
nor moral liberty, and that they do not labor. If it is
demonstrated that they possess the *primary and creative
faculties,* respect their human person, for it is sacred.

In the " Creation of Order in Humanity," you say :

" Specifically, labor satisfies the desire of our personality, which tends invincibly to make a difference between itself and others, *to render itself independent, to
conquer its liberty* and its character."

Prove then that women have no special work, and, if
facts contradict you, acknowledge that, it inevitably
tends to *independence,* to *liberty.*

Do you deny that they are your equals because they
are less intelligent as a whole than men ? In the first
place, I contest it ; but I need not do so, you yourself resolve this difficulty in the " Creation of Order in Humanity : "

" The inequality of capacities, when not caused by

constitutional vices, mutilation or want, results from
general ignorance, insufficient method, lack or falsity of
education, and divergence of intuition through lack of
sequence, whence arises dispersion and confusion of ideas.
Now, all these facts productive of inequality are essentially abnormal, therefore the inequality of capacities is
abnormal." -

Unless you prove that women are mutilated by Nature, I do not exactly see how you can escape the consequences of your syllogism : not only has feminine inferiority the same sources as masculine ignorance, but
public education is refused to women, the great professional schools are closed to them, those who through
their intellect equal the most intelligent among you have
had twenty times as many difficulties and prejudices to
overcome.

You wish to subordinate women because in general
they have less muscular force than you ; but at this rate
the weak men ought not to be the equals of the strong,
and you combat this consequence yourself in your first
" Memoir on Property," where you say :

" Social equilibrium is the equalization of the strong
and the weak."

If I have treated you with consideration, it is because you are an intelligent and progressive man, and
because it is impossible that you should remain under
the influence of the doctors of the Middle Age on one
question, while you are in advance of the majority of
your cotemporaries on so many others. You will cease
to sustain an illogical series that is without foundation,
remembering, as you have said so well in the " Creation
of Order in Humanity : "

" That the greater part of philosophical aberrations

and chimeras have arisen from attributing to logical series a reality that they do not possess, and endeavoring
to explain the nature of man by abstractions."

You will acknowledge that all the higher animal species are composed of two sexes;

That in none is the female the inferior of the male,
except sometimes through force, which cannot be the basis of human right;

You will renounce the androgynus, which is only a
dream.

Woman, a distinct individual, endowed with consciousness, intellect, will and activity like man, will be
no longer separated from him before the laws.

You will say of all, both men and women, as in your
first " Memoir on Property : "

" Liberty is an absolute right, because it is to man
what impenetrability is to matter, a condition *sine qua
non* of existence. Equality is an *absolute right*, because
without equality, there is no society."

And you will thus show the second degree of socia-
ability, which you yourself define, " the recognition in
another of a personality *equal* to our own."

I appeal therefore from Proudhon drunk with theology
to Proudhon sobered by facts and science, moved by the
sorrows and disorders resulting from his own systems.

I hope I shall not encounter his Herculean club raised
against the holy banner of truth and right; against woman,— that being physically so weak, morally so strong,
who, bleeding, and steeped in gall beneath her crown of
roses, is just on the point of reaching the top of the
rough mountain where progress will shortly give her
her lawful place by the side of man. But if my hopes
are deceitful, mark me well, M. Proudhon, you will find

me standing firmly in the breach, and, whatever may be
your strength, I vow that you shall not overthrow me.
I will courageously defend the right and dignity of your
daughters against the despotism and logical error of
their father, and the victory will remain mine, for, definitively, it always belongs to truth."

Proudhon replied by the following letter in the *Revue
Philosophique*:

"To MADAME d'HÉRICOURT.

"Well, Madam, what did I tell you in my
last letter?

"I consider the sort of crusade that is being carried
on at this time by some estimable ladies in both hemispheres in behalf of their sex, as a symptom of the general revolution that is being wrought; but nevertheless
as an exaggerated symptom, an infatuation that proceeds
precisely from the inferiority of the sex and its incapacity to understand and to govern itself.

"I begin by withdrawing the word *infatuation*, which
may have wounded you, but which was not, as you
know, intended for publicity.

"This point adjusted, I will tell you, Madam, with
all the respect that I owe you as a woman, that I did
not expect to see you confirm my judgment so speedily
by your petulant appeal.

"I was at first at a loss to know whence came the
discontent that impelled the bravest, the most distinguished among you, to an assault on paternal and marital supremacy. I said to myself, not without disqui-
tude, What is the matter? What is it that troubles
them? With what do they reproach us? To which
of our faculties, our virtues, our prerogatives; or else of

our failings, our perfidies, our calamities, do they aspire? Is this the cry of their outraged nature, or an
aberration of their understanding?

"Your attack, joined to the studies which I immediately commenced on the subject, came at last to solve
the question.

"No, Madam, you know nothing of your sex; you
do not know the first word of the question that you and
your honorable confederates are agitating with so much
noise and so little success. And, if you do not comprehend this question; if, in your eight pages of reply to
my letter, there are forty paralogisms, it results precisely,
as I have told you, from your *sexual infirmity*. I mean
by this word, the exactness of which is not, perhaps, irreproachable, the quality of your understanding, which
permits you to seize the relation of things only as far as
we, men, place your finger upon them. You have in
the brain, as in the body, a certain organ incapable by
itself of overcoming its native inertia, and which the
masculine spirit alone is capable of setting in motion;
and even this does not always succeed. Such, Madam,
is the result of my direct and positive observations; I
make them over to your obstetrical sagacity, and leave
you to calculate therefrom the incalculable consequences
to your thesis.

"I will willingly enter into an elaborate discussion
with you, Madam, on this obscure subject, in the *Revue
Philosophique*. But— as you will comprehend as well as
I — the broader the question, the more it affects our most
sacred, social, and domestic interests, the more important is it that we should approach it with seriousness
and prudence.

"The following course, therefore, appears to me indispensable : In the first place, you have promised us a book, and I await it. I need this work to complete my documents and to finish my demonstration. Since I had the honor of receiving and replying to your letter, I have made earnest and interesting studies on woman, which I ask only to rectify if they are erroneous ; as I also desire to set a seal on them if, as I have every reason to presume, your publication brings me but one confirmation more.

" I have verified by facts and documents the truth of all the assertions which you call on me to retract, namely :

" That the difference of sex raises up between man and woman a separation ANALOGOUS — I did not say equal — to that which the difference of races and species establishes between animals ;

" That by reason of this separation or difference, man and woman are not *associates ;* I did not say that they could not be anything else ;

" That, consequently, woman can only be a *citizen* in so far as she is the wife of a citizen ; as we say *Madame la Presidente* to the wife of a President : which does not imply that no other rôle exists for her.

" In two words, I am in a position to establish, by observation and reasoning, the facts, that woman, being weaker than man with respect to *muscular force*, as you yourself acknowledge, is not less inferior to him with respect to INDUSTRIAL, ARTISTIC, PHILOSOPHICAL and MORAL POWER ; so that if the condition of woman in society be regulated, as you demand for her, by the same justice as the condition of man, it is all over with her, she is a slave.

" To which I add, immediately, that this system is

3

precisely what I reject: the principle of pure, rigorous right, of that terrible right which the Roman compared to an unsheathed sword, *jus strictum*, and which rules individuals of the same sex among themselves, being different from that which governs the relations between individuals of different sexes.

" What is this principle, differing from justice, and which, notwithstanding, would not exist without justice; which all men feel in the depth of their souls, and of which you women alone have no idea? Is it love? nothing more? I leave it to you to divine. And if your penetration succeeds in clearing up this mystery, I consent, Madam, to sign you a certificate of genius; *Et eris mihi magnus Apollo*. But then you will have given me the cause.

" Such, Madam, in a few words, are the conclusions to which I have arrived, and which the reading of your book surely will not modify. Notwithstanding, as it is absolutely posssible that your personal observations may have led you to diametrically opposite results, good faith in the discussion and respect for our readers and ourselves exact that, before entering upon the controversy, a reciprocal interchange of all the documents that we have collected should be made between us. You may take cognizance of mine.

" One other condition, which I entreat you, Madam, to take in good part, and from which I shall not depart under any pretext, is that you shall choose yourself a male sponsor.

" You, who have declared yourself so energetically on this point, would not wish your adversary to make the least sacrifice to gallantry in so serious a discussion; and you are right. But I, Madam, who am so far from

admitting your pretensions, cannot thus release myself
from the obligations which manly and honorable. civility
prescribes towards ladies ; and as I propose, besides, to
make you serve as a subject of experiment ; as, after
having made the autopsy of five or six women of the
greatest merit for the instruction of my readers, I count
also on making yours, you will conceive that it is quite
impossible for me to argue from you, of you, and with
you, without exposing myself at every word to a violation of all the rules of conventionality.

" I know, Madam, that such a condition will annoy
you ; it is one of the disadvantages of your position to
which you must submit courageously. You are a plain-
tiff, and, as a woman, you affirm that you are oppressed.
Appear, then, before the judgment seat of incorruptible
public opinion with this tyrannous chain which rouses
your ire, and which, according to me, exists only in
your disordered imagination. You will be but the more
interesting for it. Besides, you would deride me if,
while sustaining the superiority of man, I should begin
by according to you the equality of woman by disputing
with you on an equal footing of companionship. You
have not counted, I imagine, upon my falling into this
inconsistency.

" You will not lack for champions, besides. I expect
of your courtesy, Madam, that he whom you shall select
as my antagonist, who will sign and affirm all your arti
cles, and assume the responsibility of your affirmations
and replies, shall be worthy of both you and me ; so
that, in fine, I shall not have a right to complain that
you have pitted me against a man of straw.

" What has most surprised me, since this hypothesis
of the equality of the sexes, renewed by the Greeks as

well as by many others, has become known among us,
has been to see that it numbered among its partisans
almost as many men as women. I sought a long time
for the reason of this strange fact, which I at first attributed to chivalric zeal; I think now that I have
found it. It is not to the advantage of the knights. I
shall be glad, Madam, for their sake and yours, if this
serious examination should prove that the new emancipators of woman are the most lofty, the broadest, and
the most progressive, if not the most masculine minds
of the age.

" You say, Madam, that women have a weakness for
soldiers. It is doubtless on this account that you have
lashed me soundly. *He who loveth, chasteneth.* When
I was three years and a half old, my mother, to get rid
of me, sent me to a school-mistress of the neighborhood,
an excellent woman, called Madelon. One day she
threatened to whip me for some piece of mischief. It
made me furious. I snatched her switch from her hand,
and flung it in her face. I was always a disobedient
subject. I shall be glad, therefore, to find that you do
not assume towards me castigating airs, which it does
not belong to a man to return; but I leave this to your
discretion. Strike, redouble the blows, do not spare me;
and if I should chance to grow restive under the rod,
believe me none the less, Madam, your affectionate servant and compatriot,

" PROUDHON."

Taking up the discussion in turn, I replied as follows, in the ensuing February number : —

I am forbidden, sir, to answer your letter in the inde-

corous style which you have deemed proper to assume
towards me :

By respect for the gravity of my subject ;

By respect for our readers ;

By respect for myself.

You find yourself ill at ease in the Popilian circle
that has been traced around you by the hand of a woman ; all understand this, I among the rest. Ill-armed
for defence, worse armed, perhaps, for attack, you would
like to escape; but your skill as a tactician will avail
you nothing ; you shall not quit the fatal circle till vanquished, either by me, or by yourself, if you confess
your weakness on the point in litigation, by continuing
to refuse a discussion under flimsy pretexts, or, lastly,
by public opinion, which will award to you the quality
of inconsistency, the least desirable of all to a dialec-
tician.

This being understood, I must tell you that, personally, I am satisfied that you should attack, in *the rights
of woman*, the cause of justice and progress. It is an
augury of success to this cause ; you have always been
fatal to all that you have sought to sustain.

It is true that your attitude in this question makes
you *the ally of the dogmatism of the Middle Age ;* it
is true that the *official representatives* of this dogmatism avail themselves, at the present time, of your arguments and your name to maintain their influence over
women, and through them over men and children ; and
this in order to revive the past, to stifle the future. Is
this your intention ? I do not believe it. You are, in
my eyes, a subverter, a destroyer, in whom instinct
sometimes gets the better of intellect, and from whom
it shuts out a clear view of the consequences of his

writings. Formed for strife, you must have adversaries; and, in default of enemies, you cruelly fall on those who are fighting in the same ranks with yourself. In all your writings, one feels that the second part of education — that which inspires respect and love of woman — is completely wanting in you.

Let us come to your letter.

You reproach me with having made *forty paralogisms;* it was your duty at least to have cited one of these. However, let us see.

You say : between man and woman there is a separation of *the same nature as that which the difference of race establishes between animals.*

Woman, by nature and destination, is *neither associate, nor citizen, nor functionary.*

She is, until marriage, only *apprentice,* at most, *under-superintendent* in the social workshop ; she is a *minor* in the family, and *does not form a part of the commonwealth.*

You conceive of no destiny for her outside of the household : she can be only *housewife* or *courtesan.*

She is incapable *of understanding and of governing herself.*

To make a paralogism is to draw a conclusion from false premises ; now did I conclude from such in saying :

In order that all these paradoxes may become truths, you have to prove :

That man and woman are not of the same race ;

That they can be reproduced separately ;

That their common product is a mixed breed or a mule ;

That difference of races corresponds to difference of rights.

You have to define for us an association, and also the nature of a citizen or a functionary.

You have to prove that woman is less useful than man in society;

That, at the present time, she is necessarily a house-wife, when she is not a courtesan ;

That she is destitute of intellect, that she knows nothing of government.

You pretend that woman has not a right *to demand for herself special legislation.*

Was I guilty of a paralogism in pointing out to you that it is not she, *but you*, who demand this, since you lay down as a principle the inequality of the sexes before human law?

All that you say relatively to the *pretended* inferiority of woman and the conclusions which you draw from it applying to human races inferior to our own, it would be easy for me to demonstrate that the consequence of your principles is the *re-establishment of slavery.* The nearest perfect has the right to take advantage of the weakest, instead of becoming his educator. An admirable doctrine, full of the spirit of progress, full of generosity ! I compliment you most sincerely on it.

You say that labor specialized is the great emancipator of man; that labor, conscience, liberty, and reason, find only in themselves their right to exist and to act ; that these pure forces constitute the human person, *which is sacred.*

You lay down the principle that the law is the same for all ; so that, to establish exceptions, it would be necessary to prove that the individuals excepted are *above* or *beneath* the human species.

You say that social equilibrium is the equalization of the strong and the weak ; that all have the same rights, not through that which distinguishes them from each other, but through *that which is common to them,—the quality of human beings.*

Was I guilty of paralogisms in saying to you :

Then you cannot, by reason of her weakness or even of a supposed inferiority, exclude woman from equality of right : your principles interdict it, unless you prove :

That she is superior or inferior to the human species, and that she does not form a part of it ;

That she is destitute of conscience, of justice, and of reason; that she does not labor, that she does not execute specialties of labor.

It is evident, that your doctrine concerning general right is in contradiction to your doctrine concerning the right of women ; it is evident that you are very inconsequent, and that, however skillful you may be, you cannot extricate yourself from this embarrassment.

In what you call an answer, there are a few passages that are worth the trouble of pausing to consider.

You ask *what impels the bravest, the most distinguished among us to an assault on paternal and marital supremacy.*

You do not comprehend the movement, or you would have said *masculine supremacy.*

In my turn, I ask you :

What would have impelled Proudhon, a Roman slave, to play the part of Spartacus ?

What would have impelled Proudhon, a feudal serf, to organize a Jacquerie ?

What would have impelled Proudhon, a black slave, to become a Toussaint L'Ouverture?

What would have impelled Proudhon, a Russian serf, to take the character of Poutgachef?

What would have impelled Proudhon, a citizen of '89,

to overthrow the privileges of the nobility and the clergy?

What would impel Proudhon . . . but I will not touch on reality.

What would Proudhon have replied to all the holders of *prerogatives* and *supremacy*, who would not have failed on their part to have put to him the naïve question: "Ah! what does this vile slave, this unworthy serf, this audacious and stupid citizen want of us, then? *To which of our faculties, our virtues, our prerogatives does he aspire? Is this the cry of his outraged nature, or an aberration of his understanding?*"

The answer that Proudhon would make, is that which will be made to him by all women who have attained majority.

There is in the brain of woman, say you, an organ which the masculine mind alone is capable of setting in motion. Render the service then to science of pointing it out and demonstrating its manner of working. As to the other organ of which you speak, it is its inertia, doubtless, that has caused it to be defined by some, *parvum animal furibondum, octo ligamentis alligatum.* Before choosing anatomical and physiological facts as proofs of your assertions, consult some learned physician; such is the counsel given you, not only by my *obstetrical, but also by my medical sagacity.*

You offer to acquaint me with your *direct* and *positive* observations. What, Sir! has it been possible for you in a few weeks to delve into the depths of the healthy and the diseased organization! to go through the whole labyrinth of functions implicated in the questions. It is more than miraculous; despite my good will, I cannot believe it, unless you prove that you are

a *prophet* in communication with some deity. Shall I
tell you what I really think? It is that you have studied these matters neither *directly* nor *indirectly*, and
that it belongs to me to tell you *that you do not understand woman; that you do not know the first word of
the question.* Your five or six *purely* moral and intellectual autopsies prove only one thing; namely, your
inexperience in physiology. You have naïvely mistak-
en the scalpel of your imagination for that of science.

With regard to autopsies, you tell me that you are
awaiting my promised work, in order to make mine. It
would be doubtless a great honor to be stretched on
your dissecting table in such good company as you
promise me, but the instruction of my future readers
does not permit me to enjoy this satisfaction. I shall
not send my book to press until your own shall have ap
peared, for I, too, intend to make your autopsy; dissect
me therefore now; I promise you on my side that I
will perform my duty conscientiously, properly and del-
icately.

" Woman," you say, " being weaker than man with
respect to *muscular force*, is not less inferior to him with
respect to INDUSTRIAL, ARTISTIC, PHILOSOPHICAL AND
MORAL POWER ; so that if the condition of woman in
society be regulated, as you demand for her, *by the
same justice as the condition of man*, it is all over with
her ; she is a slave."

Terrible man, you will be then always inconsistent,
you will always contradict yourself and facts !

What do you hold as the basis of right ? *The simple
quality of being human*; everything that distinguishes
individuals disappears before right. Well ! even though
it were true that women were inferior to men, would

it follow that their rights were not the same? According to you, by no means, if they form a part of the human species. There are not two kinds of justice, there is but one; there are not two kinds of right, there is but one in the absolute sense. The recognition and respect of individual autonomy in the lowest of human beings as well as in the man and woman of genius is the law which should preside over social relations; must a woman tell you this!

Let us now examine the value of your series of *man and woman*.

With respect to the reproduction of the species, they form a series; this is beyond dispute.

As to the rest, do they form a series? No.

If it were a law that woman is *muscularly* weaker than man, the strongest woman would be weaker than the weakest man; facts demonstrate the contrary daily.

If it were a law that women are inferior to men in *industrial power*, the most skillful woman would be inferior in industrial pursuits to the least skillful man; now facts demonstrate daily that there are women who are excellent manufacturers and excellent managers; men who are unskilled in and unsuited to this kind of pursuits.

If it were a law that women are inferior to men in *artistic power*, the best female artist would be inferior to the most indifferent male artist; now facts daily demonstrate the contrary; there are more great female than male tragedians; many men are mediocre in music and painting, and many women, on the other hand, remarkable in both respects, etc., etc.

What follows from all this? That your series is false, since facts destroy it. How did you form it? The pro-

cess is a curious study. You chose a few remarkable
men, in whom, by a convenient process of abstraction,
you beheld *all* men, even to cretins; you here took a
few women, without taking into account in the slightest
degree any differences of culture, instruction, and surroundings, and compared them with these eminent men,
taking care to forget those that might have embarrassed
you ; then, deducing generals from particulars, creating
two entities, you drew your conclusions. A strange
manner of reasoning, truly ! You have fallen into the
mania of *imposing rules on Nature, instead of studying
Nature's rules*, and deserve that I should apply your
own words to you : " The greatest part of the philosophical aberrations and chimeras have arisen from attributing to logical series *a reality that they do not possess, and endeavoring to explain the nature of man by
abstractions.*"

Still, if this were to strengthen your doctrines concerning the *basis* of right, it might be comprehended ;
but it is to overthrow them !

You transform yourself into a Sphinx, to propose to
me a riddle. " What is that right," you say, " *which
is not justice, and which, notwithstanding, would not
exist without it*, which presides over the relations of
both sexes, the *jus strictum* governing only individuals
of the same sex. If you divine it, you will have given
me the cause."

It is not necessary to be *the great Apollo*, to divine
that it is the *right of grace, of mercy*, towards an inferior that is not armed with strict right.

If I have divined rightly, you have simply begged
the question by supposing *that resolved which I dispute*.
I maintain that there is only one *right*, that *one single*

right presides over the rights of individuals and of sexes, and that the right of mercy belongs to the domain of sentiment.

You wish it proved that the new emancipators of woman are the most elevated, the broadest, and the most progressive minds of the age. Rejoice, your wish is accomplished: a simple comparison between them and their adversaries will prove it to you.

The emancipators, taking woman in the cradle of humanity, see her marching slowly towards civil emancipation. The intelligent disciples of progress, they wish, by extending a fraternal hand to her, to aid her in fulfilling her destiny.

The non-emancipators, denying the historical law, regardless of the progressive and parallel movement of the populace, woman, and the industrial arts towards affranchisement, wish to thrust her back far beyond the Middle Age, to the days of Romulus and the Hebrew patriarchs.

The emancipators, believing in individual autonomy, respecting it, and recognizing it in woman, wish to aid her to conquer it. Judging of the need that a free being has of liberty by the need that they have of it themselves, they are consistent.

The non-emancipators, blinded by pride, perverted by a love of dominion as unbridled as unintelligent, desire liberty only *for themselves*. These egotists, so suspicious of those that menace their own freedom, wish half the human species to be in their chains.

The emancipators have enough heart and ideality to desire a companion with whom they can exchange sentiment and thought, and who can improve them in some respects and be improved by them in others; they love and respect woman.

The non-emancipators, without ideality, without love, chained to their senses and their pride, despise woman; and wish to have in her only a *female, a servant, a machine to produce young ones.* They are *males, they are not yet men.*

● The emancipators desire perfection of the species, in a three-fold point of view : physical, moral, and intellectual. They know that races cannot be improved without selecting and perfecting the mothers.

The non-emancipators are bent upon something quite different from the improvement of the species : let their children be lacking in intelligence, malicious, ugly, or deformed ; they think much less of this than of being *masters.* Do they know enough of physiology to have reflected that the faculties *depend on organization,* that organization is capable of modification, that modifications are transmitted, that woman has a great share in this transmission, a greater share, perhaps, than that of man ? It is therefore *essential* to place her in a condition to perform this great function in the manner most useful to humanity.

The emancipators desire humanity to go forward, to vibrate no longer between the past and the future; they know the influence that women possess, first over children, then over men ; they know that woman cannot serve progress *unless she finds it to her interest to do so ;* that she will find it so only through liberty ; that she will love it only if her intellect is elevated by study, and her heart purified from the petty selfishness of home by the predominating love of the great human family. As they desire the end sincerely, they sincerely desire the means ; so long as half the human race shall labor as it is doing to destroy the edifice constructed by *a few members* of the other half; so long as half the human race, *the one that secretly governs the other*, shall have its face turned towards the past, the landmarks that point to the future will be threatened with being torn up. Do you consider it a crime in the emancipators to comprehend this, to seek to conjure down the peril ; and do you consider a virtue in the non-emancipators the foolish pride that places a cataract over their eyes ?

A few words more, and I shall have done. You would rather, you say, that I should not assume castigating airs with you. But have you really the right to complain of it, you who have constituted yourself the chief whipper-in of the economists and the socialists ? I shall never go so far towards you as you have gone towards them. You must resign yourself to my abrupt, sometimes harsh style. I am implacable towards whatever appears to me false and unjust ; and were you my brother, I should not war against you less sharply ; before all ties of affection and family, should come the love of justice and humanity.

I owe now to my readers and to you, sir, the exposition of the thesis that I undertake to sustain ; for the phrase, *the emancipation of women* has been, and is, quite variously interpreted.

With respect to *right*, man and woman are equal, whether the equality of faculties be admitted or rejected.

But for a truth to be useful, it must be adapted to the surroundings into which we seek to introduce it.

Absolute right being recognized, the practice of it remains. In practice, I see two kinds of rights : woman is ripe for the exercise of one of them ; but I acknowledge that the practice of the second would be at present dangerous, by reason of the education that the majority of them have received. You comprehend me, without making it necessary for me to explain myself more clearly in a Review in which social and political subjects are interdicted.

The directors of the *Revue* having informed me that my adversary refused to continue the discussion, I made the following recapitulation of his creed, concerning the rights and nature of woman.

To the editors of the *Revue* *Philosophique et Religieuse :*

You inform me that M. Proudhon will not reply to the questions that I have put to him ; I have neither the means nor the wish to constrain him to do so. I shall not inquire into the motives of his determination ; my business now is only to make an exposition of his creed, which may be summed up in this wise :

" I believe that between man and woman, there is a separation of the same nature as that which the difference of race places between animals ;

" I believe that, by nature and by destination, woman is neither associate, nor functionaay, nor citizen ;

" I believe that, in the social workshop, she is, until her marriage, only apprentice, at most under-superintendent ;

" I believe that she is a minor in the family, art, science, manufactures, and philosophy, and that she is *nothing* in the commonwealth ;

" I believe that she can only be housewife or courtesan ;

" I believe that she is incapable of understanding and of governing herself ;

" I believe firmly that the basis of the equality of rights is in the simple quality of being human ; now, woman being unable to have rights equal to those of man, I affirm that she does not belong to the human species."

Is Proudhon conscious how far his creed is in opposition to science, to facts, to the law of progress, to the tendencies of our own age, and does he dare to attempt to justify it by proofs ?

Does he feel that this creed classes him among the abettors of the dogmatism of the Middle Age, and does he recoil before such a responsibility ?

If this were the case, I should praise him for his prudent silence, and it would be my warmest desire that he should keep it forever on the question that divides us. To treat a subject, it is necessary to love and understand it ; I dare not say that Proudhon does not love woman, but I do affirm that he does not understand her ; he sees in her nothing more than the female of man ; his peculiar organization seems to render him unfit for the investigation of such a subject. He promises, in the work that he is preparing, to treat of the sphere and the rights of women ; if his doctrine has for its basis the paradoxical affirmations of his creed, I hope that he will this time take pains to rest them at least upon the semblances of proofs, which I shall examine with all the attention of which I am capable.

By shrinking from discussion, he cannot escape my criticism.

The two studies of Proudhon are simply the development of this creed.

I promised to dissect the author ; therefore, I shall do so.

Let me not be reproached with being pitiless; Proudhon has deserved it.

Let me not be reproached with being a reasoning machine; with such an adversary, one should be nothing else.

Let me not be reproached with being harsh; Proudhon has shown a harshness and injustice with respect to women, even the most illustrious, that exceed all bounds. If I am harsh, I will endeavor on my part not to be unjust.

I

Well, M. Proudhon, you have sought war with women! War you shall have.

You have said, not without reason, that the Comtois are an obstinate race; now, I am your countrywoman; and as woman generally carries virtues and failings farther than man, I intend to outdo you in obstinacy.

I have raised the banner under which your daughters will one day take shelter if they are worthy of the name they bear; I will hold it with a firm hand and will never suffer it to be struck down; against such as you, I have the heart and claws of a lioness.

You begin by saying that you by no means desired to treat of the inequality of the sexes, but that half a dozen insurgent women with ink-stained fingers having defied you to discuss the question, you will establish by facts and documents the *physical, intellectual and moral inferiority of woman;* that you will prove that her emancipation is the same thing as her prostitution, and will take her defence in hand against the rambling talk of a few impure women whom sin has rendered mad. — *Vol.* III., p. 337.)

I alone, by shutting you up in a circle of contradictions, have dared defy you to discuss the question; I sum up, therefore, in my own person, the few impure women whom sin has rendered mad.

Insults of this sort cannot touch me; the esteem, the regard, the precious friendship of eminently respectable men and women suffice to reduce unworthy insinuations to naught. I should not notice them, with such contempt do they inspire me, were it not necessary to tell you that the time has gone by when one might hope to stifle the voice of a woman by attacking her purity.

If you do not ask the man who demands his rights and seeks to prove their legitimacy, whether he is upright, chaste, etc., no more have you the right to ask the question of the woman who makes the same claim.

Were I therefore so unfortunate as to be the vilest of mortals as regards chastity, this would not at all lessen the value of my claim.

I greatly dislike any justification, but I owe it to the sacred cause that I defend, I owe it to my friends, to tell you that the moral education which my sainted, lamented mother gave me, together with scientific studies, serious philosophy, and continual occupation, have kept me in what is commonly called the right path, and have strengthened the horror that I feel for all tyranny, whether it be styled man or temperament.

You accuse your biographer of having committed an indignity in directing an accusation against a woman, because this woman was your wife; do you not commit an indignity yourself in insulting many others?

And if you blame those who calumniate the morals of Proudhon because he is not of their opinion, in what light do you think that men will regard your calumni-

ous insinuations against women, because they do not
think like you?

You claim that we have no morality, because we lack
respect towards the dignity of others; who has set us
this detestable example more than you? You, who style
yourself the champion of the principles of '89 — who
are the men and women whom you attack?

They who are in different degrees, and from different
stand points, in favor of these principles.

Your anger has no bounds against George Sand, our
great prose writer, the author of the bulletins of the republic of '48. You depreciate Madame de Staël, whom
you have not read, and who was in advance of most of
the masculine writers of her epoch.

Two scaffolds are erected, two women mount there-
on: Madame Roland and Marie Antoinette. I, a woman, will not cast insult on the decapitated queen, dy-
ing with dignity and courage; no, I bow before the
block, whatever head may lay on it, and wipe away my
tears. But, Marie Antoinette died the victim of the
faults that her princely education had caused her to commit against the modern principles; while Madame Roland, the chaste and noble wife, died for the revolution,
and died blessing it.

Whence comes it that you greet the queen with your
sympathies, while you have nought but words of blame
and contempt for the revolutionist? And the men that
belong to the great party of the future, how do you
style them?

The Girondins, *effeminate;*

Robespierre and his adherents, *eunuchs;*

The gentle Bernardin de St. Pierre, *effeminate;*

M. Legouvé and those who think like him concerning the emancipation of women, *effeminate;*

M. de Girardin, *absurd;*

Béranger, a pitiable author, and effeminate; Jean Jacques, not only the prince of *effeminates,* but *the greatest enemy of the people and the revolution* — he who was evidently the chief author of our " French Revolution."

Are we not justified in asking you, whether you are for or against the Revolution ?

M. Proudhon, you have forfeited your right to all consideration, since you have none for those who have neither offended you or offered you provocation, those who have never pretended to reduce you to servitude ; men have lacked courage; they ought to have stopped you when you began to descend to insulting personalities ; what they have not done, I, a woman, will do, fearing nothing, or no one, except my own conscience.

Proudhon, the greatest enemy of the people, is the writer who, treading under foot reason and conscience, science and facts, calls to his aid all the ignorance, all the despotism of the past, to mislead the spirit of the people with respect to the rights of half the human species.

Proudhon, the greatest enemy of the revolution, is he who shows it to women as a toy ; who detaches them from its holy cause by confounding it with the negation of their rights ; who attacks and vilifies the advocates of progress ; who dares, in fine, in the name of the principles of general emancipation, to proclaim the social annihilation and the conjugal servitude of one entire half of humanity.

Behold the enemy of the people and of the revolution !

II.

I had proceeded thus far in my reply when, pausing to take breath and to reflect, I grew calm.

What! said I to myself, have I then no more sense than to take in earnest that shapeless thing honored by the name of theory by the good people who are so bewildered by the noise of Proudhon's drum and tamtam that they see stars at noon-day and the sun at midnight? Let me be calm, let me not give to the affair more importance than it possesses; and since I must set forth this thing to my readers, let me do it in a fitting tone. We will leave Proudhon to explain himself in his own words.

No sooner had I taken this good resolution, than I evoked M. Proudhon, and said to him in all humility: Master, I come to you that you may define for me the nature of woman, and also something of the nature of man.

PROUDHON. You do well, for I alone am capable of instructing you: listen then to me.

" The complete human being, *adequate to his destiny,* I speak of the physical, is the male, who, through his virility, attains the highest degree of muscular and nervous tension comporting with his nature and end, and thence, the maximum of action in labor and in battle.

" Woman is a DIMINUTIVE of man, lacking one organ to become a pubescent youth.

" She is a *receptacle for the germs that man alone produces*, a place of *incubation*, like the earth for the seed of the wheat; an *organ inert* in itself, and purposeless with respect to the woman. Such an organization — *presupposes the subordination of the subject.*

"In herself, I speak still of the physical, woman has no reason to exist ; *she is an instrument of reproduction* which it has pleased nature to choose in preference to any other.

"Woman, in this first count, is inferior to man : *a sort of mean term between him and the rest of the animal kingdom.*" — *Justice,* Vol. III., etc.

And remark that I am not alone in my opinion :

"Woman is not only different from man," says Paracelsus, "she is different because she is lesser, because her sex constitutes for her one faculty less. Wherever virility is wanting, the subject is imperfect ; wherever it is taken away, the subject deteriorates. Woman lacks nothing in the physical point of view except *to produce germs.*

"Likewise, in the intellectual point of view, woman possesses perceptions, memory and imagination, she is capable of attention, reflection, and judgment ; what does she lack ?

"The power of producing germs, that is, ideas.—*Id.*

Now, follow my reasoning closely : It being admitted that *strength has some weight in the establishment of right ;* it being admitted, on the other hand, that woman is one third weaker than man, she will then be to man, in physical respects, as two is to three. Consequently, in the social workshop, the value of the products of woman will be one third less than that of the products of man ; therefore, in the division of social advantages, the proportion will be the same : *thus says justice.*

"Man will always be stronger and will always produce more," *which signifies that man will be the master, and that woman will obey, dura lex, sed lex."—Id.*

Besides, reflect that woman falls to the charge of man during gestation ; her physical weakness, her infirmities, her maternity, exclude her *inevitably* and *judicially* from all political, doctrinal and industrial direction.—*Id.*

We will now proceed to the second point. But first, mark well that woman, like all else, is autonomic ; woman, considered apart from the influence of man, is the thesis ; woman, considered under the influence of man, is the antithesis ; it is the thesis that we are now examining. Let us therefore approach the *thetic* woman in the intellectual relation.

We will first admit the principle that *thought is proportional to force ;* whence we have a right to conclude that man posseses a stronger intellect than woman. Thus we see man alone possessing genius. As to woman, she is nothing in science ; we owe to her no invention, *not even her distaff and spindle.* She never *generalizes*, never *synthetizes ;* her mind is anti-metaphysical ; *she cannot produce any regular work, not even a romance ; she composes nothing but medleys, monsters ;* " she makes epigrams, satire ; does not know how to express a judgment in set terms, nor assign its causes ; it was not she who created abstract words, such as cause, time, space, quantity, relation. *Woman is a true table rapping medium.*"— *Id.*

I have already told you that woman does not produce intellectual germs any more than physical germs ; her intellectual inferiority tells upon the quality of the product as much as upon the intensity and duration of the action and, as in this feeble nature, the defect of the idea results from the lack of energy of the thought, it may be truly said that woman possesses a mind *essentially* false, of irremediable *falsity.*

"Disconnected ideas, contradictory reasonings, chimeras taken for realities, unreal analogies erected into principles, a tendency of mind inclining inevitably towards annihilation : such is the intellect of woman."

Yes, woman " *is a passive, enervating being, whose conversation exhausts like her embraces. He who wishes to preserve entire the strength of his mind and body will flee her.*" — *Id.*
she would not emerge from the bestial condition."

" *Without man, who is to her prophet and word,*

AUTHOR. Calm yourself, Master, and tell me whether it is true that you have dealt harshly with literary women.

PROUDHON. Literary women! As if there were any! " The woman author does not exist ; she is a contradiction. The part of woman in literature is the same as in manufactures ; she is useful where genius is no longer of service, like a needle or a bobbin.

" By cutting out of a woman's book all that is borrowed, imitated, gleaned, and common-place, we reduce it to a few pretty sayings ; philosophy on nothing. To the community of ideas, woman brings nothing of her own, any more than to generation."

AUTHOR. Ah! I understand : you mean that, in the character of author, the woman of genius does not exist. But in this respect, among the number of men that write how many are there who have genius, and who never borrow from any one ?

PROUDHON. I grant that there are many effeminate men ; which does not alter the fact that woman would do better *to go and iron her collars* than to meddle with writing; for, " it may be affirmed without fear of calumny, that the woman who dabbles with philosophy

4

and writing destroys her progeny by the labor of her
brain and her kisses which savor of man; the safest
and most honorable way for her is to renounce home
life and maternity; destiny has branded her on the
forehead; made only for love, the title of concubine if
not of courtesan suffices her."— *Id.*

Let us now consider the *thetic* woman in the moral
point of view. We will admit in the first place the
principle *that virtue exists in the ratio of strength and
intellect,* whence we have a right to conclude that man
is more virtuous than woman. Do not laugh; it disturbs my ideas. I go further; man alone is virtuous;
man alone has the sense of justice; man alone has the
comprehension of right. Tell me, I pray you, " what
produces in man this energy of will, this confidence in
himself, this frankness, this daring, all these powerful
qualities that we have agreed to designate by the single
word, morality. What inspires him with the sentiment
of his dignity, the scorn of falsehood, the hatred of injustice, the abhorence of all tyranny? Nothing else
than the consciousness of his strength and reason."

AUTHOR. But then, Master, if man is all this, why
do you reproach the men of our times with lack of courage, of dignity, of justice, of reason, of good faith?
When I take up in minute detail the terrible charges
which you have fulminated against the masculine race,
I can make nothing of the meaning of the tirade you
have just uttered.

PROUDHON. Consider what you irreverently name a
tirade, as the necessary check to feminine immorality.

It is only to set forth the truth that of all the differences that separate her mind from ours, the conscience
of woman is the most trifling, her morality is of a dif-

ferent nature; what she regards as right and wrong is not identically the same as what man himself regards as right and wrong, so that, relatively to us, *woman may be styled an immoral being.*

" *By her nature she is in a state of constant demoralization,* always on this side or that of justice. . . . Justice is insupportable to her. . . . Her conscience is anti-judicial."

She is aristocratic, loves privileges and distinctions; " in all revolutions that have liberty and equality for their object, women make the most resistance. They did more harm in the revolution of February than all the powers of the masculine reaction combined.

" Women have so little judicial sense that the legislator who fixed the age of moral responsibility at sixteen for both sexes, might have delayed it till forty-five, for women. Woman's conscience is *decidely of no value till this age.*"

In herself, woman is *immodest.*

It is from man therefore that she receives modesty, " which is the product of manly dignity, the corollary of justice.

" Woman has no other inclination, no other aptitude than love.

" In affairs of love, the initiative belongs truly to woman."— *Justice, Vol.* III., pp. 364, 366.

AUTHOR. How many persons you will astonish, Master, by revealing to them that *modesty comes from man;* that consequently all the young girls who have been seduced, all the little girls whose corruptors and violators are punished by the courts, are but jades, who, through their initiative, have caused men to forget their character as inspirers of chastity !

You enlighten me, illustrious Master ; and I shall at once draw up a memorial to demand that all seduced and violated women and girls shall be punished as they deserve ; and that, to console the seducers, suborners, corruptors and violators, poor innocent victims of feminine ferocity, for having sinned against the *corollary of justice and the product of manly dignity,* rose-trees shall be forced to blossom, in order that the *maires* of the forty thousand communes of France and Algeria may crown them winners of the roses.

PROUDHON. Jest as you please ; woman is nevertheless so perverse in her nature, that, through inclination, she seeks men who are ugly, old, and wicked.

AUTHOR. Is not this somewhat exaggerated, Master ?

PROUDHON. (Forgetting what he has just said,) "Woman always prefers a pretty, finical puppet to an honest man ; a beau, a knave can obtain from her all that he desires ; she has nothing but disdain for the man who is capable of sacrificing his love to his conscience."

You see what woman is : " *unproductive by nature, inert, without industry or understanding, without justice, and without modesty,* she needs that a father, a brother, a lover, a husband, a master, a man, in fine, should give her that magnetic influence, if I may thus term it, which will render her capable of manly virtues, of social and intellectual faculties."— *Id.*

And as "all her philosophy, her religion, her politics, her economy, her industry are resolved in one word : Love ;

"Now shall we make of this being belonging wholly to love, an overseer, an engineer, a captain, a merchant, a financier, an economist, an administrator, a scholar, an artist, a professor, a philosopher, a legislator, a judge, an orator, the general of an army, the head of a State?

" The question carries its answer within itself." — *Id.*

I have laid down and proved my thesis, I am about to draw my conclusions.

" Since in economical, political and social action, the strength of the body and that of the mind concur and are multiplied, the one by the other, the physical and intellectual value of the man will be to the physical and intellectual value of woman as 3×3 is to 2×2, or as 9 to 4.

" In the moral, as in the physical and intellectual point of view, her value (that of woman,) is also as 2 to 3.

" Their share of influence, compared together, will be as $3 \times 3 \times 3$ is to $2 \times 2 \times 2$ or as 27 to 8.

" According to these conditions, woman cannot pretend to counterbalance the virile power; her subordination is inevitable. Both by nature, and before justice, she does not weigh the third of man."—*Id.*

Do you understand clearly?

AUTHOR. Very clearly. Your theory, if theory there be, is only a tissue of paradoxes; your pretended principles *are contradicted by facts*, your conclusions *are equally contradicted by facts;* you *affirm* like a revelator, but you *never prove*, as a philosopher should do. There is so much ignorance and senseless metaphysics in all that you say, that I should rather give you credit for bad faith than be compelled to despise you.

I have listened to you patiently while you have said to me, in saying it of all women:

You are inert, passive, you possess the germ of nothing;

You are a mean term between man and beast, you have no right to exist ;

You are immoral, immodest, imbecile, aristocratic, the enemy of liberty, equality and justice.

In your turn, endeavor to listen to me calmly, while I refute your allegations by facts, by science and by reason.

III.

There is, by your own confession, but one good method of demonstration ; that of basing every affirmation *upon well established facts, not contradicted by others, legitimately deduced.*

Let us see how you have followed this method.

In order to prove that the *thetic* woman, or woman considered apart from the influence of man, is such as you depict her, it is necessary that you should bring us face to face with an assemblage of such women, and afterwards, with another assemblage composed of men who have never been subjected to the influence of women, that we may verify for ourselves the native activity of the latter and the native inertness of the former. Have you had at your disposal, can you place at ours these proofs *de facto ?*

No ; and if you neither have them nor can procure them, what is your thesis, if not the illusion of a brain sick with pride and with hatred of woman ?

1. You say : man alone produces physical germs. Anatomy answers : *It is woman that produces the germ ;* the organ that performs this function in her, as in all other females, is the ovary.

2. You say : woman is a diminutive of the man ; she is an imperfect male ; anatomy says : *man and wo-*

man are two distinct beings, each one complete, each
one furnished with a special organism, the one as necessary as the other.

3. You say with Paracelsus, of whom this is not
the only absurdity: *where virility is wanting, the sub-*
ject is imperfect; where it is taken away, the subject
deteriorates. Mere good sense replies: the being can
only be incomplete or deteriorate *when it differs from its*
type; now the type of woman is feminity not *mascu-*
linity. . . . If, like you, I were a lover of paradox, I
would say: *man is an imperfect woman,* since it is the
woman that produces the germ; his part in reproduction is very doubtful, and science may even learn some
day to dispense with it. This is Auguste Comte's paradox; it is worth as much as yours.

To prove that woman is only an imperfect male, it is
necessary to establish by facts that man on being deprived of virility, finds the organs developed in him peculiar to woman, becomes qualified for conception, gestation, delivery, and giving suck. Now I have never
learned that any keeper of a seraglio had been transformed into an odahlic; have you?

4. You say: the organs peculiar to woman are inert, and purposeless with respect to herself; physiology
answers: the labor that these organs accomplish is immense; pregnancy and the crisis that terminates it are
incontestable proofs of this. The influence of these organs makes itself felt, not only on the general health,
but in the intellectual and moral order. Pathology, no
less eloquent, depicts to us the grave disorders produced
among women by forced continence, incontinence, the
excessive or perverted vitality of these organs which you
pretend are inert.

5. You say: woman is the soil, the place of incubation for the germ. Anatomy has told you in reply that the woman alone produces the germ. Read my reply to your friend Michelet on the subject of the resemblance of children and you will know what facts add to the answer of science. Your affirmation is no less absurd in the presence of these facts than that of a simpleton who should pretend that the soil in which the seed of the carnation or the ˙oak is deposited, has the property of causing rosebushes or palm trees to spring up.

From this *false* supposition that woman has not physical germs, you conclude that she is destitute of intellectual and moral germs. . . . And do you really dare accuse woman of thus *taking false analogies for principles ?*

Grant that when a man indulges in them thus wantonly, and mistakes them for principles, we ought to be more inclined to laugh than to be vexed.

6. You say that intellectually and morally, woman is in herself, nothing.

Now, if I am not mistaken, you admit that our functions have our organs for their basis, and you place the functions of intellect and morality in the brain, according to Gall, or similary.

Well, Anatomy tells you: in both sexes, the cerebral mass is similar in composition and, adds Phrenology, in the number of organs. Biology adds: the law of development of our organs is *exercise*, which supposes action and reaction, the result of which is the augmentation of the volume, consistency and vitality of the organ exercised.

The point in question then, to convince your readers

of the truth of your affirmations, is to prove that *the two sexes are subjected to the same exercise of the brain and to the same stimulus,* and that despite this identity of education, woman constantly remains inferior. Have you proved this? Have you ever thought of doing so? No. For if you had, your theory would have fallen to to the ground, since you would have been forced to acknowledge that man and woman cannot be alike, for we say to man from his infancy: resist, struggle;

To woman: yield, always submit.

To man: be yourself, speak your thoughts boldly, ambition is a virtue; you can aspire to everything.

To woman: dissemble, calculate your slightest word, respect prejudices; modesty, abnegation, such is your lot; you can attain to naught.

To man: knowledge, talent, courage will open every career of life to you, will make you honored by all.

To woman: knowledge is useless to you; if you have it, you will pass for a pedant, and if you have courage, you will be disdainfully called *virago.*

To man: for you are instituted lyceums, universities, special schools, high prizes; all the institutions through which your intellect can be developed; all the libraries in which is accumulated the knowledge of the past.

To woman: for you is history in madrigals, the reading of prayer-books and novels. You have nothing to do with lyceums, special schools, high prizes, anything that would elevate your mind and enlarge your views; a learned woman is ridiculous!

Man must display the knowledge that he often possesses but superficially, woman must hide what she really possesses.

Man must appear courageous when he is often but a

4*

coward; woman must feign timidity when in reality she is not afraid.

For where man is reputed great and sublime, woman is found ridiculous, sometimes odious.

If you had verified as you should have done, these diametrically opposite systems of training, the one tending to develop and ennoble the being, the other to degrade it and render it imbecile, instead of writing such absurdities, you would have said to yourself: woman must really have the initiative to resist the iniquitous system of repression that weighs upon her; she must have great elasticity to show herself so often superior to the majority of men in intellect, and *always in morality*.

I am curious to know what you males would be if subjected to the same system as we. Look at those who have not studied like you, and tell me whether they are not in general beneath uncultivated women. Look then at the men who have received a feminine education; have they not all the affectation, all the narrowness of mind of silly women?

Look, on the contrary, at those women who, through the wish of their teachers or their own energy, have been subjected to masculine discipline, and tell me, on your conscience, whether they do not equal the most intelligent, the firmest among you?

7. You say: intellectual force is in proportion to physical force. *Facts* reply: great thoughts, useful works, date from the period when the physical forces began to decline. *Facts* say also: the athletic temperament, which is the most vigorous, is *the least intellectual*: statuaries fully comprehend this, and sculpture Hercules with a large body and a small head.

8. You say that morality is in a direct ratio to physical and intellectual force combined. This pleasantry we will not refute; every one knows too well that these things have no relation, and that facts contradict your assertion.

9. You say: woman being one third weaker, should have in social labor one third the privileges of man.

Upon what elements do you base this proportion? In order to establish it, did you carry a dynamometer about through our districts and measure the strength of each man and of each woman?

But were your affirmation true, is naught but *strength* employed in labor? Then, great economist, what do we do with *skill?* What Samsonian muscles are needed to keep books, dispense justice, measure cloth, cut and sew garments, etc. !

And what is the end of civilization if not to shift the employ of our strength from ourselves to machinery that we may be at liberty to use only our intellect and skill?

10. You say: the infirmities, the weaknesses, the maternity of woman, and her aptitude for love, exclude her from all functions; she is *judicially and absolutely* excluded from all political, industrial and doctrinal direction.

She cannot be a political leader. . . . Yet history shows us numerous empresses, queens, regents and sovereign princesses who have governed with wisdom and glory, and have shown themselves far superior to many male sovereigns, unless Maria Theresa, Catherine II, Isabella and Blanche of Castile, and many others, are but myths.

Woman cannot be a legislator. . . . All the women whom I have just cited have been so, and many more beside.

Women càn be neither philosophers nor professors.

Hypatia, massacred by the Christians, taught Philosophy with luster ; in the Middle Age and later, Italian women filled chairs of ·Philosophy, Law and Mathematics, and excited admiration and enthusiasm ; in France, at the present time, the Polytechnists are making great account of *the geometrician*, Sophie Germain, who has taken it into her head to study Kant.

Woman cannot be a merchant or an administratrix. . Yet a great portion of the feminine population devote themselves to trade, or fill commercial positions. It is even admitted that the prosperity of commercial establishments is almost always due to the administrative genius of woman.

Woman cannot be an overseer, a foreman of a workshop. . . . Yet a host of women superintend workshops, invent, improve, carry on manufactures alone, and contribute, by their taste and activity, to thè increase of the national wealth and the industrial reputation of France.

Woman cannot be artist. . . . Yet every one knows that the greatest literary artist of our age is a woman, George Sand ; yet every one bows before Duchesnois, Mars, Georges, Maxime, Ristori, Rachel, Dorval ; yet every one pauses before the beautiful paintings of Rosa Bonheur ; yet since the revival of the fine arts, every century has registered many celebrated women.

We meet women everywhere, working everywhere, competing with man. . . . Yet Proudhon pretends that she can be nowhere, that she is excluded from every place absolutely and *judicially;* that if she governs and legislates like Maria Theresa, it is a contradiction ;

That if she philosophises like Hypatia, it is a contradiction ;

That if she commands an army and wins victories like the wife of the conqueror of Calais ; if she fights like Jeanne d'Arc, Jeanne Hachette, Madame Garibaldi and thousands of others, it is a contradiction ;

That if she is merchant, administratrix, superintendent of a workshop, like thousands of women, it is a contradiction ;

That if she is learned like Dr. Boivin, Sophie Germain, and many others, if she is a professor as are many among us, it is a contradiction.

The thesis sustained by Proudhon is, as we have just seen, contradicted by *science* and by *facts*. We ask ourselves whether it is possible that he is ignorant of the simplest notions of Anatomy and Biology ; we ask ourselves whether it is possible that he is so far blind as not to see that woman *is in reality* all that he pretends that she *absolutely and judicially* cannot be in his absurd and insulting theory ; and we conclude that the author is struck with gnorance and voluntary blindness.

Your reproaches are pleasant ; from the origin of society, man has been the master ; now, the ancient world sunk beneath the weight of slavery, usury, and the most shameless vices ; the modern world seems doomed to perish through inequality and its sad consequences, you yourself acknowledge that injustice *caused by your sex* exists every where in the world, and you say that man has judicial sense !

And, in the face of the inequality and oppression created by men, of their love of puerile distinctions, of the base deeds which they commit for a bit of ribbon, you accuse women of loving inequality and privileges !

They may love them, *like you*, but they are better than you, if not more just; they pray for the vanquished, you kill him!

I do not deny that women did much harm to the Revolution of February, for they are as intelligent as men, and have great influence over them. But what did this Revolution do for them, I pray?

Mark me well, you and all those who are blind enough, proud enough, despotic enough to resemble you, and remember what I say.

Woman is like the people : she desires no more of your revolutions, which decimate us for the benefit of a few ambitious babblers.

She will have liberty and equality for all men and women, or she will take care that no one shall have them.

We, Women of Progress, openly declare ourselves adversaries of whoever shall deny the right of woman to liberty.

Our sisters of the people, indignant at their exclusion from the popular assemblies, say to you : you have lured us long enough, it is time that this should end. We will no longer suffer ourselves to be ensnared by your high-sounding words of Justice, Liberty, and Equality, which are only false coin so long as they are applied to but half the human species. Do you wish to save the perishing world? Call woman to your side. If you will not do this, let us alone, insipid phraseologists; you are naught but ambitious hypocrites; we do not wish our husbands to follow you, and they will not.

IV.

PROUDHON. Let us consider woman in the antithesis. I have said that woman, considered apart from
masculine influence, is *nothing*.

AUTHOR. Yes, Master, because this is a pure creation of your thought.

PROUDHON. But woman, considered under the influence of man, is half of the human being, and *I sing lit-
anies in her praise*.

AUTHOR. Then you make woman re-enter humanity
through the door of Androgyny, in order to restore to
her her share of rights. . . . This is absurd ; no matter.

PROUDHON. Not so ! not so ! Woman have rights !
Never, so long as I am Proudhon ! She is indeed the
complement of man, who, without her, would be only
a brute.

AUTHOR. Ah ! my learned Master, how do these
things harmonize in your brain ? You have said hitherto that *woman owes everything to man*, you tell me
now that, without woman, man would be only a brute.
Is he not then, *adequate to his destiny*, as you have affirmed ? And if woman is nothing without him, and he
nothing without woman, I can see no longer upon what
you rest in making him the guide of this poor unfortunate.

PROUDHON. I need not explain myself, such is my
idea. I am simply comparing the respective qualities of
the sexes, and, as I find, they are *incommutable*.

AUTHOR. Ah ! I catch a glimpse of your meaning ; then you do not weigh them in the balance since
they are not alike, and, being unable to prejudice the
rights of woman, you leave her free.

PROUDHON.   What! what!   Woman free!   Horrible!   Are you resolved to throw me into convulsions?
Woman, however eminent may be her talents, should
serve man in silence and in all humility.

AUTHOR.   Frankly, Master, all this appears to me
nonsense, which, satanic as you are, you cannot yourself understand in the least.

PROUDHON.   Listen without interrupting me further,
if you wish to comprehend me.

" Without feminine grace, *man would not have
emerged from the brutality of the early ages ; he would
violate his female, smother his little ones, and give
chase to his fellows in order to devour them.*

" *Woman is the conscience of man personified,* the
incarnation of his youth, *his reason and his justice, of
all within him that is purest, most sacred, most sublime.*
— *Justice, Vol.* III., etc.

" The ideality of his being, she becomes to him a
principle of animation, a gift of strength, of prudence,
of justice, of patience, of courage, of sanctity, of hope,
of consolation, without which he would be incapable of
sustaining the burden of life, of preserving his dignity,
of enduring himself, *of fulfilling his destiny.*

" It is through her, through the grace of her divine
word, that man gives life and reality to his ideas, by
bringing them back unceasingly from the abstract to the
concrete.

" *The auxiliary on the side of justice,* she is the angel of patience, of resignation, of tolerance, the guardian of his faith, the mirror of his conscience, the source
of his devotion.   Vanquished, guilty, it is still in the
bosom of woman that he finds consolation and pardon."

Man has strength, woman beauty.   Through her

beauty, she should be the expression of Justice, "and
the attraction that draws us to it. . . . *She will be
better than man.* . . . She will be the motor of all
justice, all knowledge, all industry, all virtue." — *Id.*

Also, "beauty is the true destination of the sex; it
is its natural condition, its state."— *Id.*

Woman is the soul of everything; " without her, all
beauty fades; nature is sad, precious stones lose their
luster, all our arts, children of love, become insipid,
half of our labor is without value.

" If, with respect to vigor, man is to woman as 3 to
2, woman, with respect to beauty, is to man as 3 to 2.

" If, from the body, we pass to the mind and conscience, woman, through her beauty, will be revealed
with new advantages."— *Id.*

The mind of woman is *more intuitive, more concrete,
finer than that of man;* " it seems to man, and is in fact,
more circumspect, more *prudent*, more reserved, *wiser*,
more equable; it was *Minerva*, the protectress of Achil-
les and Ulysses, who appeased the fury of the one, *and
shamed the other of his paradoxes and profligacies;* it
is the Virgin whom the Christian litany calls *the seat
of wisdom.*

" The quality of the feminine mind has the effect of
serving the genius of man as a radiator, by reflecting
his thoughts at an angle which makes them appear more
beautiful if they are correct, more absurd if they are
false; consequently, of simplifying our knowledge and
condensing it into simple propositions, easy to seize upon
as simple facts, and the intuitive, aphoristic, imaged
comprehension of which, *while giving woman a share
in the philosophy and the speculations of man,* makes
their memory clearer to him, their digestion more easy.

. . . *There is not a man among the most learned, the most inventive, the most profound, who does not feel a sort of refreshment from conversation with women.* . .

" Popularizers are generally minds of the feminine type ; but man does not like to be subservient to the glory of man, and provident Nature has assigned this part to woman. .

" Let her speak, then, *let her write, even, I authorize and invite her to do so ;* but let her do it according to the measure of her feminine intelligence, since it is on this condition that she can serve us, and *please* us, *otherwise I withdraw the permission.*

" Man has strength ; but that constancy of which he boasts overmuch, he derives especially from woman. . . Through her he endures, and learns true heroism. *Upon occasion, she can set him the example of it ;* she will be, then, *more sublime than he.*

" Woman will render the law kind, and will convert this two-edged sword into an olive branch. . . . . There is no justice without tolerance ; now, it is in the exercise of tolerance that woman excels ; by the sensibility of her heart and the delicacy of her impressions, by the tenderness of her soul, by her love, in fine, she will blunt the sharp angles of justice, destroy its asperities, of a divinity of terror make a divinity of peace. Justice, the mother of Peace, would be only a cause of disunion to humanity, were it not for this tempering which she receives especially from woman." — *Id.*

And what chastity does woman possess ! With what constancy she awaits her betrothed ! What continence she observes during the absence or sickness of her husband ! Ah ! " woman alone knows how to be modest. . . . . Through this modesty, which is her most precious prerogative, she triumphs over the transports of man, and ravishes his heart."— *Id.*

And what wisdom in her choice of the companion of her life !

" She desires man to be strong, valiant, ingenious ; she turns from him if he is mincing and delicate."—*Id.*

Now, my unloved, indocile, and very irreverent disciple, let us recapitulate.

Woman, with respect to physical, intellectual and moral beauty, is to man as 3 to 2 ; " thus it may be said, indeed, that between man and woman there exists a certain equivalence, arising from their respective comparison, in the two-fold point of view of strength and beauty ; if, by labor, genius, and justice, man is to woman as 27 to 8, in her turn, by graces of form and mind, by amenity of character and tenderness of heart, she is to man as 27 to 8. . . . But these respective qualities are incommutable, cannot be the subject of any contract. . . .

" Now, as every question of preponderance in the government of human life is within the jurisdiction either of the economical order, or of the philosophical or judicial order, it is evident that superiority of beauty, even of that which is intellectual and moral, cannot create a compensation for woman, whose condition is thus made fatally subordinate."— *Id.*

Do you understand me now ?

AUTHOR. I understand that this is pure sophistry, a thing easily demonstrated ; that if your *thesis* is absurd, your *antithesis*, however complimentary it may be, is quite as much so ; that you have piled contradictions upon contradictions, and that it is a sad spectacle to me to see so strong and fine an intellect as yours abandon itself to such practices.

You shall judge for yourself whether my reproaches
and regrets are well founded.

In the *Thesis* you say : man alone is in himself intelligent and just, he alone is adequate to his destiny.
Woman has no reason for existing; without man, she
would not emerge from the bestial condition.

In the *Antithesis :* without woman, who is the principle of animation of man, the motive power of all science, of all art, of all industry, of all virtue — without
woman, who renders justice possible, thought compre-
hensible and applicable, man, far from being in himself
just, intelligent, a worker, would be but a brute, *who
would violate his female, strangle his little ones, and
pursue his fellow men in order to devour them.*

What follows from these divergent affirmations ?
That if woman alone is inadequate to her destiny, man
alone is inadequate to his, and that the adequateness of
both is caused by the synthesis of their respective qualities.

It also follows, by your own admission, that man
receives as much from woman as she receives from him,
since, if he rescues her from the bestial state, she rescues him from the state of brute ferocity.

It follows, lastly, by your own admission, that there
is equivalence between the respective qualities of the
two sexes.   Only you pretend that these qualities cannot be measured by each other, and cannot therefore be subject for contract, and that the qualities of
man being more important to the social state than those
of woman, the latter should be subordinated to the
former.

Tell me, is there commutability between the qualities
that distinguish men from each other ?

Between the man of genius and the humble rag-picker?

Between the philosopher who elevates the human mind and the porter who does not even know how to read?

Between the brain that discovers a great natural law and the one that reflects on nothing?

To answer affirmatively is impossible: for we only compare things of the same nature.

Now, if there can be no commutability between individuals so different, is there not, according to your system, subject for social contract between them?

Why then do you claim that these men should be *equal socially?*

Why then do you admit that they may associate things in a private contract which cannot be subjected to a common measure?

There is no need to be learned in philosophy or economy to know *that any contract whatsoever is an admission of personal insufficiency;* that we would not enter into partnership with others if we could dispense with them; and that in general the design of the contracting parties is *to establish commutability where it has not been established by the nature of things.*

To a common work, one brings his idea, another his hands, a third, his money, a fourth, custom: if each of the parties had had all these combined, no one would have thought of forming a partnership: a happy insufficiency brought them together, and caused them to establish equivalence between the shares of capital which could not be subjected to a common measure.

Were it true, therefore, that the qualities of the sexes differ as you pretend, then, as through this same difference, they are *equally* necessary to the collective work, they are *essentially* subject to contract, and *equivalent.*

But do they differ as you say? You know the answer of *science* and *facts.* We will not return to it. All your distinctions of beauty and strength are only imaginary classifications. We all know that of eighteen millions of Frenchmen, at the present time, we have a few men of genius, absorbed in specialties, a few more men of talent, perhaps not four philosophers, mediocrities in abundance, and an immense host of cyphers. It is mockery, therefore, to establish the right of prepotency of a sex from qualities which, on the one hand, do not exist in each of its members, and, on the other, are often found in the highest degree in the sex which it is claimed to reduce to subjection.

Besides, did your sex possess the qualities which you ascribe to it, to the exclusion of mine; since, by your admission, there would be neither civilization, nor science, nor art, nor justice, without the qualities you term peculiar to woman; and since, without these qualities, man would be only a brute and an anthropophagus, it thence follows that woman is *at least* the equivalent of man, if not his superior.

Let us now notice a few of your contradictions.

1st *Thesis.* Woman is a sort of mean term between man and the rest of the animal kingdom.

Antithesis. No; woman is the idealisation of man, in that which is purest and most sublime in him.

2d *Thesis.* Woman is an inert creature, devoid of understanding, that has no reason for existing.

Antithesis. No; woman is the animating principle of man; without her, he could not fulfil his destiny; she is the motive power of all justice, all science, all industry, all civilization, all virtue.

3d *Thesis.* Woman does not know how to express an opinion in set terms, or to assign reasons for it; she has only disconnected ideas, erroneous reasonings; she mistakes chimeras for realities, composes nothing but medleys, monsters.

Antithesis. No; the intellect of woman is finer than that of man; she has a wiser, more prudent, more reserved mind; she is the foil of masculine ideas. She is Minerva shaming Ulysses for his paradoxes and profligacies; she is the seat of wisdom.

4th *Thesis.* Without the magnetic influence of man, woman would not emerge from the bestial state.

Antithesis. Without the magnetic influence of woman, man would be but a ferocious beast.

5th *Thesis.* The woman who philosophises and writes, destroys her progeny; she had better go iron her collars; she is good for nothing but to be concubine or courtesan.

Antithesis. Woman should participate in the philosophy and speculations of man, and popularize them by her writings.

6th *Thesis.* The conversation of woman exhausts, enervates; he who wishes to preserve intact the force of his mind and body, will flee her.

Antithesis. The conversation of woman refreshes the most eminent men.

7th *Thesis.* Woman has an infirm conscience; she is immoral, anti-judicial; she is worth nothing as to moral responsibility until forty-five years of age.

Antithesis. Woman is the mirror of the conscience of man, the incarnation of this conscience; through her alone justice becomes possible; she is the guardian of morals; she is superior to man in moral beauty.

8th *Thesis.* Woman is without virtue.

Antithesis. Woman excels in tolerance; through her, man learns constancy and true heroism.

9th *Thesis.* Woman is immodest: she takes the initiative in affairs of love.

Antithesis. Woman alone knows how to be modest; in principle, there are no impure women; woman calms the sensual passions of man.

10th *Thesis.* Woman prefers an ugly, old, and wicked man.

No; woman prefers a pretty, mincing puppet, a beau.

Antithesis. No; woman wishes man strong, valiant, ingenious; she turns from him when he is but a pretty, mincing puppet, a beau.

I might go on thus to a hundred, and then make a cross to begin another hundred. Can it be possible that you trifle in this manner with your readers?

PROUDHON. The contradiction is not in my thought, but only in the terms. The woman of my thesis is she who has not been subjected to masculine magnetism, to which the woman of my antithesis, on the contrary, has been subjected.

AUTHOR. You would have reason to laugh at us, should we take such an answer in earnest. What! have you seen women outside of society, who would have taken men for monkeys?

Have you proved that in this menagerie, they think falsely, they write badly, they are worth nothing as to conscience until forty-five years of age?

That there, in the absence of men, the women take the initiative in affairs of love?

That the conversation of these women exhausts, enervates the men who are not there?

That these women prefer the old, ugly and wicked men, or the pretty, mincing puppets, who are not at their disposal ?

If the woman of your thesis is the one who has not been subjected to masculine influence, why do you take the women whom you attack from among those who have been subjected to it ?

Your contradictions, Master, are genuine and fair contradictions. For you as for us, there is but one woman : she who lives in the society of man, who has, like him, faults and vices, and who influences him as much as she is influenced by him : the other has never existed except in the brain of mystics and of victims of hallucination.

But we will leave this.

I have been told that you have spoken of love : it would seem to me impossible, did I not know your audacity.

PROUDHON. I have spoken of it, as well as of Marriage.

AUTHOR. Well! let us make a little excursion into these two territories. We will first speak of Love.

V.

PROUDHON. Love! . . . It wearies and annoys me greatly. I have never yet been able to make my ideas agree on this subject.

I at first defined love : " the attraction of the two sexes towards each other with a view to reproduction," adding that this attraction becomes purified by the adjunction of the Ideal. I even made a most beautiful discovery with respect to this, namely : that there is a sexual division because it is impossible to idealize anything but the objective.— *Vol.* III.

AUTHOR. How you run on! Then all of the animal and vegetable species in which the sexes are separated have an ideal in love? An ideal in the brain of a horse or a mare may pass, since there is a brain; but where will you lodge that of the male and female flower?

PROUDHON. On my honor, I never thought of asking myself that question. We will return, if you please, to the definition of human love. I say, then, that love is an attraction given with a view to reproduction; notwithstanding, I think, also, that to love, properly called, progeny is odious. — *Id.*

AUTHOR. But this is a contradiction . . .

PROUDHON. Am I to blame for that! You know, that in my eyes, man and woman form *the organ of justice, the humanitary Androgynus.* Now I affirm that love is the moving power of justice, because it is this that attracts towards each other the two halves of the couple. It is through love, therefore, that the conscience of man and woman is opened to the knowledge of justice, which does not hinder it from being " the most powerful fatality by which nature could have found the secret of obscuring reason within us, of afflicting the conscience, and of chaining the free will."— *Id.*

AUTHOR. The moving power of justice, the sentiment which opens the conscience of the sexes to justice, and which forms the judicial organ, disturbs the reason and afflicts the conscience! But this is a contradiction.

PROUDHON. Once more, am I to blame for it? Love, sought for itself, renders man unworthy, and woman vile; and stop! " love, even when sanctioned by justice, I do not like." — *Id.*

AUTHOR. Have you not said that without the love inspired in man by the beauty of woman, there would

be neither art, nor science, nor industry, nor justice;
that man would be only a brute?

PROUDHON. Ah! I have said much more! . . .
This love, the motor of justice, the father of civilization, is, notwitstanding, *the abolition of justice*, which
exacts that it should be cast aside as soon as its office of
motor is performed. The impulse, the movement given,
it must be dispensed with. In marriage, it should play
the smallest part possible; " all amorous conversation,
even between betrothed lovers, even between husband
and wife, is indecorous, destructive of domestic respect,
of the love of labor and the practice of social duty." A
marriage of pure inclination is nearly allied to shame,
and " the father that gives his consent to it is deserving
of censure."— *Id.*

AUTHOR. A father deserving of censure because he
unites those who yield to the motive power of justice!

PROUDHON. Let young people marry without repugnance, that is right . . . But " when a son, a daughter, to satisfy inclination, tramples under foot the wishes
of the father, disinheritance is his first right and most
sacred duty."— *Id.*

AUTHOR. Thus love, the motor of justice, the cause
of civilization, the necessity for reproduction, is at the
same time a thing of shame which should be feared and
banished from marriage, and that, in certain cases, deserves disinheritance! . . . May the gods bless your
contradictions, and posterity pass lightly over them!

PROUDHON. I can say nothing more satisfactory on
the subject; but, let us talk of marriage; I am strong
indeed on that point.

Every function supposes an organ; man is the organ
of liberty; but justice exacts an organ composed of two

terms: the couple. It is necessary that the two persons that compose it should be dissimilar and unequal, "because, if they were alike, they would not be completed by each other; they would be two beings wholly independent, without reciprocal action, incapable, through this cause, to produce justice. . . . In principle, there is no difference between man and woman, except a simple diminution of energy in their faculties.

"Man is stronger, woman is weaker, that is all. . . . Man is the power of that of which woman is the ideal, and reciprocally, woman is the ideal of that of which man is the power."— *Id.*

Androgyny laid down, I define marriage to be: " the sacrament of justice, the living mystery of universal harmony; the form given by nature itself to the religion of the human race. In a lower sphere, marriage is the act by which man and woman, elevating themselves above love and the senses, declare their wish to be united according to the law, and, as far as in them lies, to pursue the social destiny, by laboring for the Progress of Justice.

"In this family religion, it may be said that the father is the priest, the wife the god, the children the people. . . . *All are in the hands of the father*, fed by his labor, protected by his sword, subjected to his government, *within the jurisdiction of his court*, heirs and continuers of his thought. . . . *Woman remains subordinate to man*, because she is an object of worship, and because there is no common measure between the force and the ideal. . . . Man will die for her, as he dies for his faith and his gods, but he will keep for himself the command and the responsibility."— *Id.*

In result, the spouses are equal, since there is com

munity of fortune, of honor, of absolute devotion ; "*in principle and practice* . . . this equality does not exist, *cannot exist.* . . . The equality of rights supposing an equilibrium between the advantages with which Nature has endowed woman and the more powerful faculties of man, the result would be that woman, instead of being elevated by this equilibrium, would be denaturalized, debased. By the ideality of her being, woman is, so to speak, beyond price. . . . That she may preserve this inestimable charm, which is not a positive faculty in her, but a quality, a manner, a state, she must accept the law of marital power : *equality would render her odious*, would be the dissolution of marriage, the death of love, *the destruction of the human race.*

"And the glory of man consists in reigning over this admirable creature, in being able to say : she is myself idealized, she is more than I, and, notwithstanding, would be nothing without me. . . . In spite of this or on account of this, I am and ought to remain the head of the community ; if I yield the command to her, she becomes debased and we perish."— *Id.*

Marriage should be monogamous, " because conscience is common between the spouses, and because it cannot, without being dissolved, admit a third participant."— *Id.*

It should be indissoluble, because conscience is immutable, and the spouses could not procure an exchange *without being guilty of sacrilege.* If they are obliged to separate, " the deserving one needs only to heal the wounds made in his heart and conscience, the other has no longer the right to aspire to marriage, but must be content with concubinage."— *Id.*

What do you think of this theory ?

AUTHOR.   Hitherto I have refused to believe in the god Proteus ; but on contemplating you, Master, I abjure my incredulity.

You appear to us first under the garb and form of Manou, and we discuss his physiology ;

You appear to us next, successively, in the shape and vestments of Moses, St. Thomas Aquinas, and St. Bonaventure; you are incarnated for a moment in Paracelsus;

Lastly, you put on the Roman toga, over which you wrap the ungraceful robe of Auguste Comte.

All this is too old, too unsightly for our age. . . . Have you really nothing better to give us than the resurrection of the Roman law at the glorious time when Cincinnatus ate his dish of lentils stark naked ?

PROUDHON.   What! do you dispute that marriage by *confarreation is not the masterpiece of the human conscience ?*

AUTHOR.   Do I dispute it ?   Yes, indeed, and many other things beside.   But tell me, what meaning do you give to the words *sacrament* and *mystery*, that sound so hollow and false from your lips ?

PROUDHON.   Despite all my explanations concerning marriage, there nevertheless remains a mystery with respect to it.   This is all I can tell you in elucidation. You must comprehend that "marriage is an institution *sui generis*, formed at the same time at the tribunal of human justice by contract, and at the spiritual tribunal by sacrament, and which perishes as soon as the one or the other of these two elements disappears."— *Id.*

You must also comprehend that " marriage is a function of humanity, outside of which love becomes a scourge, the distinction of the sexes has no longer any meaning, the perpetuation of the species becomes a real injury to the living, *justice is contrary to nature and the plan of the creation is absurd.*"— *Id.*

AUTHOR. The plan of the creation absurd, and justice contrary to nature without marriage! What does this mean in plain language?

PROUDHON. What! Is your intellect so feeble that it does not comprehend that, without marriage, there is not, there cannot be justice?

AUTHOR. Then marriage is necessary to all?

PROUDHON. No; but " all participate in it and receive its influence through filiation, consanguinity, adoption which, universal in its essence, in order to act, has no need of cohabitation. . . . In the animic or spiritual point of view, marriage is to each of us a condition of felicity. . . . Every adult, healthy in mind and body, whom solitude or abstraction has not sequestered from the rest of mankind, loves, and by virtue of this love, contracts marriage in his heart. . . . Justice, which is the end of love, and which can be obtained either by domestic initiation, by civic communion, or, lastly, by mystical love," suffices "for happiness in every condition of age and fortune."— *Id.*

And do not confound marriage with any other union, with concubinage, for example, " which is the mark of a feeble conscience." I do not however condemn the concubinary, for " society is not the work of a day, virtue is difficult to practise, without speaking of those to whom marriage is *inaccessible*."— *Id.*

In my opinion, it is for the interest of woman, of children, and of morals, that concubinage should be regulated by legislation. Every child should bear the name of the concubinary father, who should provide for his subsistence and for the expenses of his education;

" the forsaken concubine should also have a right to an indemnity, unless she has been the first to entèr into another concubinage."— *Id.*

But it is not from concubinage, but from marriage that all justice, all right proceeds. This is so true, that if you " take away marriage, the mother is left with her tenderness, but without authority, without rights : *she can no longer do justice to her son;* there is illegitimacy, a first step backward, a return to immorality."— *Id.*

AUTHOR. All that you have just said concerning love, marriage, justice and right, contains so many equivocations, errors, sophisms, and so much pathos, that nothing less than a huge volume -would suffice to refute, after first explaining you. We will content ourselves, therefore, with dwelling on the principal points.

VI.

1. The Androgynus, by definition, is a being combining the two sexes. Now marriage does not make of man and woman *a single being ;* each preserves his individuality ; your humanitary Androgynus is not therefore worth the trouble of discussion; it is only a fantasy.

2. Every organ supposes a function, it is true, but what *facts* authorize you to say that the married couple is the organ of justice ? Especially when you take the trouble to contradict yourself, in admitting that justice is produced outside of marriage ; that there is no need of being married to be just?

The organ of justice, like all other organs, is in each of us ; it is the moral sense which comes into action when the point in question is the appreciation of the moral value of an act, or to apply to our own conduct the moral science accepted by the reason of the age.

3. According to you, equilibrium is *equality; equality is justice :* there is, therefore, a contradiction on your part in exacting of two beings, endowed each with liberty, will and intellect, that they should acknowledge themselves *unequal* to produce *equality.*

4. To affirm, as you have done, that progress is the realization of the ideal through free will ; that, consequently, the ideal is superior to the reality, and that man progresses because he suffers himself to be guided by it ; then to affirm that woman is the ideal of man and that, notwithstanding, she is *less* and should *obey,* is a double contradiction. If the point from which you start be admitted, logic would exact that man should permit himself to be guided by woman. But what is the use of discussing a thing that is devoid of meaning to the intellect ? If man, according to you, represents in reality strength, reason, justice, woman being the idealization of man, would therefore represent the greatest strength, the loftiest reason, the most sublime justice. . . . Do you pretend to say this, you who affirm the contrary ?

5. To say that marriage is an institution *sui generis,* a *sacrament,* a *mystery,* is to affirm what ? And what enlightenment do you fancy that you have given us ? Are you fully sure of comprehending yourself better than we comprehend you ? I doubt it.

6. Can you demonstrate why, in an association between strong, intelligent men, and weak, narrow-minded men, justice exacts *equality,* respect for the dignity of all, and declares the slave *debased* who submits ; whilst in the association of man and woman, *identical in spe-*

5*

cies according to you, the woman who is always, according to you, the weak and narrow-minded being, would be *debased* and would become *odious* by equality?

Can you explain also how, in a couple which stands for the producer of justice or equality, this equality *would be the death of love and the destruction of the human race?*

·Grant that such a farrago of nonsense and contradictions presents as many unfathomable *mysteries* as your marriage.

We will say nothing of divorce : we leave it to modern reason and conscience whether the dissolution of morals and of the family, due in a great measure to the indissolubility of marriage, does not give cause that it should be granted. What reasons do you give, besides, to support your opinions? An absurdity: that the rupture of marriage is *sacrilege ;* an affirmation contradicted by facts : that conscience is immutable.

8. Between the bastard and his mother, there is no justice, say you. Your conscience is younger by two thousand and some hundred years than the modern conscience. In the work of reproduction, the task to be performed with reference to the new being, is divided between the parents. On the woman, as the more vital, more elastic, and more resisting, devolves the more perilous part of this task. You shall risk your life to form humanity from your own substance, says Nature to her. To the man it belongs to pay his debt to his children by erecting the roof under which they take shelter, by bringing the food which you elaborate or prepare for them. To him it belongs to accomplish his duty towards his sons by the use of his strength, as you accomplish yours by supplying them with your blood and your milk.

Your rights over the child arise, adds conscience, from his incapacity to take care of himself, from the duties which you fulfil towards him, from the obligation under which you are placed to form his reason and conscience, and to make him a useful and moral citizen.

Well, what happens most of the time, in cases of illegitimacy? That the father having weakly, cruelly, contrary to all justice, deserted his task, the mother performs double duty towards her children : *she is at once father and mother.*

And it is when this mother has a *double* right that you dare to say that she has *none !* that between her and her son there is no justice ! In truth, I should rather live among savages than in a society that thinks and *feels* like you.

A mother has an incontestable right over her child, for she has risked her own life to give it birth : the father acquires rights over it only when ever he fulfils his duty; when he does not fulfil it, he has no right; thus says reason. In this question, marriage signifies nothing. If I were illegitimate, and my father had basely abandoned me, I should despise and hate him as the executioner of my mother ; as a man without heart and conscience, a vile egotist ; and I should doubly love and respect her who had been at once my mother and my father. Such are the dictates of my conscience, my reason, and my heart.

9. What is your marriage, *the first form given by Nature to the religion of the human race,* in which woman is an idol who does the cooking and mends the stockings of her priest ?

What is this institution, in which man is reputed to

defend his wife and children with his sword, whom the law defends, even against him?

In which man is reputed to support by his labor those who often labor more than he, or who bring him a dowry?

The wife and children are under the jurisdiction of the tribunal of man! May the gods preserve us from this frightful return to the manners and customs of the patriarchs and Romans. Women and children are under the jurisdiction of the social tribunal, and it is safer for them: the French wife has not at least to fear that her Abraham will sacrifice her little Isaac, nor that her domestic despot, leaving the child on the ground, like the ancient Roman, will thus condemn it to death. Society has a heart and generous proctors who, happily, no longer see the family tribunal in the same light as Proudhon. It is true that our author is an Epimenides, awaking after a sleep of more than two thousand years.

I have finished, Master; have you anything more to say?

PROUDHON. Certainly. I have to speak of the sphere of woman. This sphere is " the care of the household, the education of childhood, the instruction of young girls under the superintendence of the magistrates, the service of public charity. We dare not add the national festivals and spectacles, which might be considered as the seed-time of love.

" Man is the worker, woman the housewife.

" The household is the full manifestation of woman.

" For woman, the household is an honorable necessity.

" As all her literary productions are always reduced to a domestic novel, the whole value of which is to serve, through love and sentiment, to the popularization of justice, so her industrial production is brought back in conclusion, to the labors of the household; she will never depart from this circle."— *Id.*

AUTHOR. Pardon my astonishment, Master, that woman, whose mind is *irremediably false*, who is *immoral*, who composes nothing but *medleys, monsters*, who *takes chimeras for realities, who does not even know how to write a novel*, knows how, notwithstanding, by your own admission, to write a novel in order to popularize justice through sentiment and love. She therefore comprehends, feels, and loves justice?

I remark next, that the cares of the household are *labor;*

That education is *labor;*

That the service of public charity is *labor*

That the arrangement and superintendence of festivals and spectacles presume varied *labors;*

That to popularize justice through a domestic novel is *labor;*

Whence it follows that woman is a *worker*, that is, a useful producer; she differs from man, therefore, merely in the kind of production; and we have only to ascertain whether the labor of woman is as useful to society as that of man. I charge myself, when you like, with establishing this *equivalence* by *facts*.

I remark, in the second place, that the education of childhood, the instruction of young girls, the service of public charity, the arrangement of festivals and spectacles, the popularization of justice by literature, do not form a part of the labors of the household; and that woman, therefore, is not *merely housewife*.

. I remark, thirdly, that our female superintendents, merchants, artists, accountants, clerks, and professors, are no more housewives than your male superintendents, merchants, artists, book keepers, clerks, and professors; that our female cooks and waiting-maids are no more housewives, than your male cooks, bakers, confectioners, and footmen; that, in all these functions, and in many others, women equal men, which proves that they are not less fitted than you for employments that do not pertain to the household, and that you are not less adapted than they to those that do pertain to it. Rude facts thus stifle your affirmations, and show us that woman may be *something else than housewife or courtesan.*

Lastly, Master, what is the position of all women relatively to all men?

PROUDHON. Inferiority; for the entire feminine sex fills the place with regard to the other sex, in certain respects, of the wife with regard to the husband: this proceeds from the sum total of the respective faculties.

AUTHOR. So there is neither liberty nor equality even for the woman who has not a father or husband?

PROUDHON. " The truly free woman is the woman who is chaste; the chaste woman is she who experiences no amorous emotion for any one, *not even for her husband.*"—*Vol.* III.

AUTHOR. Such a woman is not chaste: she is a statue. Chastity being a *virtue,* supposes the dominion of the reason and the moral sense over an instinct: the chaste woman, therefore, is she who controls a certain instinct, not she who is destitute of it. I add that the woman who yields herself to her husband without attraction, plays the part of a prostitute. I knew well that you understood nothing either of love or of woman!

Shall we, in conclusion, compare your doctrine con-

cerning the right of woman with that which you profess concerning right in general ?

PROUDHON. Willingly . . . since I cannot do otherwise.

AUTHOR. Do you admit that woman is identical in
species with man ?

PROUDHON. Yes, only her faculties are less energetic.

AUTHOR. I grant you this for the sake of discussion.
Expound your general theory concerning right, I will
apply it to woman, and you shall draw the conclusion.

VII.

PROUDHON. " The law regulating only human relations, *it is the same for all*; so that, to establish exceptions, it will be necessary to prove that the individuals
excepted are of superior order, or inferior to the human
species."— *Creation of Order in Humanity.*

AUTHOR. Now you admit that woman is neither
superior nor inferior to the human species, but is identical in species with man ; the law is therefore the same
for her as for man.

PROUDHON. I draw the contrary conclusion, *because
man is the stronger.*

AUTHOR. A contradiction, Master.

PROUDHON. " Neither figure, nor birth, nor *the
faculties*, nor fortune, nor rank, nor profession, nor talent, *nor anything which distinguishes individuals apart*,
establishes between them a difference of species : all being men, and the law only regulating human relations,
it is the same for all."— *Id.*

AUTHOR. Now, woman is in essence identical with
man ; she differs from him only in manners and quali-

ties which, according to you, by no means make her differ in essence; once more, therefore, the law is the same for her as for man.

PROUDHON. It is logical; but I conclude the contrary, *because man is the stronger.*

AUTHOR. A contradiction, Master.

PROUDHON. " Social equilibrium is the equalization of the strong and the weak. So long as the strong and the weak are not equal, they are *strangers,* they cannot form an alliance, they are *enemies.*"— 1st *Memoir on Property.*

AUTHOR. Now, according to you, man is the strong and woman the weak of an identical species; social equilibrium ought therefore to *equalize* them, that they may be neither strangers nor enemies.

PROUDHON. It is logical; but I claim that they should be *made unequal* in society and in marriage. Man should have the prepotence, *because he is the stronger.*

AUTHOR. A contradiction, Master.

PROUDHON. " From the identity of reason in all men, and the sentiment of respect which leads them to maintain their mutual dignity at any cost, follows equality before justice." — (*Justice, Vol.* III, etc.) All are born free: between individual liberties there is no other judge than equilibrium, *which is equality;* the identity of essence does not permit the creation of a hierarchy. — *Vol.* II, the whole of the 8th *Study.*

AUTHOR. Now, woman is in essence identical with man. She is born free; between her and man there is, therefore, no other judge than equality; it is not permissible, therefore, to establish a hierarchy between them.

PROUDHON. It is logical. But I conclude, on the contrary, that it is necessary to create a hierarchy between the sexes, and to give the prepotence to man, *because he is the stronger.*

AUTHOR. A contradiction, Master.

PROUDHON. " The dignity of the human soul consists in being unwilling to suffer any one of its powers *to subordinate* the others, to require all to be at the service of the collective whole; this is morality, this is virtue. Whoever speaks of harmony or agreement, in fact, necessarily supposes terms in opposition. Attempt a hierarchy, a prepotence ! *you think to create order, you create nothing but absolutism.*" — *Justice, Vol.* II.

AUTHOR. Woman, according to you, forms with man an organism, that of justice. Now, according to you, the two halves of the androgynus have different qualities, which are required to harmonize with each other in equality under pain of creating absolutism instead of order ; the feminine faculty is therefore required to form an equipoise with the masculine faculty.

PROUDHON. It is logical; but I conclude that the dignity of the humanitary androgynus lies in subjugating the feminine faculty and creating despotism, *because man is the stronger.*

AUTHOR. A contradiction, Master.

PROUDHON. " Justice is the respect spontaneously felt for and *reciprocally guarantied* to human dignity, in *whatever person* and whatever circumstance it may be found compromised." — *Justice, Vol.* I.

AUTHOR. Now, woman is a human being, possessing a dignity which should be respected and guarantied by the law of reciprocity ; therefore one cannot be wanting in respect to feminine dignity without being wanting in justice.

PROUDHON. It is logical; but although woman is a
human being, identical in species with man, and although I believe that there is no other basis of right
than equality, I nevertheless affirm that the dignity of
woman is inferior to that of man, *because he is the
stronger.*

AUTHOR. A contradiction, Master.

PROUDHON. " Right is to each the faculty of exacting from others respect for human dignity in his person," duty is " the obligation of each to respect this
dignity in another." — *Justice, Vol.* I.

AUTHOR. Now, woman being identical in species,
man possesses a dignity *equal* to hers; therefore she
should be respected in her dignity, that is, in her person, her liberty, her property, her affections ; this is her
right as a human being, and man cannot deny it without failing in justice and in his duty.

PROUDHON. It is logical. But I claim that woman
has not the right which my principles attribute to her ;
that man alone has rights, *because man is the stronger.*

AUTHOR. A contradiction, Master.

PROUDHON. " Liberty is an *absolute* right, because it
is to man what impenetrability is to matter, a condition
sine qua non of existence." — 1st *Memoir on Property.*

AUTHOR. Now, woman is a human being, she has
therefore an *absolute* right to liberty, which is her condition *sine qua non* of existence.

PROUDHON. It is logical. But I conclude, on the
contrary, that woman has no need of liberty ; that this
condition *sine qua non* of existence for our species, does
not regard one half of the species ; that man alone cannot exist without liberty, *because he is the stronger.*

AUTHOR. A contradiction, Master.

PROUDHON. "Equality is an absolute right, *because without equality, there is no society.*" — *Id.*

AUTHOR. Now, woman is a human and social being; she has an absolute right, therefore, to this equality, without which she would be but a Pariah in society.

PROUDHON. It is logical. But I nevertheless conclude from this that woman has no more right to equality than to liberty. That, although of the same species as man, and consequently amenable to the law of equality, nevertheless she is not amenable to it, and should be unequal and in subjection to man, *because he is the stronger.*

AUTHOR. Fie, Master! To contradict yourself thus is disgraceful to your reputation. It would be better to maintain that woman has not the same rights as man, because she is of a different species.

PROUDHON. Woman is bound to feel that she does not possess a dignity equal to that of man; in the association formed between them to produce justice, *the notions of right and duty shall be no longer correlative.* Man shall have all rights, and shall accept only such duties as it shall please him to recognize.

AUTHOR. Reflect that man, after having denied the dignity and the right of woman, will labor to stultify her more and more in the interest of his despotism!

PROUDHON. That does not concern me: the family should be immured: the husband is priest and king therein. If, as in the case with all liberty oppressed, the woman grows restive, we will tell her *that she does not know herself, that she is incapable of judging and ruling herself;* that she is a cypher; we will outrage her in her moral worth; we will deny her intellect and activity: and by dint of intimidating her, we will succeed in forcing her to be silent : for man must remain master, *since he is the stronger !*

AUTHOR.   Deny and insult us, Master, this does us no harm : the lords of the Middle Age employed this method with their serfs, your sires . . . we are now indignant at them.   Slaveholders employed and still employ this method with the blacks, and the civilized world is indignant at them, slavery is restricted, and is on the way to disappear.

Meanwhile, I point out your contradictions to my readers ; your authority over minds will be thereby lessened, I hope.

Those who claim, in accordance with the major of the preceding syllogisms, that you found right upon identity of species, an abstraction of individual qualities ; that you believe right and duty correlative ; that you desire equality and liberty, will be quite as nearly right as those who claim, in accordance with the conclusion of the same syllogisms, that you base right upon force, superiority of faculties ; that you accept inequality and despotism, deny individual liberty and social equality, and do not believe in the correlation of right and duty.

If it is painful to you to have fallen into contradictions so monstrous, believe that it is not less painful to me to be forced, in the interest of my cause, to point them out to the world.

Having taken in hand the cause of my sex, I was under obligations to parry your attacks by turning against yourself your allegations against us.

It was necessary to do this, not by denials and declamations which prove nothing, or by affirmations without proofs, according to your method of proceeding ; but by opposing to you science and facts ; by making use only of the rational method which you extol without employing it, by charging you often with contradicting yourself when proofs *de facto* would have demanded too much detail and time.

You accuse women of *taking chimeras for realities*. I have proved to you that you deserve this reproach, since your theory is in contradiction to science and facts.

You accuse women of *erecting unreal analogies into principles.* . . . I have proved that you have done so as well, in deducing from the *pretended* absence of physical germs in woman, the absence of intellectual and moral germs.

You accuse woman of *reasoning wrongly.* . . . I have brought you face to face with your own principles, that you might draw from them contradictory conclusions.

You accuse woman of creating nothing but *medleys, monsters.* . . . The anatomy of your theory proves that you know how to do so quite as well.

You accuse woman of lacking intellect, of want of justice, virtue, chastity. . . . I appeal from you to yourself, and you say positively the contrary.

Where you are fantastic, contradictory, I, *a woman*, appeal to logic.

Where you are wanting in method, I, *a woman*, employ scientific and rational method.

Where you contradict your own principles, I appeal to these same principles to judge and condemn you.

Which of us two is the more reasonable and more rational?

My modesty suffers, I acknowledge, at the thought that I have played the part of *Minerva shaming Ulysses of his paradoxes and·his profligacies.*   At last, this tiresome part is ended !

I have addressed so many harsh things to you in so firm and resolute a tone, that I should be sorry to quit you without a few friendly words coming from my heart. You ought to be fully convinced of my sincerity, for you see that you have to deal with a woman who shrinks from no one; who is never intimidated, however great may be her opponent, or whatever name he may bear. You may be my adversary: I shall never be your enemy, for I regard you as an honest man, a vigorous thinker, one of the glories of France, one of the great men of our Comté, always so dear to the heart of her children; lastly, one of the admirations of my youth. You and I belong to the great army that is assaulting the citadel of abuse, and endeavoring to mine and sap it; I do not shun this solidarity. Is it so necessary that we should fight? Let us live in peace; ·I can entreat it of you without stooping, since I do not fear you. Understand one thing that I tell you without bitterness: that you are incapable of understanding woman, and that by continuing the struggle, you will inevitably range her under the banner of the anti-revolutionists.

Your pride has set enmity between you and woman, and you have bruised her heel: no one would be more sorry than I to see her crush your head.

CHAPTER III.

What thought Auguste Comte, who died in September, 1857.

To solve this question, it is necessary first to divide the man into two parts; not as the wise king Solomon designed to divide the child disputed for by two mothers, but in thought, by making of him two distinct men; a philosopher and a revealer.

M. Comte, who denied and insulted his master, Saint Simon, is only the popularizer of his recently edited works : so much for the rational phase.

What belongs to him exclusively is a socio-religious organization, which cannot be the work of a healthy mind.

What belongs to him exclusively, is a heavy, dry, insulting style, arrogant to the point of being revolting, loaded and overloaded with adjectives and adverbs.

What belongs to him exclusively, are a few ideas that he has submerged in volumes, containing not less than from seven hundred and fifty to eight hundred pages, in small type. I do not advise you to peruse them, readers, unless in your heart and soul you believe yourself deserving of many years of purgatory, which you prefer to expiate on the earth . . . I do not know whether I ought to say above or below, since astronomy has reversed the positions of the material and spiritual worlds.

The disciples of Comte are divided into two schools: that of the Positivist Philosophers, and that of the Priesthood.

The first reject the religious organization of Comte, and are in reality nothing but the children of modern Philosophy, and very estimable adversaries of that nebulous thing which is called Metaphysics. We could not therefore have them in sight in this article; so, let not M. Littré and his honorable friends frown in reading us: we are about to find fault only with the high priest and his priesthood.

The doctrine of Comte concerning woman being connected with the whole of his religious system, let us first say a word about this system.

There is no God; there is no soul: the object of our adoration should be Humanity, represented by the best of our species. . . .

There are three social elements: woman, priest, and man.

Woman is the moral providence, the guardian of morals:

Had it not been for the wholly mystical love, I willingly believe, that Comte had for Madame Clotilde de Vaux, it is probable that woman would not have been the *moral Providence;* thanks to this love, she is nothing less than this. We will see that neither is she anything more.

Of a nature superior to that of man (in the opinion of Comte), she is nevertheless subject to him, in consequence of a philosophical paradox which we need not refute here.

The function of woman is to render man *moral;* a task which she can perform well only in private life; all social and sacerdotal functions are therefore interdicted her.

She should be *preserved from labor,* should renounce dowry and inheritance; man is charged with maintaining her; daughter, she is supported by her father or her brothers; wife, by her husband; widow, by her sons. In default of her natural maintainers, the state, *on the requisition of the priesthood,* provides for her wants.

Marriage is instituted for the perfecting of the married couple, above all, for that of the man: the reproduction of the species has so little to do with its end, that the progress of science permits us to hope that, some day, woman will be able *alone* to reproduce humanity, so as to realize and to generalize the hypothesis of the Virgin Mother. Then it will be possible to regulate human production, by entrusting to none but the most deserving women the task of conceiving children and bringing them into the world, especially members of the priesthood.

Divorce is not permitted, and widowhood is eternal for both sexes.

Such, in brief, is the Comtist doctrine concerning woman, marriage and procreation. As the reader might suspect us of malicious exaggeration, we entreat him to read attentively the following pages, emanating from the pen of the originator of the system.

According to him, women have never demanded their emancipation; the men who claim it for them are, after

Comte's usual courteous style, nothing but *utopists
corrupted by retrogression.* " All transitional ages,'
he says, " have given rise, like our own, to sophistica
aberrations concerning the social condition of woman.
But the natural law which assigns to the effective sex
an existence essentially domestic, has never been mate-
rially altered. . . . Women were then (in antiquity)
too low to reject worthily, even by their silence, the doc-
toral aberrations of their pretended defenders. . . . But
among the moderns, the happy liberty of the western
women permits them to manifest a decisive repugnance
which is sufficient, in default of rational ratification, to
neutralize these wanderings of the mind, *inspired by the
intemperance of the heart.*

" Without discussing unreal retrograde utopias, it is
of importance to feel, the better to appreciate real order,
that if women should ever obtain this temporal equality
demanded, without their consent, by their pretended
defenders, their social guaranties would suffer thereby
as much as their moral character. For they would find
themselves thus subjected, in the majority of occupations, to an active daily competition which they could
not sustain, while at the same time the practical rivalry
would corrupt the principal sources of mutual affection.
Man should support woman, such is the natural law of
our species."— *Politique Positive,* t. I.

" It is necessary to consider the just independence
of the affective sex as founded upon two connected conditions, its universal affranchisement from labor outside
the household, and its free renunciation of all wealth. . .

" Domestic priestesses of humanity, born to modify
by affection the necessary reign of force, they should
shun, as radically degrading, all participation in command."— *Id.* t. IV.

" The moral degradation appears to me still greater when woman enriches herself by her own labor. The continued eagerness of gain makes her then lose even that spontaneous kindness which preserves the other type in the midst of its dissipations.

" No worse industrial chiefs can exist than women." — *Caté. Pos.*

So ladies, ye who prefer labor to prostitution, who pass days and nights in providing for the wants of your family, it is understood of course that you *are degraded;* a woman ought not to do anything ; respect and honor belong to idleness.

You, Victoria of England, Isabella of Spain, — you command, therefore you *are radically degraded.*

M. Comte pretends that masculine superiority is incontestable in all that concerns the properly called " source of command . . . that the intellect of man is stronger, more extended than that of woman.

" A healthy appreciation of the universal order will make the affective sex comprehend how important *submission* is to dignity.

" The priesthood will make women feel the merit of *submission*, by developing this *admirable* maxim of Âristotle : *the chief strength of woman consists in surmounting the difficulty of obeying ;* their education will have prepared them to comprehend that all dominion, far from really elevating, necessarily degrades them, by depreciating their chief worth so as to expect from strength the ascendancy which is due to love alone." — *Ibid.*

Here are a few pages from the system of Politique Positive, t. IV., which are too curious not to interest the reader.

" The better to characterize feminine independence, I think it best to introduce a bold hypothesis, which human progress perhaps will realize, although it is my business neither to examine when nor how.

" If the masculine apparatus contributes to our generation only after a simple excitement, derived from its organic destination, the possibility may be conceived of replacing this stimulant *by another or several others, of which the woman would dispose at will.* The absence of such a faculty among the neighboring species cannot be sufficient to interdict it to the most eminent and most modifiable race. . . .

" If feminine independence can ever reach this limit, in accordance with the sum total of moral, intellectual, and even material progress, the social function of the affective sex will be found notably improved. Then all fluctuation between the animal appreciation which still prevails, and the noble doctrine systematized by positivism, would cease. The most essential production (that of our species) would become independent of the caprices of a perturbating instinct, the normal repression of which has hitherto constituted the principal obstacle to human discipline. Such a privilege would be naturally found transferred, with full responsibility, to the organs best fitted to its use, alone capable of guarding themselves from vicious impulses, so as to realize all the advantages that it permits."

Which means in good English, my female readers, that perhaps the time will come when you will create children without the co-operation of these gentlemen ; that this function will be confided to those among you who shall be most worthy of it, and that they will be held responsible for the imperfection of the product.

" Thenceforth," resumes the author, " the utopia of
the Virgin Mother will become to the purest and most
eminent an ideal goal, directly suited to sum up human
perfection, thus carried even to systematizing procreation, while ennobling it. . . . Success depends most of
all on the general development of the relations between
the soul and the body, its continued search (that of the
problem of fruitful virginity) will worthily institute the
systematic study of vital harmony, by procuring to it at
once the noblest aim and the best organs."— *Ibid.*

Translated : the study of the relations of the brain
with the body will lead us to discover the means of pro-
creating children without the co-operation of man ; this
is the noblest aim of this study, as the faculty of being
a virgin mother should be the ideal which the purest
and most eminent women should seek to attain.

" Thus," continues M. Comte, " I am led to represent the utopia of the Virgin Mother as the synthetic
résume of positive religion, all the phases of which it
combines."— *Ibid.*

Translation : To procreate children without the concurrence of man, *sums up positive religion, and combines all its phases.*

This may be very fine, but as to being *rational* and
positive — what do you think, readers ?

" The rationality of the problem," adds the author,
" is founded upon the determination of the true office
of the masculine apparatus, designed especially to sup-
ply to the blood an excitative fluid, capable of strength-
ening all the vital operations, whether animal or organic.
In comparison with this general service, the special use
of the fecundative stimulus becomes more and more
secondary in proportion as the organism is elevated. It

may thus be conceived that in the noblest species, this
liquid ceases to be indispensable to the awakening of the
germ, which may result artificially from several other,
and even from material sources, especially from a better
reaction of the nervous upon the vascular system."—*Ibid.*

All this would be possible, I grant, *if* the fluid of
which you speak, High Priest, had, above all, the general function which you attribute to it ;

If the reproduction of our species by the co-operation
of the two sexes were not a *law ;*

If we could preserve a species while destroying its
law ;

If facts did not contradict the possibility of the hypothesis.

Now, to place an *if* before a natural law and the phe-
nomena which are its expression, is only a gross absurdity : we explain laws, we do not reform them without
profoundly modifying the being that they govern ; we
do not destroy without destroying this being : for the
individual being is *the law in form.*

The author dwells as follows on the consequences of
the absurd hypothesis.

" Thence it may be conceived that civilization not
only disposes man better to appreciate woman, but aug-
ments the participation of this sex in human reproduction, which ought, finally, *to emanate from it alone.*

" Regarded individually, such a modification ought to
improve the cerebral and corporal constitution of both
sexes, by developing therein continued chastity, the importance of which has been felt more and more by universal instinct, even during irregularities.—p. 277.

" Considered domestically, this transformation would
render the constitution of the human family more in

conformity with the general spirit of sociocracy, by completing the just emancipation of woman, thus made, even physically, independent of man. The normal ascendancy of the affective sex would be no longer contestable with respect to children *emanated from it exclusively.*

" But the principal result would consist in perfecting the fundamental institution of marriage (the improvement of the married couple without sexual motive), the positive theory of which would then become unexceptionable. Thus purified, the conjugal tie would experience an amelioration as marked as when Polygamy was replaced by Monogamy : for we should generalize the utopia of the Middle Age, in which Maternity was reconciled with Virginity.

" Regarded civilly, this institution alone permits the regulation of the most important of productions, which can never become sufficiently susceptible of sytemazition, so long as it shall be accomplished in delirium and without responsibility.

" Reserved to its best organs, this function would perfect the human race by better determining the transmission of ameliorations due to external influences, both social and personal. . . . . Systematic procreation coming to remain more or less concentrated among the better types, the comparison of the two cases would give rise not only to valuable enlightenment, but also to an important institution which would procure to sociocracy the principal advantage of theocracy. For the development of the new mode would soon cause a non-hereditary caste to spring up, better adapted than the common populace *for the recruital of spiritual and even temporal chiefs,* whose authority would then rest on a truly *superior* origin, which would not shun investigation.

All these indications will suffice to show the value of the utopia of the Virgin Mother, destined to procure to Positivism a synthetic résume, equivalent to that which the institution of the Eucharist furnishes to Catholicism." — *Ibid.*

It is much to be feared, alas! that the disciples of this great man, however ardent seekers of *vital harmony* they may be, will never find.the *synthetic résume* of Positivism, the *equivalent* of the Eucharist: and it will be a great pity: to order children as we order shoes, and leave them on the mother's hands when they do not suit, would be very convenient.

And what, I ask you, will the future leaders of humanity do, if they can only obtain respect and obedience on the condition of proving that they are *sons of virgins?*

But we will not jest with so grave a personage as the High Priest of Humanity: we will only say in passing, that never was atheist seen to show himself more profoundly a Christian through contempt for works of the flesh. Hear what he says on page 286 of the work before cited:

" Useless to individual conservation, the sexual instinct co-operates only in an *accessory and even equivocal* manner to the propagation of the species. Philosophers truly freed from superstition should regard it more and more as tending above all to disturb the principal design of the vivifying fluid. But without waiting for the feminine utopia to be realized, we may determine, *if not the atrophy, at least the inertia of this cerebral superfœtation*, with more facility than is indicated by the insufficient efforts of theologism. While positive education will make the vices of such an instinct everywhere felt, and *will raise up the continued hope of its desuetude*, the whole final system ought naturally to institute a revulsive treatment with respect to it, more efficacious than Catholic austerities. For the universal aspiration of domestic existence and of public life will develop the sympathetic faculties to such a degree, that sentiment, intellect, and activity will always concur to stigmatize and repress the most perturbing of selfish propensities."

Despite all this *aspiration*, and all these stigmas, do not trust to it, High Priest! Be advised by me, use camphor, and plenty of it; scatter it everywhere as a certain Amphitryon scattered nutmeg.

It is in prevision of the excommunications hurled by you against this *vile*, this *useless* instinct, that Nature has been prodigal of camphor.

Upon the whole, you see, my female readers, that if M. Comte believes us weaker than man in body, mind, and character, in return, he believes us better.

We are moral providence, guardian angels: he dreams of affranchisement for us through the subversion of a natural law.

But meanwhile he places us under the yoke of man by exempting us from labor;

He rivets our chains by persuading us cajolingly to despoil ourselves of our property;

He says to us in the gentlest voice imaginable: never command: it would degrade you;

Your great strength is in obeying him whom *it is your destiny to direct.*

You will be naught in the temple, naught in the state ·

6*

In the family, you are domestic priestesses, the auxiliaries of the priesthood.

Three sacraments out of nine are refused you : that of destiny, because, for you, it is confounded with that of marriage ; that of retirement, because you have no profession ; lastly, that of incorporation, because a woman cannot, in herself, merit a personal and public apotheosis.

If you have been worthy auxiliaries, you shall be interred near those whom you shall have influenced, like their other useful auxiliaries : the horse, the dog, the cow, and the ass ; and mention shall be made of you when honors shall be paid to the member of humanity to whom you shall have belonged.

Shall we refute such doctrines ? No. Our answer to them finds a fitter place in the article devoted to M. Proudhon, who has drawn largely from the doctrine of M. Comte.

As to the priests who continue the teachings of their master, it suffices to refer them to what I said to M. Comte in the Revue Philosophique of December, 1855.

The women of the present time are in general intelligent, because they receive an education superior to that of their mothers. The majority of them devote themselves to an active life either in the arts or the trades ; men acknowledge them as their competitors in these, and even confess that they are superior in management. No man, worthy of the name, would dare contest that woman is his equal, and that the day of her civil emancipation is close at hand.

Women, on their side, more independent and more deserving, without having lost anything of their grace and gentleness, no longer accept the famous axiom :

man should support woman; still less do they accept the *admirable* maxim of Aristotle, fit for the slaves of the gyneceum. Be sure that every *true* woman will laugh at the raiment of clouds which you pretend to give her, at the incense with which you wish to asphyxiate her; for she cares no longer for adoration. She wishes to carry her intellect and activity unfettered into spheres suited to her aptitudes; she wishes to aid her brother, man, in clearing up the field of theory, the domain of practice; she claims that every human being is the judge of his own aptitudes; she does not recognize in any man or in any doctrine the right of fixing her place, and of marking out her road. Through the labor of war was the patriciate constituted; through peaceful labor was servitude emancipated; *through labor*, also, does woman claim to conquer her civil rights.

Such is what many women are, what they wish to be to-day; see if it is not madness to seek to revive the gyneceum and the atrium for these women, impregnated with the ideas of the eighteenth century, wrought upon by the ideas of '89 and of the modern reformers. To say to such women that they shall have no place in the state, nor in marriage, nor in science, nor in art, nor in the trades, nor even in your subjective paradise, is something so monstrous that I cannot conceive, for my part, how aberration could go so far.

You will no longer find an interlocutress to say: " that a woman can scarcely ever deserve a personal and public apotheosis . . . that views involving the fullest experience and the profoundest reflection are *naturally interdicted* to the sex whose contemplations can scarcely go beyond the circle of private life *with success* . . . that *the moral degradation of woman is still greater when she enriches herself by her own labor* . . . that there are no worse industrial chiefs than women. . . . " And if any woman behind the times should be so imbecile and immodest as to hold such language, all men of any worth whatever would regard her only with disdain.

But you, who wish to annihilate woman, from what principle do you draw such a consequence? That she is an affective power, you say . . . yes, but, as to that, man is such, likewise; and is not woman, as well as he, alike intellect and activity? By reason of a purely accidental predominance, can one half of the human species be banished beyond the clouds of sentimentality? And ought not all serious discipline to tend to develope, not one phase of the being, but the ponderation, the harmony of all its phases? Want of harmony is the source of disorder and deformity. The woman who is solely sentimental commits irreparable errors; the man who is solely rational is a species of monster, and the person in whom activity predominates is but a brute. Since you believe in Gall and Spurzheim, you know that the encephalon of the two sexes is alike, that it is modifiable in both, that all education is founded on this modificability; why has it never occurred to you that if man *en masse* is more rational than woman, it is because education, laws and custom have developed in him the anterior lobes of the brain; while in woman, education, laws and custom develop especially the posterior lobes of this organ; and why, having established these facts, have you not been led to conclude that, since organs are developed only in consequence of the excitants applied to them, it is probable that man and woman, subjected to the same cerebral excitants, would be de-

veloped in the same manner, with the shades of difference peculiar to each individuality; and that for woman
to be developed harmoniously under her three aspects,
she must manifest herself socially under three aspects?
Be sure, sir, your principle is thrice false, thrice in
contradiction to science and reason; in the presence of
the physiology of the brain, all theories of classification
fall to the ground: before the nervous system, women
are the equals of men: they can be their inferiors only
before muscular supremacy, attacked by the invention
of powder, and about to be reduced to dust by the triumph of mechanism.

I should say many more things to you, sir, were not
this critical sketch too long already; but imperfect
though it may be, having to my mind only the meaning
of a woman's protest against your doctrines, I shall
pause here.

CHAPTER IV.

LEGOUVÉ.

The inheritor of a name which commands respect, Ernest Legouvé, an elegant, eloquent, and impassioned author, has written a Moral History of Women, whence exhales a perfume of purity and love which refreshes the heart and calms the soul.

In every page of this book, we detect the impulse of an upright heart and lofty mind, indignant at injustice, oppression, and moral deformity. The author has deserved well of women, and it is with pleasure that I seize the opportunity of thanking him in the name of those who, at the present time, are struggling in various countries for the emancipation of half the human race.

What is the object of Legouvé's work? We will let him tell it himself.

" The object of this book is summed up in these words : to lay claim to feminine liberty in the name of the two very principles of the adversaries of this liberty: tradition and difference (of the sexes), that is to say, to show in tradition progress, and in difference equality.

God created the human species double, we utilize but half of it ; Nature says two, we say one ; we must agree with Nature. Unity itself, instead of perishing thereby, would only then be true unity ; that is, not the sterile absorption of one of two terms for the benefit of the other, but the living fusion of two fraternal individualities, increasing the common power with all the force of their individual development.

" The feminine spirit is stifled, but not dead. . . . We cannot annihilate at our pleasure a force created by God, or extinguish a torch lighted by his hand ; but turned aside from its purpose, this force, instead of creating, destroys; this torch consumes instead of giving light.

" Let us then open wide the gates of the world to this new element : we have need of it."

Then, examining the position of women, the author adds : " No history presents, we believe, more iniquitous prejudices to combat, more secret wounds to heal.

" Shall we speak of the present ?   As daughters, no public education for them, no professional instruction, no possible life without marriage, no marriage without a dowry.   Wives — they do not legally possess their property, they do not possess their persons, they cannot give, they cannot receive, they are under the ban of an eternal interdict.   Mothers — they have not the legal right to direct the education of their children, they can neither marry them, nor prevent them from marrying, nor banish them from the paternal house nor retain them there.   Members of the commonwealth, they can neither be the guardians of other orphans than their sons or their grand-sons, nor take part in a family council, nor witness a will ; they have not the right of testifying in the state to the birth of a child !   Among the working people, what class is most wretched ? Women.   Who are they that earn from sixteen to eighteen sous for twelve hours of labor? Women. Upon whom falls all the expense of illegitimate children? Upon women. Who bear all the disgrace of faults committed through passion? Women."

Then, after showing the position of rich women, he continues: " And thus, slaves everywhere, slaves of want, slaves of wealth, slaves of ignorance, they can only maintain themselves great and pure by force of native nobleness and almost superhuman virtue. Can such domination endure? Evidently not. It necessarily falls before the principle of natural equity; and the moment has come to claim for women their share of rights and, above all, of duties; to demonstrate what subjection takes away from them, and what true liberty will restore to them; to show, in short, the good that they do not and the good they might do."

The history of the past shows us woman more and more oppressed in proportion as we trace back the course of centuries. " The French Revolution (itself), which renewed the whole order of things in order to affranchise men, did nothing, we may say, for the affranchisement of women. . . . '91 respected almost all of the feminine disabilities of '88, and the Consulate confirmed them in the civil code."

This, in Legouvé's opinion was the fault of the philosophy of the eighteenth century, for " woman is, according to Diderot, a courtesan; according to Montesquieu, an attractive child; according to Rousseau, an object of pleasure to man; according to Voltaire, nothing. . . . Condorcet and Sieyès demanded even the political emancipation of woman; but their protests were stifled by the powerful voices of the three great continuers of the eighteenth century, Mirabeau, Danton, and Robespierre."

Under the Consulate, "feminine liberty had no more decided enemy (than Bonaparte:) a southerner, the spirituality of woman was lost on him; a warrior, he saw in the family a camp, and there required, before all else, discipline; a despot, he saw in it a state, and there required, before all else, obedience. He it was who concluded a discussion in council with these words: *There is one thing that is not French; that a woman can do as she pleases.* . . . Always man (in the thought of Bonaparte), always the honor of man ! As to the happiness of woman, it is not a single time in question (in the civil code.)"

It is in behalf of the weakness of women, it is in behalf of tradition which shows them constantly subordinate, it is in behalf of their household functions, that the adversaries of the emancipation of women oppose it. "To educate them is to deform them; and they do not want their playthings spoiled," says M. Legouvé, ironically. He then continues in a serious strain : "What matters tradition to us ? What matters history to us ? There is an authority more powerful than the consent of the human race : *it is the Right.* Though a thousand more centuries of servitude should be added to those which have already passed, their accord could not banish the primordial right which rules over everything, the absolute right of perfecting one's self which every being has received from the sole fact that he has been created."

To those who base their opposition on the domestic functions of woman, he answers: "If there (in the household) is their kingdom, then there they should be queens ; their own faculties assure them there of authority, and their adversaries are forced, by their own principles, to emancipate them as daughters, as wives, as mothers. Or, on the contrary, it is sought to extend their influence, to give them a rôle in the state, *and we believe that they should have one :* well; it is also in this dissimilarity (between the two sexes), that it is fitting to seek it. When two beings are of value to each other, it is almost always because they differ from, not because they resemble each other. Far from dispossessing men, the mission of women therefore would be to do what men leave undone, to aspire to empty places, in short, to represent in the commonwealth the spirit of woman."

As is evident, Legouvé demands the civil emancipation of woman in the name of the eternal Right, in the name of the happiness of the family, in the name of the commonwealth ; their long standing oppression is an iniquitous fact, and he casts blame on all who have perpetuated it. This blame from a man of heart and justice may perhaps have some weight with those women who are so much accustomed to bondage that they do not blush at it — that they even no longer feel it !

In his first book, " The Daughter," which is divided into seven chapters, Legouvé takes the child from her birth ; he shows her made inferior in the ancient religions and systems of legislation by Menu, by Moses, at Rome, at Sparta, at Athens, and under the feudal régime ; and he asks why, even in our days, the birth of a daughter is received with a sort of disfavor. It is because she will neither continue the name nor the works of her father, says he ; it is because her future gives rise to a thousand anxieties. "Life is so rude and so uncertain for a girl ! Poor, how many chances of misery ! Rich, how many chances of moral suffering !

If she is to have only her labor for a maintenance, how
shall we give her an occupation that will support her in
a state of society in which women scarcely earn wherewith not to die? If she has no dowry, how can she
marry in this world in which woman, never representing anything but a passive being, is forced to buy a husband? . . . From this *début*, and in this child's cradle,
we have found and caught a glimpse of all the chains
that await women : insufficiency of education for the
rich girl ; insufficiency of wages for the poor girl ; exclusion from the greater part of the professions ; subordination in the conjugal abode."

In the second chapter, the author shows by what
gradations the daughter, deprived of the right of inheritance, has come in our times to share equally with her
brothers ; then, passing to the right of education, he
answers those who pretend that to give a solid education
to woman would be to corrupt her and to injure the
family : " The diversity of their nature (man and woman) being developed by the identity of their studies, it
may be said that women would become so much the
more fully women in proportion as they received a masculine education.

" Well ! it is in the name of the family, in the name
of the salvation of the family, in the name of maternity,
of marriage, of the household, that a solid and earnest
education must be demanded for girls. . . . Without
knowledge, no mother is completely a mother, without
knowledge no wife is truly a wife. The question is not,
in revealing to the feminine intellect the laws of nature,
to make all our girls astronomers or physicians ; do we
see all men become Latinists by spending ten years of
their life in the study of Latin? The question is to

strengthen their minds by acquaintance with science; and to prepare them to participate in all the thoughts of their husbands, all the studies of their children. . . . Ignorance leads to a thousand faults, a thousand errors in the wife. The husband who scoffs at science might have been saved by it from dishonor."

Insisting upon the rights of woman, the author adds: " As such (the work of God) she has the right to the most complete development of her mind and heart. Away then with these vain objections, drawn from the laws of a day! It is in the name of eternity that you owe her enlightenment." Further on, he exclaims indignantly: " What! the state maintains a university for men, a polytechnic school for men, academies of art and trades for men, agricultural schools for men — and for woman, what has it established? Primary schools! And even these were not founded by the State, but by the Commune. No inequality could be more humiliating. There are courts and prisons for women, there should be public education for women; you have not the right to punish those whom you do not instruct!" M. Legouvé demands, in consequence, public education for girls in athenæums, " which, by thorough instruction with respect to France, her laws, her annals, and her poetry, shall make her women French women in truth. The country alone can teach love of country."

Ancient religions and systems of legislation punished misdemeanors and crimes against the purity of women severely (says M. Legouvé in his fourth chapter). Our code, profoundly immoral, does not punish seduction, and punishes corruption only derisively, and violation insufficiently. To declare void the promise of marriage is fearful immorality; to permit no investigation of pa-

ternity and to admit that of maternity, is as cruel as it
is immoral. If the solicitude of the legislator for property be compared with his solicitude for purity, we
shall soon see how little the law cares for the latter.
" The law recognizes as criminal only a single kind of
robbery of honor, *violation*, but it defines, pursues and
punishes two kinds of robbery of money, *larceny* and
fraud; there are thieves of coin, there are no sharpers
in chastity."

When a man has seduced a girl fifteen years old
under promise of marriage, he has " a right to come
before a magistrate and say : This is my signature, it is
true ; but I refuse to acknowledge it ; a debt of love is
void in law."

The indignant author exclaims, further on : " Thus,
therefore, on every side, in practice and in theory, in
the world and in the law, for the rich as for the poor,
we see abandonment of public purity, and a loose rein
to all ungoverned or depraved desires. . . . Manufacturers seduce their workwomen, foremen of workshops
discharge young girls who will not yield to them, masters corrupt their servant maids. Of 5083 lost women,
enumerated by the grave Parent-Duchâtelet at Paris in
1830, 285 were servants, seduced by their masters, and
discarded. Clerks, merchants, officers, students deprave
poor country girls and bring them to Paris, where they
abandon them, and prostitution gathers them up. . . .
At Rheims, at Lille, in all the great centres of industry,
are found organized companies for the recruital of the
houses of debauchery of Paris."

With the indignation of an upright man, M. Legouvé
adds : " Punish the guilty woman if you will, but punish also the man ! She is already punished ; punished

by abandonment, punished by dishonor, punished by
remorse, punished by nine months of suffering, punished
by the burden of rearing a child : let him then be smit-
ten in turn ; or else, it is not public decency that you
are protecting, as you say, it is masculine sovereignty,
in its vilest form : seigniorial right !

"Impunity assured to men doubles the number of
illegitimate children. Impunity fosters libertinism ;
libertinism enervates the race, wastes fortunes and
blights offspring. Impunity fosters prostitution ; prostitution destroys the public health, and makes a profession of idleness and license. Impunity, in short, sur-
renders half the human race as a prey to the vices of
the other half: behold its condemnation in a single
word."

In the fifth chapter, the author finding, with reason,
that girls are married too young, desires that they
should not enter upon family duties until twenty-two
years old ; works of charity, solid studies, innocent
pleasures, and the ideal of pure love will suffice to keep
them pure till this age. "If the young maiden learns
that nothing is more fatal to this divine sentiment (love)
than the ephemeral fancies which dare call themselves
by its name ; if she perceives in it one of those rare
treasures which we win only by conquering them, which
we keep only by deserving them ; if she knows that the
heart which would be worthy to receive it must be purified like a sanctuary and enlarged like a temple ; then
be sure that this sublime ideal, engraven within her,
will disgust her, by its beauty alone, with the vain
images that profane or parody it ; idols are not wor-
shipped when God is known."

" What is marriage ? " asks M. Legouvé.

" The union of two free beings, forming an alliance ,in order to perfect themselves through love." Neither antiquity nor the Middle Age considered it in this light. The father, in ancient times, transmitted to the husband his right of property in his daughter in consideration of a certain sum. At Athens, the daughter, even when married, formed part of the paternal inheritance, and was bound to leave her husband to espouse the heir. At Rome, the father, after having given his daughter in marriage, had the power to take her back and to espouse her to another. Among the barbarians, she belonged to him who paid the *mundium* to her father. Under the feudal system, the law disposed also of the daughter without her consent. The French Revolution emancipated her in this respect; she is required now to consent to her marriage; but the customs of the age take from her the benefit of this emancipation; she is married too young to know what she is doing, and interest almost always determines her parents to give her in marriage. For woman to profit by her legal emancipation, she should be at least twenty-two years old when she marries; she should make her choice freely; and her relatives should content themselves with keeping her apart from those whom she ought not to choose, and should only enlighten and counsel her; for on the love between the married couple depends the happiness and virtue of the wife.

Examining next the origin of the dower, the transferral of the dowry, the betrothal and the marriage, he shows the *mundium* paid at first to the father or the brother; then later, to the maiden, becoming, with the rest of the nuptial gifts, the origin of the dower, which he wishes to see made obligatory in modern times. Passing to the dowry, he proves that, becoming by degrees a custom among the Romans, it was at first the property of the husband; then, as the world progressed, it became the property of the wife. Our code fully protects the dowry; but the law should oblige wealthy parents to endow their daughters so that they can marry. In olden times, a maiden was betrothed by pledges exchanged by the father and the man who asked her in marriage; at a later date the pledge was given to the maiden instead of the father, and the law intervened to render obligatory promises of marriage. At the present day, in France, there are no longer betrothed, but future spouses.

In his second book, the author distinguishes the beloved one from the mistress, the adoration of pure from that of sensual love; the first produces goodness, patriotism, and respect for woman; the second regards her only as an object of pleasure and of disdain. Antiquity had no knowledge of pure love; the Middle Age, which comprehended it, was divided equally between it and sensual love; to-day, we have learned to comprehend that the two loves should be united; that the beloved and the mistress should make one in the person of the wife.

The third book, " The Wife," is divided into seven chapters.

The subordination of woman in marriage, with contempt for the mother, arose from two erroneous ideas: the inferiority of her nature; her passivity in the reproduction of the species, in which she performed the part of the earth with respect to the reception of germs. Modern science has destroyed these bases of inferiority by demonstrating: 1st, that the human germ, before

taking its definitive form, passes, in the bosom of its
mother, through progressive degrees of animal life;
2d, that in all species, both animal and vegetable, the
females are the conservers of the race, which they bring
to their own type.

Among the Romans, two forms of marriage placed
the wife, soul, body and estate, *in the hands* of her husband; in a third form, which left her in her father's
family, she received a dowry, inherited, and administered
her property. Barbarism and feudality made the wife
a ward, the husband an administrator, and a step was .
taken towards the equality of the spouses by the institution of *acquéts*, or property belonging to both, though
obtained by but one. To-day, the maiden is married
sometimes under the dotal system, occasionally under
that of' the separation of property, and chiefly under
that of communion of goods. This last, which is the
rule, permits the husband to dispose of the property of
his partner, to sell the household furniture, to take possession of the very jewels of his wife to adorn his mistress. " Thus, this law respects no dignity, no delicacy,
nothing whatever," says M. Legouvé. The omnipotence of the husband is a crime of the law in every
point of view; it is in manifest violation of the modern
principle, which exacts that all authority shall be limited
and placed under surveillance. " To surrender to the
husband the fortune of the wife is to condemn her to an
eternal moral minority, to create him absolute master of
the actions and almost of the soul of his companion."
The author next addresses himself to those who pretend
to justify marital omnipotence by the incapacity of woman : " In vain do facts protest against this alleged incapacity; in vain does reality say : To whom is the

prosperity of most of our commercial houses due?   To
women. Who establish, who superintend the thousands
of establishments of millinery and objects of taste?
Women. By whom are the boarding-schools, the farms,
often even, the manufactories, sustained?   By women.
It matters not, the Code denies to the wife the foresight
to preserve, the judgment to administer, even the maternal tenderness to economize, and the marriage certificate becomes the expression of this disdainful phrase:
the most reasonable woman never attains the good sense
of a boy fourteen years of age." How shall we set to
work to remedy this iniquitous and shameful state of
affairs? The property of the partners should be divided
into three shares: one for the wife, to be placed at her
disposal five years after marriage, one for the husband,
and a third common to both, to be administered by the
husband under the direction of a family council, which
council, in case of incapacity or waste, shall have the
right provisionally to take away the management from
him, to entrust it to his wife.

If anything is iniquitous and revolting, it is the power
of the husband over the person and the actions of his
wife ; the right over her of correction, still tolerated in
our days.   There must be a directing power in the
household ; the husband must be the depositary of this
power, which should be limited, and controlled by the
family council.   Legal omnipotence demoralizes the
husband, who believes in the end in the lawfulness of his
despotism.   It is said·that custom establishes precisely
the contrary of what the laws prescribe : this is generally true, but it is at the expense of the moral character of the wife, thus forced to have recourse to artifice.
" Restore liberty to women, since liberty is truth ! "

exclaims Legouvé. " This will be, at the same time, to
affranchise man. Servitude always creates two slaves :
he who holds the chain and he who wears it."

Antiquity, the Middle Age, and the centuries nearer
our own, punished the adultery of the wife severely,
even cruelly, yet did not admit that a man could become
guilty of this offence with respect to his spouse. Our
present code acknowledges, indeed, that the husband
can commit adultery, but only in case he maintains his
mistress under the conjugal roof; the wife is an adulte-
ress everywhere, and is punished severely ; as to the
husband, his punishment is a farce. " Such impunity,"
says M. Legouvé, " is not only injurious to order, it is
an insult to public morals, *it is a lesson of debauchery,
given by the law itself.*" If, by adultery, the wife
wounds the heart of an honorable man, introduces false
heirs into the family, she at least can abstract nothing
from the common fortune ; while the husband, in the
same case, can ruin the family, while increasing the
number of natural children and provoking his wife to
wrong by his neglect and brutality. The husband, besides, is more criminal than the wife, for he seeks adultery, while, on the contrary, it comes to the wife under
a thousand attractive forms. Notwithstanding, the
adultery of the woman deserves greater punishment
than that of the man.. . . . Ah! M. Legouvé, is this
logic ?

The Oriental wife was and is still, a slave, a genera-
trix ; the Roman wife was something more than this ;
the wife of the Middle Age owed her body to her husband, but the Courts of Love had decided that her affections could, nay, should belong to another. To-day,
the ideal of marriage is enlarged ; we comprehend that

it is the fusion of two souls, a school for mutual perfection, and that the two spouses should belong wholly to each other.

We have been led to this new ideal of the conjugal union by the civilizing struggles of the church against divorce and repudiation. In its nature, marriage is indissoluble, but in the existing state of things in which the ideal is but very exceptionally realized, the legislator has deemed it right to render possible the separation of the spouses: this measure is immoral and unfortunate both for the partners and for their children. The only remedy for family difficulties is *divorce*, a question with which the church has nothing to do.

The whole of the last chapter of the third book is a condemnation of fickleness in love, and an affirmation of the indissolubility of marriage and of the sanctity of the conjugal tie.

The fourth book, " The Mother," comprises six chapters.

Until a late day, it was believed that woman was only the soil in which man, the creator of the species, deposited the human germ. Modern science has overthrown this false doctrine, and elevated woman by demonstrating these three incontestable facts: 1st, that, dating from the moment of conception, the human germ passes through successive degrees of animal life until it acquires its proper form ; 2d, that the female sex is the conserver of the race, since it always brings them to its own type, as well in the human as in the animal and vegetable species ; 3d, that woman is physiologically of a nature superior to man, since it is now demonstrated that the higher the respiratory apparatus is placed in the organism, the more elevated is the species in the scale of beings; and that woman breathes from the upper, and man from the lower part of the lungs.

Maternity does not give to women rights over their children, but contributes, notwithstanding, to their emancipation; thus, in India, a woman who had borne sons could not be repudiated, and at Rome, a woman emerged from tutelage at maternity.

It is iniquitous to give the paternal authority to the father alone; the mother should have an equal right with him over her children. Supremacy of direction belongs indeed to the father, but this direction should be limited and superintended by a family council, and transferred to the mother in case of the unworthiness of her spouse.

The education of the children belongs of right to the mother, because she understands them best, and because it is necessary that she should acquire that entire influence over her sons which she will need afterwards to counsel and to console them. Public education is not fit for boys until they have attained their twelfth year; younger, it is injurious in its results to their character. The author demands that the maternal grand-parents shall not be made inferior in guardianship, as is the case now in the law; and he considers it as sacrilege not to give to the mother an equal right with respect to consent to the marriage of their children.

Legitimate maternity is happiness to the rich woman; want, often grief, to the poor woman. Illegitimate maternity is to women of all ranks a source of sorrow, shame and crime. To the rich girl it is dishonor, an eternal bar to marriage; to the poor girl it is poverty, shame if she keeps her child; crime, if she destroys it. Yet the law dares grant impunity to the corrupter, to

the seducer, to the man who has not hesitated to sacrifice to a moment of passion the whole future of a woman, the whole future of a child ! The State ought to
come to the aid of all poor mothers, because it is for its
interest that the race should be strong and vigorous, and
because mothers are the preservers of the race. Let
the genius of women be set to work ; let infant schools
and infant asylums be founded in every quarter of
France.

The Hindoo widow was burned ; the Jewish widow
was bound to re-marry certain men designated by the
law ; the Grecian and the Gothic widow passed under
the guardianship of her son, and the latter could not
even re-marry without his permission ; the Christian
widow was condemned to seclusion ; none of these women had any rights over their children. The French
code restores full liberty to the widow, renders to her
the right of majority, appoints her the guardian and
directress of her children ; it is a preliminary step to
liberty in marriage.

The fifth book, *Woman*, is divided into five chapters.

All antiquity oppressed woman, although it recognized in her something superior, and made her a priestess or a prophetess. The Christian woman of the early
ages, who alone could dethrone the Pagan woman, not
only endured martyrdom as courageously as man, but
was distinguished for her great charity, for the purity
and lucidity of doctrine which rendered her the counsellor of learned men. We do not know, in reality, to
what heights woman can attain ; we cannot judge her
by what she is to-day, since she is the work of the eternal oppression of man. " Who can say whether many

of the ills that rend society, and of the insoluble problems that trouble it, may not be caused in part by the
annihilation of one of the two forces of creation, the
ban placed on female genius? Have we a right to say
to half the human kind: you shall not have your share
in life and in the state? Is it not to deny to them (to
women) their title of human beings? Is it not to dis-
inherit the state itself? Yes, woman should have her
place in civil life," concludes Legouvé.

Woman and man are equal, but different. To man,
belong synthesis, superiority in all that demands comprehensive views, genius, muscular force; to woman, belong
the spirit of analysis, the comprehension of details, imagination, tenderness, grace. Man has more strength of
reason and body, woman more strength of heart, with a
marvelous perspicacity to which man will never attain.
The division thus fixed, what ought woman to do?

In the family, the task of the wife is the management
of domestic affairs, the education of the children, and
the comfort of the husband, of whom she should be the
inspiration. By the side of the eminent man, yet in
the shade, there is always a woman; this career of hid-
den utility and of modest devotion is the one best suited
to woman. In civil life there are several fields of occupation which they may enter with success: art, literature, instruction, *administration*, medicine. "Modesty
itself demands that we should call in women as physicians, not to men, but to women; for it is an abiding outrage upon all purity that their ignorance should forcibly
expose to masculine curiosity the sufferings of their sisters. . . . Nervous diseases, especially, would find in
feminine genius the only adversary able to understand
and combat them." The author says that it is the duty

of society to see that poor women do not work for one-third or one-fourth the wages of men; and that, in manufactures, they have not the most dangerous and least remunerative labors. " Parent-Duchâtelet," says he, " attests that of three thousand lost women, *only thirty-five had an occupation that could support them,* and that fourteen hundred had been precipitated into this horrible life by destitution. One of them, when she resolved on this course, *had eaten nothing for three days.*" M. Legouvé thinks it shameful that men should enter into competition with women in the manufacture of articles of dress and taste.

In the fifth and last chapter, the author recognizes the remarkable capacity of women in administration, of which he cites numerous examples. He demands that they should have the superintendence of prisons for women, hospitals, charitable institutions, the legal guardianship of foundlings, the management, in short, of all that concerns social charity, because they will acquit themselves in it infinitely better than men. But he refuses to them all participation in political acts and in all that concerns the government, because they have no aptitude for things of this nature. Finally, he concludes thus: " Our task is finished; we have examined the principal phases of the life of women, in the character of daughters, wives, mothers, and women, comparing the present with the past, and endeavoring to indicate the future; that is, by pointing out the bad, verifying the better, seeking the best.

" What principle has served us in this as a guide? Equality in difference.

" In the name of this principle, what ameliorations have we demanded in the laws and customs?

" For daughters:

" Reform in education.

" Laws against seduction.

" The postponement of the marriageable age.

" The actual participation of the betrothed parties in the execution of their contract.

" Abolition of the formal request to the father of consent to marriage, which is an insult to the father and an injustice to the child.

" For wives :

" An age of legal majority.

" Administration, and the right of disposing of a portion of their private property.

" The right to appear in law without the consent of their husbands.

" The limitation of the power of the husband over the person of the wife.

" The creation of a family council, charged with controling this part of the power.

" For mothers :

" The right of government.

" The right of direction.

" The right of education.

" The right of consent to the marriage of their children.

" A law requiring the investigation of paternity.

" The creation of a family council to decide on serious disagreements between father and mother.

" For women :

" Admission to guardianship and the family council.

" Admission to all professions.

" Admission within the bounds of their capabilities and duties to public offices."

It is evident that Legouvé has but one end, that of advancing the emancipation of women a single step; he does not demand all that he believes just, but all that seems to him mature and possible.

We should thank him for his prudence: he has brought over many men to our cause, and has prepared them to hear the voice of woman, speaking loudly and firmly by her right as a wife and a human being, as a worker and a member of the social body.

By the side of Legouvé, outside the social schools, are a phalanx of just and generous men who have written in our favor. We thank them all for their good words.

CHAPTER V.

On page 42 of his pamphlet, "Liberty in Marriage," De Girardin says, with great reason: "Man is born of woman. Everything, therefore, that benefits woman will benefit man.

"To fight and conquer for her is to fight and conquer for himself."

Inspired by these excellent sentiments, the celebrated publicist has investigated the causes of the slavery and degradation of woman, and the means of paralyzing them.

Every child has for its father the husband of its mother : this, according to M. de Girardin, is the principle of two great wrongs : the servitude of the married woman ; the inequality of children before the law, which classes them as legitimate and illegitimate.

That children may become equal, that woman may be affranchised from the yoke of man, it is necessary, says the author, to substitute the system of maternity for that of paternity ; to modify Marriage, and to render woman independent through the institution and universalizing of the dower.

We will let M. de Girardin expound the rest of his

doctrine himself. " We must choose," says he, " between these two systems:

" Between the system of *presumed* paternity, *which is the system of the law*, and the system of maternity, *bearing its proof within itself, which is the system of Nature;* the latter is in conformity with incontestable truth, the former is condemned by undisputed statistics. The system of paternity is *inequality of children before the mother and before the law; it is woman possessed and not possessing;* . . . it is no longer the legal slavery of woman, *but is still conjugal servitude."—Liberty in Marriage.*

" Without equality of children before the mother, equality of citizens before the law *is only an imposture,* for evidently and incontestably, this equality does not exist for 2,800,000 children, who, arbitrarily entitled illegitimate, are placed outside of common right in violation of natural law."—*Id.*

According to De Girardin, the logical consequences of the system of maternity would be:

The abolition of civil marriage;

The mother's name alone given to the child;

The inheritance placed solely in the maternal line.

" Marriage," says he, "is a purely individual act, and, as regards its celebration, a purely religious act.—

" Marriage is an act of faith, not of law: it is for faith to govern it, *not for law to make rules for it.*

" As soon as the law intervenes, it intervenes *without right,* without necessity, *without utility.*

" For one abuse that it pretends to avert, it gives rise to innumerable others which are worse, and from which society afterwards suffers seriously, without taking into account the cause that produced them.

" Legal liberty in marriage is durable love in the household ; indissolubility of marriage is habitual love outside of the household."— *Id.*

With respect to inheritance and dowry, the author expresses himself thus :

" To inherit at the death of the mother, because maternity and certitude are two equipollent terms, and to · receive a support from the father, because paternity and doubt are two inseparable terms ; such is the true law of Nature."— *Id.*

In De Girardin's opinion, woman has the same rights as man to liberty and equality ; the sexes are equal, not through *similitude* but *equivalence* of faculties and functions ; man produces, acquires, woman administers, economizes ; it belongs therefore to man to provide for the expenses of the household. It is his duty, on uniting himself to a woman, to settle on her an inalienable dower that will permit her to perform her maternal functions properly, and to escape from the vices that frequently result from want and abandonment.

To the objection that the wages of the working people are insufficient to satisfy this duty, the generous publicist replies : Well, raise the rate of wages by excluding from industrial occupations the women and children that lower it by competition with men. And if this measure be not sufficient to balance receipts and expenses, increase the wages, for " there is no consideration weighty enough to make me admit that, in order not to diminish the profits of some men, others shall be eternally condemned to insufficient wages ; and that to shelter some women from violation, others shall be necessarily devoted to prostitution."— *Id.*

In comparing the lot of the wife under the two systems, De Girardin expresses himself thus :

" Under the system of paternity, the wife, loaded
with the gifts of fortune, sinks under the weight of an
idleness which most frequently inflames and disorders
her imagination. She does not know what to do to
employ her time. Woman does nothing because man
does everything.

" The wife who has brought no dowry and received
no dower, sinks under the weight of a toil contrary to
nature which obliges her, through economy, to separate
herself from her child a few days after giving it birth,
and to put it away from her to nurse, for the consideration of five or six francs a month ; to go to work in one
direction while her husband works in the other, and not
to rejoin him till evening, when each returns from the
workshop which has kept them absent from their household all day : if this is what is called the family, *is it
indeed worth all the stir that is made about it ?*

" Under the system of maternity, on the contrary,
the richer a woman is, the further she is removed from
idleness ; for not only has she her children to nurse, to
rear, to instruct, and to watch over, but she has also to
administer her fortune which will one day be theirs.

" To preserve this fortune, to increase it still more :
here is wherewith to occupy her leisure, to calm her
imagination, to place her under curb. It is wrong to
suppose women not qualified for the management of
business ; they excel in it, however little may have been
their practice or application.

" Long enough has man been the personification of
war, of slavery, of conquest; it is the turn of woman
to be the personification of peace, of liberty, of civilization.

" In this new system (*that of maternity*), each of the

two has his part: to man labor, the genius of enterprise; to woman economy and the spirit of foresight.

" Man speculates, woman administers ;

" Man acquires, woman preserves ;

" Man brings in, woman transmits ;

" The dowry remains the attribute of the father, the inheritance becomes the privilege of the mother ;

" Each of the two thus exercises the function that is *natural* to him, and in conformity with the essence of things."— *Id.*

A number of women have asked whether De Girardin recognizes political right for women. He says nothing about it, either in his work " Liberty in Marriage," or in his " Universal Politics." But when a man writes that :

" Woman, belonging to herself, and being dependent only on her reason, has the same rights as man to liberty and equality."

That " universal suffrage should be *individual* and *direct.*"

That " every holder of a general insurance has a right to be a party to it."

It is evident that we may deduce, without any great stretch of logic, that, woman being *free and equal to man,*

Woman being comprised in universality,

Woman holding, like man, her policy of insurance, has a right, like man, to be elector, to be eligible to office, and to vote *individually and directly.*

Now, as M. de Girardin is not one of those who recoil from the consequences of their principles, we are led to believe that he admits to woman the exercise of political right for woman.

I have been told that, in 1848, one of those pitiable individuals who have neither intellect enough to be logical, nor justice enough to comprehend the oppressed, was haranguing before M. de Girardin against the claims of certain women to enter political life. " Why not?" asked M. de Girardin. "Do you believe that Madame de Girardin would deposit a less intelligent vote in the electoral urn than that of her footman?"

If this anecdote be true, the opinion of the publicist concerning the political right of woman is not doubtful.

La liberte dans le marriage has raised a tempest of indignation, to a greater or less degree feigned, among the prudes ; and for some time it required courage openly to proclaim one's self the (feminine) champion of the author.

Abolish marriage ! cry some, veiling their faces with an air of offended modesty.

Make a speculation of love ! exclaim others who, apparently, have preserved their holy innocence and baptismal ignorance.

Come, ladies, we might say, — a truce to conventional delicacy and sentimentality. Let men suffer themselves to be deceived by our mask, nothing is more natural ; but what is the use of playing the farce among women ?

M. de Girardin does not really suppress marriage ; he changes it in some respects, but leaves it intact in a religious point of view. If his system should be adopted, therefore, you might be married in the presence of the clergymen of your respective faiths, precisely as was done some seventy years ago, and you would have no fewer scruples than your grandmothers, who believed themselves then sufficiently married.

On the other hand, in suppressing civil marriage, the author does not interdict such and such particular stipulations; if therefore you hold in any degree to the religion of the Code, it will be lawful for you to stipulate in your notarial contract :

1. That you will be submissive to your husbands ;

2. That you will permit them to manage your fortune, even contrary to your interests and to those of your children ;

3. That without authority from them, you will neither go to law, nor undertake anything, nor sell anything, nor receive anything, nor give anything away ;

4. That, so long as they shall live, you renounce all authority over your children ; that they can, if they please, take them from you, banish you from them, have them reared by whoever they choose, even by their mistress, finally, give them in marriage contrary to your will ;

5. That you recognise their right to carry elsewhere their love, their attentions, their fortune and your own ; provided that this does not happen under your roof ;

6. That, lastly, you grant their right, if, abandoned by them, you attach yourself to another, to drag you before the bar, to dishonor you, to imprison you with thieves and prostitutes ; that even in such case you declare them excusable in killing you.

Yes, ladies, you might stipulate all this, for M. de Girardin disputes no one the rights of lacking dignity and being imbecile ; of what then do you complain ?

You reproach M. de Girardin with wishing to make a speculation of love ! Be good enough to tell me what you call the greater part of the marriages of the

present time, in which men have the heartlessness to
speculate even on death!—in which they ask how much
a young girl has, what are her expectations, and *how
old are her parents.*

Answer, women:

Is it true that the great majority of seduced women
are incapacitated, through shame and poverty, from
rearing their children?

That what you call a first fault, drives the greater
part of them to make a traffic of their charms?

That the great majority of men forget, after satisfying their passion, both the woman whom they have
led astray, and the innocent creature that owes its life
to them?

Is it true that the horrible and cruel selfishness of
men and the insane confidence of women produces annually a fearful number of so called illegitimate children, the greater part of which people the prisons, the
galleys, and the public brothels?

Is it true, lastly, that this same selfishness and this
same confidence are the cause of thousands of human
lives being criminally sacrificed?

And if all this shame, all these griefs, all these crimes
are true?

If there are so many women seduced and heart-
broken;

If there are so many children abandoned;

If there are so many infanticides;

If the law does not protect the woman deceived and
made a mother;

If this law does not compel the seducer to any reparation;

If public opinion leaves to the victim all the shame;

Why do you reproach a man for reminding a young girl that from love may proceed maternity?

For telling her that she ought to provide in advance for the child that may be born, in order that it may not be cast upon public charity, and that she herself may not risk falling into those sinks of impurity that are the shame and degradation of our sex?

Do you reproach a man then for taking our part against the selfish and animal passions of his sex, and against the impunity accorded them by the laws?

Do you reproach him for taking in hand the cause of morals and health, in opposition to the degradation of soul and body?

A young girl stipulate the sale of her person! say you? what essential difference do you find between this kind of contract, and those that are made to-day before the notary on the occasion of a marriage?

Did not most among you, ladies, purchase your husbands with so much dowry, so much income, so much *expectations?* And if these husbands of yours did not think it shameful to be sold, and if you do not esteem them less for it, be good enough to tell me from what principle you judge it shameful for a young girl to do the same in order to rear her children, and to live without prostituting herself?

For my part, I do not see.

Ladies, you are grown-up children: men feign to have contempt for the woman who thinks of her interests in love . . . . . because they wish, if possible, to keep their money, that is all.

Is this to say that I admit all the ideas of M. de Girardin? No.

I admit with him, that woman can only be free and

the equal of man, in so far as she is a wife, through a change in marriage. ·

That, in the state of insecurity in which she is placed with respect to wages and to maternity outside of marriages, woman *does well* to take measures to prevent man from shifting the obligations of paternity from himself to her.

I would willingly admit that the child should bear the mother's name only, if men did not object so strongly to it. The child, belonging to both, should bear both names, and choose, at majority, the one that he preferred; or else the daughters should bear the name of the mother and the sons that of the father, from the time of majority.

I readily admit the equality of children before the mother and the law; for bastardy is meaningless in nature and is social iniquity. But what I do not admit, is the ideal M. de Girardin has formed with regard to the respective functions of each sex:

The exclusion of woman from active occupations;

The universalizing of the dower;

Lastly, family education.

To say that man represents labor, the genius of enterprise, that he speculates, acquires, brings in, — that woman represents economy, the spirit of foresight, — that she administers, preserves, transmits, is to establish a series which does not appear to me at all in conformity with the nature of things, since it is notorious that a great number of women do what M. de Girardin attributes to the other sex, and *vice versâ*.

Functions, to be properly performed, should be the result of aptitudes. Now Nature, except in what concerns the reproduction of the species, does not appear to have classed these according to the sexes. Since the origin of society, we have attempted to do it, but history is at hand to reveal to us that, in acting thus, we have only succeeded in tyrannizing over the sturdy minorities that have given the lie to such pretensions. Now, M. de Girardin, admitting a false series, *à priori*, is led without perceiving it to forge chains for all women whom Nature has not made in conformity with the conventional order which he wishes to see realized.

To exclude woman from active occupations in order to confine her to the cares of the household is to attempt an impossibility, to close the way to progress, and to replace woman beneath the yoke of man. It is to attempt an impossibility, because there are branches of manufactures that can be executed only by women; because many women who would not marry, or who would be left portionless widows without resources, could only remain pure by devoting themselves to some active employment which, notwithstanding, would be interdicted to them. To see woman in the household alone, is to view her from a contracted stand point, which retards the advent of her liberty. It is to close the way to progress, because there are social functions which will never be well performed until woman shall participate in them, and social questions that will never be resolved until woman shall stand by the side of man to elucidate them. It is to replace woman beneath the yoke of man, because it is in human nature to rule and domineer over those whom we provide with their daily bread.

To wish to erect the dower into an institution, is to wish to restore one of the most lamentable phases of the Past at the moment when Humanity is marching to-

wards the Future — that which shows us woman pur-
chased by man.   The universalizing of the dower
would be therefore a criminal attempt on the liberty
and moral dignity of woman.   Lastly, to claim that
every mother ought to educate her children herself appears to us to propose as great impossibility as social
danger.

If every well constituted woman, is fit to bring children into the world and to nourish them with her milk,
very few are capable of developing their intellect and
heart, for education is a special function, requiring a
particular aptitude, with which all mothers cannot be
endowed.

Next, family education perpetuates divergence of
opinions and sentiments, maintains prejudices, favors
the development of vanity and selfishness, and tends, by
this means, to paralyze the most noble, the most civilizing sentiment — that of universal solidarity.   Assuredly, at the present time, many motives may justify
family education, but for the good of humanity it is to
be desired that parents who sympathize in progressive
ideas should assemble their children together to form
them for social life, instead of rearing them each by
himself.

I submit this critical sketch to M. de Girardin in the
name of the principle that he has always defended: —
individual dignity and human liberty.

CHAPTER VI.

MODERN COMMUNISTS.

The Communists hold as the principle of social organization, not *the agrarian law*, as has been charged on them through ignorance or bad faith, but the enjoyment *in common* of the soil, of implements of labor, and of products. *From each one according to his strength, to each one according to his needs*, is the formula of most among them.

It is not our business to examine the social value of this doctrine, but only to show what Communism thinks of woman and her rights.

The modern communists may be divided into two classes: the religious and the political.

Among the first are the Saint Simonians, the Fusionists and the Philadelphians.

Among the second, are the Equalitarians, the Unitarians, the Icarians, etc.

The first consider woman as the equal of man. To the others, she is free; among some, with a shade of subordination.

The Unitarians, who have drawn largely from Fourier, proclaim woman free, and equal with man.

We shall speak here of only a few of the communis-

tic sects, reserving for separate articles what relates to
the Saint Simonians and the Fusionists.

The Philadelphians, admitting God and the immortality of the soul, lay down these two principles : God
is the chief of the social order ; Fraternity is the law
that governs human relations.

Religion, to the Philadelphians, is the practice of Fraternity ; Progress is a dogma, Community is the law of
the individual before God and conscience.

Touching the relations of the sexes and the rights of
woman, M. Pecqueur thus expresses himself in his
work ; *La République de Dieu*, pp. 194, 195.

" Complete equality of the man and the woman ;

The Monogamic marriage, intentionally indissoluble
as a normal condition ; such is the second practical consequence of the dogma of religious fraternity.

1. EQUALITY.

" We bring no proofs in evidence of this ; *his reason
is blotted out by prejudice and his heart chilled by
egotism*, who is not impressed at once with the truth of
equality.

" In the state of society created by the religion of
fraternity and equality, women will find, from their earliest years, *the same means and the same conditions of
development of function and of remuneration*, in short,
THE SAME RIGHTS, the same social aim to pursue as men ;
and in proportion as custom shall correspond with the
religious and moral ends of the union, will the living
law deduce the practical consequences of all order, contained in the germ in the dogma of the complete equality
of the sexes.

" 4. MONOGAMY AND INDISSOLUBILITY.

" To comprehend the lawfulness of the unlimited or indefinite monogamic marriage, it suffices to consider: 1st. the exigencies of our inmost nature, that is, the characteristics of love ; its instinctive aspiration to the union and the fusion of two beings, to duration and to perpetuity ; the necessity of possessing each other reciprocally and of having faith in this possession *in order to love each other;* in short, instinct, desire ; the irresistible and universal affections, and the joys of paternity and of the family ; 2d. the physiological conditions of generation, which exact monogamy in order to assure the reproduction and the good and progressive conservation of the species ; 3d. social and religious exigencies, which require relations of all kinds to be predetermined and regulated, that each one may be secure in his expectation and his possession, and that there may be a possibility of satisfying the fundamental propensities of our natures. . . . To claim to introduce polygamy, promiscuousness, or union for a term of years into such surroundings, (the Philadelphian society,) is evidently to decree selfishness and mere carnal pleasure, while proclaiming duty and dignity. It is inconceivable that two moral beings, once united by pure love, should ever cease to love each other, to delight in each other, or at least to endure each other, when they are presumed already to be devoted and sacrificing without distinction in their love to their brothers and sisters.

" Still less is it conceivable that their brothers and sisters would dream of diverting this reciprocal love of two members of the family to their personal advantage ; *for this would be infamy."*

8

M. Pecqueur admits, notwithstanding, that in very rare cases, divorce may be granted on account of incompatibility of temper. In such case the offending party would be excluded from the republic, and the other would be at liberty to remarry.

According to M. Pecqueur, indissolubility of marriage does not relate to the present antagonistic state of society, as he says :

" Divorce is a great misfortune, not only to the parties concerned, but to religion ; notwithstanding, in the kingdom of Cæsar in which pure justice is the question, it is the lesser evil, when the individuals are determined on a separation in fact, and are lusting after other ties. They do evil clandestinely ; they are the cause or the occasion of the temptation or the fall of others. Do what they will, the scandal is known ; so that neither society, nor the spouses, nor the children, nor morality derive benefit from the consecration of absolute perpetuity.

" It is not charitable, it is *impious* to force two beings to remain together, one of which, to say the least, maltreats, detests, takes advantage of, or domineers over the other. It is equally wrong to grant them a separation from bed and board without at the same time permitting them to yield to chaste affections when they acknowledge these in purity and liberty."

So then, to the Philadelphians, expounded by M. Pecqueur, marriage is monogamous, indissoluble by intention ; divorce is a sad necessity of the existing state of society, whilst separation is immorality. In short, woman is *free and the equal of man.*

Another communist sect, that of the Icarians, takes no notice either of the nature or the rights of women.

Its chief, M. Cabet, an ex-attorney-general, was too fully imbued with the doctrines of the Civil Code, that inelegant paraphrase of the Apostle Paul, not to be persuaded that woman ought to remain outside the pale of political right, and that she ought to be subordinate to man in general, and to her husband, good or bad, in particular.

Let us do justice however to M. Cabet's disciples; I have never found a single one of them of his opinion on this great question.

One evening in 1848, as M. Cabet was presiding over a well attended club, he was requested by a woman to put the question: *Is woman the equal of man before social and political rights?* Almost every hand was raised in the affirmative; in the negative, not a hand was raised, not a man protested against the affirmation. A round of applause followed from the galleries filled with women; and M. Cabet was somewhat disconcerted by the result. He seemed to be ignorant that the people, always eminently logical, are never guilty of quibbling to elude or to limit the principles that they have adopted.

This vote of the Cabet club was repeated in three others, in my presence. The men in paletots laughed at the demands of brave Jeanne Deroin; the men in blouses did not even smile at them.

M. Dezamy representing another shade of communism, thus expresses himself in the code of the Community; "Away with marital dominion! Freedom of alliance! *perfect equality of both sexes!* Freedom of divorce!"

He adds, under the heading; Laws for the union of the sexes, designed to prevent all discord and debauchery, page 266:

"Art. I. Mutual love, inmost sympathy, purity of heart between two beings, form and legalize their union.

" Art. II. *There should be perfect equality between the two sexes.*

" Art. III. No bond except that of mutual love can link the man and the woman together.

" Art. IV. Nothing shall prevent lovers who have separated from forming new ties as often as they shall be attracted to another person."

The ethics of M. Dezamy are not to our taste ; we prefer those of the Communist, Pecqueur ; but we are glad to prove that modern communism, divided on the questions of marriage, the family, and morals in relations of the sexes, is unanimous with respect to the liberty of woman and the equality of the sexes before the law and society.

In this, modern communism is greatly superior to that of the ancient school, practised among several nations, and taught by Plato, Morelly, etc. We recognize a sign of the times in this juster appreciation of woman, with the introduction of the principle of her rights into doctrines which formerly never took them into account.

The greater part of the Communists belong to the working class ; which proves that the people most of all feel the great truth, *that the liberty of woman is identical with that of the masses ;* and it will take more than MM. Proudhon, Comte, Michelet and their adepts, to throw cold water on their feelings and to make them retrace their steps.

SAINT SIMONIANS.

My mother, a zealous Protestant and very austere in morals, disapproved of St. Simonianism, and never per-

mitted any one to speak of it in my presence except to
condemn it ; she took great care that not a line of the
new doctrine should fall under my eyes.

Whether from a natural spirit of opposition or from
instinctive justice, I know not, but I by no means
shared in the censure that I heard expressed about me ;
one thing alone resulted from it — curiosity to become
acquainted with what were called immoral dogmas.

I was in this frame of mind when one day while with
my mother in the neighborhood of the *Palais du Justice*, I
saw a company of men advancing, clad in a graceful
costume ; they were the Saint Simonians going in a
body to defend their infant church against prosecution
at the bar. I was greatly moved by the sight ; I felt
in communion with these youth who were about to bear
testimony to their faith ; they did not seem like strangers, but as struggling for my own cause or for one that
deserved my sympathy, and tears sprang to my eyes. I
could have heartily embraced those whom I heard de-
fending them, and as heartily have assailed those who
claimed that it would be just to condemn them. My
mother being too generous to join with the latter, we de-
parted in silence. I knew, without having any knowledge of the details, that the church of St. Simon had
been dispersed.

It was not until some years after that, having made
the acquaintance of a St. Simonian lady, I was en-
abled to read the doctrinal writings and to form an idea
of the aspirations and the dogmas of the school of
St. Simon. If the nature of this work forbids me their
analysis, it cannot reproach me for expressing my sympathies for those who have had great and generous aspirations ; for those who, in a critical point of view,

have rendered real services to the cause of Progress ; for those who have brought to light the solution of the two capital problems of our epoch ; *the emancipation of woman and of the workman.* The St. Simonians have been enough assailed, enough calumniated to justify a woman who is not a St. Simonian in considering it a duty to render them justice, by acknowledging the good which they have done.

Yes, you have a right to be proud of your name of St. Simonians, you who have proclaimed the obligation of laboring without respite for the physical, moral and intellectual amelioration of the most numerous and the poorest class ;

You who have proclaimed the *sanctity* of science, art, manufactures, and labor in every form ;

You who have proclaimed the equality of the sexes in the family, the church, and the state ;

You who have preached of peace and fraternity to a world given over to wars of cannon and competition.

You who have criticised the ancient dogma, and all the evil institutions that have thence arisen ;

Yes, I repeat, you have deserved well of Progress, you have deserved well of Humanity ; and you have a right to bear with pride your great scholastic name ; for it was noble to desire the emancipation of woman, of labor, and of the laborer; it was generous to consecrate youth and fortune to it, as so many among you have done.

Through your aspirations, you have been the continuers of '89, since you dreamed of realizing what was contained in the germ in the Declaration of Rights : these are your titles of greatness ; this is why your name will not perish. But if, through your sentiments, you belonged to the great era of '89, the social form in which you claimed to incarnate your principles, belonged to the Middle Ages ; the age therefore has done right to leave you behind. Seduced by trinitarian mysticism, deluded by an erroneous historical point of view, you claimed to resuscitate hierarchy and theocracy in a system of humanity fashioned in conformity with the opposing principle ; the triumph of individual liberty in social equality. This is the reason that the age could not follow you. No more could women follow you, for they felt that they could only be affranchised through labor and through purity of morals; by ruling over, not imitating masculine passions. They felt that their power of moralization was due as much to their chastity as to their intellect ; they knew that those who make use of the most liberty in love, neither love nor esteem the other sex ; that, in general, they employ their ascendancy over it to pervert it to ruin and afflict their companions, and to dissolve the family and civilization ; that, in consequence, they are the most dangerous enemies of the emancipation of their sex ; for man, sobered of his passion, can never desire to emancipate those by whom he has been deceived, ruined and demoralized.

The St. Simonian orthodoxy is therefore, in my opinion, greatly mistaken with respect to the ways and means of realization. Shall we impute this to it as a crime ? No, indeed ! social problems are not mathematical problems; there is merit in propounding them ; courage and devotion in pursuing their solution, even when we fail completely to attain it.

We all know the spirit of the St. Simonians who first brought before the public mind of the age the question of female emancipation ; it would be ungrateful in the women who demand liberty and equality not to recognize the debt of gratitude which they have contracted toward them. It is their duty to say to their companions : the seal of St. Simonianism is the safeguard of the liberty of woman ; wherever therefore you meet a St. Simonian, you may press his hand fraternally ; you have in him a defender of your right.

Let us sketch the general outline of the St. Simonian doctrine, touching woman and her rights.

All of the St. Simonians admit that the sexes are equal :

That the couple forms the social individual ;

That marriage is the sacred bond of generations ; the association of a man and a woman for the accomplishment of a sacerdotal, scientific, artistic, or industrial work ;

All admit divorce, and transition to another union ; but some are more severe than others with respect to the conditions of divorce.

There is a division among them on the question of morals. Olinde Rodrigues and Bazard do not admit any *liaison* of love outside of marriage. M. Enfantine, on the contrary, claims the greatest liberty in love.

We should add that he gives to this opinion a fixed and provisional value only, since he says that the law of the relations of sexes can only be established in a sure and definitive manner by the concurrence of the woman ; and since, on the other hand, he prescribes continence to his closest followers, until the coming of the Woman, of which he regards himself the precursor.

In addition, to give our readers a more precise idea of the sentiments of the St. Simonians concerning woman, we will cite some passages of their writings.

" The use of woman by man still exists," says M. Enfantin ; " *this it is that constitutes the necessity of our apostleship.* This use, this subalternation *contrary to nature*, with respect to the future, results on the one hand, in falsehood and fraud ; on the other, in violence and animal passions ; it is necessary to put an end to these vices."—(*Religion St. Simonienne*, 1832, p. 5.)

" Woman, as we have said, *is the equal of man* ; She is now a slave ; it belongs to her master to affranchise her." (*Id.* p. 12.)

" There will be no definitive law and morality until woman shall have spoken." (*Id.* p. 18.)

" In the name of God," exclaims M. Enfantin in his *Appel à la Femme*, " in the name of God and of all the sufferings which Humanity, his loved child, endures to-day in her flesh ; in the name of the poorest and most numerous class whose daughters are sold to Indolence and whose sons are given up to War ; in the name of all those men and of all those women, who cast the glittering veil of falsehood or the filthy rays of debauchery over their secret or public prostitution ; in the name of St. Simon who came to announce to man and woman *their moral, social and religous equality*, I conjure woman to answer me ! " (*Entretien du 7 Décembre*, 1831.)

On his side, Bazard concludes a pamphlet, published in January, 1832, with these words :

" And we too have hastened the coming of woman ; we too summon her with all our might ; but it is in the name of the pure love with which she has imbued the heart of man, and which man is now ready to give her in return ; it is in the name of the dignity which is promised her in marriage ; it is lastly and above all, in

8*

the name of the most numerous and poorest class, *whose
servitudes and humiliations she has hitherto shared*, and
whom her enchanting voice can alone to-day have
power finally to release from the harsh imposition with
which it is still weighed down by the wrecks of the
past."

Ah! you are to a great extent right, Enfantin and
Bazard! So long as woman is not free and the equal
of man ; so long as she is not everywhere at his side,
sorrows, disorders, war, the exploitation of the weak,
will be the sad lot of humanity.

Pierre Leroux, the gentlest, best and most simple man
that I know, writes in turn in the fourth volume of his
Encyclopédie Nouvelle, article *Egalité*, the following
remarkable paragraphs :

" There are not two different beings, man and woman, there is but a single human being with two phases,
which correspond and are united by love.

" Man and woman exist to form the couple ; they are
the two parts of it. *Outside of the couple, outside of
love and marriage, there is no longer any sex;* there
are human beings of a common origin and of like faculties. Man at every moment of his life is sensation,
sentiment, knowledge ; so is woman. The definition
is therefore the same."

After having proved, according to his idea, that the
type of woman differs from that of man, he continues :

" But this type does not separate them from the rest
of humanity, and does not make of them a separate
race which must be distinguished philosophically from
man. . . . Love being absent, they manifest themselves to man as human beings, and are ranked, like
man, under the various categories of civil society."

After having observed that, however different men may be, they are therefore none the less equal, since they all are sensation, sentiment and knowledge, Pierre Leroux, applying this principle to the question of the right of woman, adds :

" From whatever side we look at this question, we are led to proclaim the equality of man and woman. For, if we consider woman in the couple, woman is the equal of man, since the couple itself is founded on equality, since love is equality in itself, and since where justice, that is, equality, does not reign, there love cannot reign, but the contrary of love.

" And if we consider woman outside of the couple, she is a being like unto man, endowed with the same faculties in various degrees ; one of those varieties in unity which constitute the world and human society."

The author says that woman should lay claim to equality only as a spouse and a human being ; that to acknowledge her as free because she has sex, is to declare her at liberty not only to use but also to abuse love ; and that the abuse of love must not be the appanage and sign of liberty.

He says that woman has sex only for him whom she loves and by whom she is loved ; that to all others she can be merely a human being.

" From this point of view," continues he, " we must say to women : you have a right to equality by two distinct titles ; as human beings and as wives. As wives, you are our equals, for love in itself is equality. As human beings, your cause is that of all, *it is the same as that of the people ; it is allied to the great revolutionary cause;* that is, to the general progress of the human kind. *You are our equals, not because you are women but because there are no longer either slaves or serfs.*

" This is the truth that must be spoken to men and
women ; but it would be to pervert this truth and to
transform it into error to say to women : You are a sex
apart, a sex in the possession of love. Emancipate
yourselves; that is, use and abuse love. Woman thus
transformed into an unchaste Venus, loses at once her
dignity as a human being and as a woman ; that is, as a
being capable of forming a human couple under the sacred law of love."

The excellent Leroux asks who does not feel, who
does not admit at the present day the equality of the sexes ?

Who would dare maintain that woman is an inferior
being, of whom man is the guide and beacon light ?

That woman is elevated by man, who is elevated only
by himself and by God ?

Who would dare maintain such absurdities to-day,
brave and upright Leroux ? P. J. Proudhon, the man
who called you *Theopompe* and *Pâlissier* — M. Michelet,
who claims that woman was created to be the most tiresome doll of her loving husband.

But to return to yourself.

You affirm that God is androgynous ; that in him co-
exist the male and female principles on the footing of
equality : that consequently, man and woman are equal
in God. I assent to this willingly, although I know absolutely nothing about it. But when you add that woman is deserving of quite as much as man, because she
has shared in all the agonizing crises of the progressive
education of the human race ;

That love, which cannot exist without the woman,
has led us from the law of slavery to that of equality ;

That consequently woman represents half in the work
of the ages ;

In this there is no mystery ; I join you therefore with all my heart in repeating to men the invitations and the lessons which you give to these ungrateful and stubborn males :

" If we are free, it is in part by woman ; let her then be made free by us.

" But is she so ?   Is she treated by us as an equal ?

" A wife — does she find equality in love and marriage ?

" A human being, does she find equality in the State ?

" This is the question.

" On the subject of woman, our civil law is a model of absurd contradictions.   According to the Roman law, woman lived perpetually under tutelage ; in this system of legislation, everything was at least in perfect harmony ; woman was always a minor.   We, on our part, declare her in a multitude of cases to be free as man.   She is no longer under general or fictitious tutelage ; her age of majority is fixed ; she is competent to inherit in her own right ; she inherits in equal proportion ; she controls and disposes of her property ; more than this, in the system of communion of goods between husband and wife, we admit the separation of property.   But let the marriage bond itself be in question, in which wealth is no longer at stake, but ourselves and our mothers, ourselves and our sisters, ourselves and our daughters ; then we are found intractable in our laws ; we no longer admit equality ; we require woman to declare herself our inferior and servant, and to swear obedience to us.

" Truly we cling more to money than to love ; we have more consideration for money-bags than for human dignity ; for we emancipate women as soon as they become freeholders ; but as soon as they become wives the law declares them our inferiors.   Here notwithstanding, that bond is in question in which the equality of man and woman is most evident; that bond in which this equality breaks forth, as it were; that bond in which it is so necessary to proclaim that without equality, the bond itself exists no longer.   Yet, by an absurd contradiction, our civil law chooses this moment to proclaim the inferiority of woman; it condemns her to obedience, makes her take a false oath, and takes advantage of love to make it outrage itself.

" I have no doubt that, to future ages, the characteristic symbol of our moral condition will be that article of our laws which sanctions in set terms inequality in love.   It will be said of us: they had so little comprehension of justice, that they did not comprehend love which is justice in even its holiest type; they had so little comprehension of love, that they did not even admit justice in it; and that in their written law, their Code, the form of marriage, the only sacrament of which they yet had any idea, instead of sanctioning equality, sanctions inequality; instead of union, disunion; instead of the love that equalizes and identifies its objects, some contradictory and monstrous relation, founded at the same time upon identity, and upon inferiority and slavery.   Yes, like those forms of the law of the Twelve Tables, that we quote now to prove the barbarity of the ancient Romans and their ignorance of justice, this article of our Code will be some day cited to characterize our grossness and ignorance, for the absence of an elevated notion of justice is as marked in it as is the absence of an elevated notion of love.

" Thence follows everything relative to the condition of woman; or rather, everything is connected with this point; for will we respect the equality of woman as a human being when we are senseless enough to deny her this quality as a wife? Is woman to-day, in so far as a human being, really treated as the equal of man? I will not enter upon this broad subject. I confine myself to a single question; what education do women receive? You treat them as you treat the people. To these too you leave the old religion that fits us no longer. They are children kept as long as possible in swaddling clothes, as though this were not the true way to deform them, to destroy at once the rectitude of their mind and the candor of their soul. Besides, what does Society do for them? To what new careers does she give them access? Yet, notwithstanding, it is evident to every thinking mind that our arts, our sciences, our manufactures will make as much new progress when women are called to take a part in them, as they did a few years ago, when they were opened to the serfs. You complain of the want and wretchedness that weighs down your systems of society; *abolish the castes that are still subsisting; abolish the caste in which you hold immured the half of the human race.*"

These few pages, my readers, give you the compass of the sentiments of the St. Simonians, both orthodox and dissenters, and justify the sympathy entertained by women who have attained *majority* for those who have so ardently pleaded their cause.

FUSIONISTS.

Louis de Tourreil, the revealer of Fusionism, is a man whom it is impossible to behold without sympathy or to hear without pleasure; he is kindly, he speaks well, and his ideas are most logically deduced; his principles once admitted, one is constrained to follow him to the end.

Tourreil expresses himself in the *Revue Philosophique* of May, 1856, on the subject of woman and her rights, as follows:

" Natnre is reduced to three great co-eternal principles or productive agents of all things. These principles are:

" The female or passive principle,

" The male or active principle,

" And the mixed or unificative principle, participating in both, which is called Love.

" God is therefore Female, Male and Androgynous, in his trinary unity.

" He is simultaneously from all eternity Mother, Father and Love, instead of being, as the theologians say, Father, Son, and Holy Spirit; three agents of like sex, incapable of producing anything.

" You will easily conceive, my dear brother, that if the masculine and the feminine sex hold the same rank in the Divine Trinity, they will be also found in the same rank in humanity. The part which the divine woman plays in Heaven, the human woman will play on Earth. . . .

" Were he (*God*) only of the masculine sex, men would say that the masculine sex alone is noble, and that woman is created merely for the service of man, as man is created for that of God. They would even question whether she had a soul, and would think that they were doing her a favor in admitting her as something in life."

After quoting the teachings of the apostle Paul with respect to woman and marriage, the author continues:

" Behold, my dear brother, the part which Christianity assigns to woman. If this doctrine therefore were followed in every point, and if it ought to be replaced by no higher one, woman would find herself condèmned in perpetuity to a subalternization humiliating to her nature.

" But Fusionism, which is the doctrine of Salvation for all, does not permit any one to be sacrificed ; for this reason, woman is the equal of man and man the equal of woman, as in God, the eternal Mother is the equal of the eternal Father, and the eternal Father is the equal of the eternal Mother."

De Tourreil believes that the Mother gives form and the Father life, two things equally necessary to constitute the being.

" Since woman is the equal of man in absolute principle," continues he, " and since she is co-eternal with him, there is injustice in subordinating her to man in the relative ; and the book of *Genesis* commits a gross error in making her proceed from man :

" If either of the two could be before the other, it would be the woman, for strictly speaking, we could conceive of the being without the life, but it would be quite impossible to conceive of the life without the being : The being without the life would be a dead being, but what would the life be without the being ? It would be a life without existence, negation, the absence of life, nothingness. Therefore, in logical order, woman is first. . . .

" Not only ought woman to be the equal of man, as we have seen, but in enunciation and classification, she should be named and classed first.

" Woman is the mould by which the species is perfected or depraved, according as the mould is good or bad. The fate of humanity depends therefore on woman, since she has all powerful influence on the fruit that she bears in her bosom.

" Pure, good, intelligent, she will produce healthy, intelligent and good beings.

" Impure, narrow, and wicked, she will produce unhealthy, unintelligent and wicked beings.

" In a word, the child will be what its mother is, for nothing can give what it has not.

" It is important therefore that woman should be developed like man, that her education should be comprehensive, that her person should be honored, respected, and tenderly cared for, in order that nothing in the social surroundings may shape it to evil.

" Destined by the Supreme Being to form the human being from her flesh, her blood and her soul, destined to nourish it with her milk and to give it its earliest education, the two acts which have the greatest influence over the individual life, woman should be considered as the chief agent of perfection. This *rôle* classes her naturally in a very elevated rank in society, and exacts of her superior perfections.

" Thus in the future she will be the image of Divine Wisdom on earth, as man will represent Divine Power.

" To man more especially will belong action ; to woman, counsel.

" Man will take the initiative in difficult enterprises ; woman will moderate or excite ardor therein.

" Man will rule the planet ; woman will embellish it.

" Man will symbolize science and manufactures ; woman will symbolize poetry and art.

" The one will always have need of the other ; they

will walk together side by side, and will find complete-
ness reciprocally in each other.

"Such, my dear friend, after a brief fashion, is the
idea which should be formed of woman. Man and woman are not two beings radically separated; both together make but a single being. To subordinate woman
to man or man to woman is therefore to mutilate the
human being, or to fail to comprehend its interests.
That humanity may be happy, neither of its halves
must suffer. And how can it help suffering if it is reduced to servitude and oppressed by the other?

"Our destiny on earth is to constitute the collective
being in his own consciousness. For this, it is necessary to realize the humanitary androgynus. Now the
humanitary androgynus necessitates first the individual
androgynus which can only be constituted by harmonious marriage.

"Marriage is therefore the great formative or deform-
ative law of the collective being, according as it is expressed by the legislator in a manner conformably or
contrary to human destiny.

"It is in marriage that the sources of good and evil
are found; would you know why?

"Because in the act that joins the man to the woman, and by which the couple are made to form but one
body, the two souls are fused by means of a reciprocal
donation, which unites the souls of the two for eternity.

"So that, after the conjunction, the soul of the woman adheres to the soul of the man and accompanies it
everywhere, while the soul of the man adheres to the
woman and never more quits it.

"Whence it follows that if the soul of the man be depraved, it depraves the woman to whom it is united, by
exercising over her a continued action, even at a dis-

tance.   So also does the depravity of the woman united
to the man deprave him without his knowing it by an
occult and permanent action.

" The souls of two depraved beings may be therefore inseparably conjoined, without thus constituting the
individual androgynus, which is the divine end of marriage or the union of the sexes.

" The individual androgynus is only possible to the
condition of unity.   But unity cannot be constituted by
evil.

" The good, the true and the perfect alone can com-
bine the conditions of unity.   The evil, the false and
the imperfect are essentially inharmonious in their nature.

" Two wicked, insincere and vicious beings will only
produce by their conjunction a still greater difference.
They will be united, but only reciprocally to torment
each other.   Unity will never be constituted by them ;
and without the constitution of unity or the individual
androgynus, it will be impossible to realize the human
destiny.

" In order that the individual androgynus may exist in
the couple, there must be perfect spiritual communion
between them ; that is, communion of thought, of feeling,
and of will.   But how can two individuals who, instead of being ruled by truth, are ruled only by their
misdirected passions, — how can these two make but
one ?   It is impossible.

" You will comprehend, my dear brother, from these
few words, how sacred is marriage, and how important
it is to contract none but harmonious unions, for the unhappiness of a lifetime often depends on an inconsiderate conjunction."

Having had several opportunities of meeting M. de

Tourreil, I asked him for some exact details in respect to the liberty of woman and marriage.

The following is an abstract of those that he has kindly given me ;

Education should be the same for both sexes ;

Woman should be at liberty to follow the vocation which comes to her from God; and of which she alone is judge ;

" In all grades and employments in the republic of God, woman should be at the side of man ;

After the age of fifty, all individuals of both sexes should be rulers and priests ;

The reproduction of the species being the work of the love of persons healthy in mind and in body, before marriage, the bride should be required to make confession to a priestess and the bridegroom to a priest, in order to be enlightened with respect to the opportuneness or unsuitableness of the union.

Dissolution of marriage should take place but in a single case, — when the husband and wife have attained to complete fusion ; that is, to feeling and knowing reciprocally that they have no longer anything to exchange. It then becomes necessary to form new ties, and, each one to labor to fuse with a new consort. In the existing condition of humanity, this fusion cannot take place ; but in the future, when we shall be nearer perfection, it will become possible several times in life.

Fusionism is, as is evident, mystical socialism.

Its votaries are gentle and good, and very tolerant towards those who do not think like them.

PHALANSTERIANS.

The motto of the Fourieristic, Societary or Phalanster-

ian school is *respect for individual liberty*, based on the
following notions :

All nature is good ; it becomes perverted only when
performing its functions in evil surroundings.

No person exactly resembling the rest, each one should
be the sole judge of his capacities, and should receive
laws only from himself.

Attractions are proportional to destinies.

If the disciples of my compatriot, Charles Fourier,
do not express themselves exactly in this wisè, all that
have written bears the imprint of these thoughts.

Are Fourier and his disciples right in believing that
the law of passional attraction *alone* is required to organize the industrial, moral and social world ?

That the primordial element of a system of society
should be the Societary or Phalansterian association ?

That the most opposite, the most diverse passions are
the conditions *sine quâ non* of harmony ?

That the compensation of labor and of competi
tion should be regulated according to Labor, Capita
and Talent ?

We are not called on to examine this here.

The only thing that need occupy us in this rapid re
view of cotemporaneous opinions is the investigation
of the sentiments and ideas of Fourier and his schoo
in that which concerns the principal object of this book
A few pages from the chief of the order, and a summary
analysis will suffice for this.

In the *Théorie des quartre Mouvements*, M. Fouriei
writes ;

" That the ancient philosophers of Greece and Rome
should have disdained the interests of women is by no
means surprising, since these rhetoricians were all ultra

partisans of the pederasty which they had brought in
high honor in *la belle antiquité*. They cast ridicule
upon the associating with women; this passion was
considered dishonorable. . . . These manners obtained
the unanimous suffrage of the philosophers who, from
the virtuous Socrates to the delicate Anacreon, affect-
ed Sodomitish love alone and contempt for women,
who were banished to the upper apartments, immured
as in a seraglio, and exiled from the society of men.

" These fantastic tastes not having found favor among
the moderns, there is reason for surprise that our philosophers should have inherited the hatred that the ancient scholars bore to women, and that they should continue to disparage the sex on account of a few wiles to
which woman is forced by the oppression which weighs
upon her; for every word or thought in conformity with
the voice of nature is made in her a crime.

" What can be more inconsistent than the opinion of
Diderot, who pretends that, to write to woman, one
has only to dip his pen in the rainbow, and sprinkle the
writing with dust from butterflies' wings? Women
might reply to the philosopher: Your civilization per-
secutes us as soon as we obey nature; we are obliged
to assume a fictitious character and to listen to impulses
contrary to our desires. To give us a relish for this
doctrine, you are forced to bring in play deceitful illusions and language, as you do with respect to the soldier whom you cradle in laurels and immortality to di-
vert his thoughts from his wretched condition. If he
were truly happy, he would welcome the plain and
truthful language which you take care not to address
to him. It is the same with women; if they were
free and happy, they would be less eager for illu-

sions and cajoleries, and it would no longer be necessary in writing to them to place rainbows and butterflies' wings under contribution.

" When it (Philosophy) rails at the vices of women, it criticises itself; this it is that produces these vices by a social system which, repressing their faculties from their infancy and through the whole course of their life, forces them to have recourse to fraud in order to yield to nature.

" To attempt to judge of women by the vicious character which they display in civilization is like attempting to judge of human nature by the character of the Russian peasant, who is destitute of all ideas of honor and liberty ; or like judging the beaver by the stupidity which they show when domesticated, whilst in a condition of liberty combined with labor, they become the most intelligent of all quadrupeds. The same contrast will reign between the women who are slaves of civilization and those who are free in the combined order ; they will surpass men in industrial devotion, in loyalty, in nobleness; but outside of the free and combined state, woman, like the domesticated beaver or the Russian peasant, becomes a being so inferior to her destiny and talents that we are inclined to despise her when judging her superficially according to appearances.

" It is a surprising thing that women should have always shown themselves superior to men when they have had it in their power to display on the throne their natural talents, of which the diadem assured them a free use. Is it not certain that of eight queens, independent and unmarried, seven will be found to have reigned with glory, while of eight kings, we count habitually seven feeble sovereigns.

. .   The Elizabeths and Catherines did not make war in person, but they knew how to choose their generals; and it is enough that these are good.   In every other branch of administration, has not woman given lessons to man?   What prince has surpassed in firmness Maria Theresa who, in a disastrous moment, when the fidelity of her subjects was tottering and her ministers were struck with terror, undertook herself alone to inspire all with new courage?   She intimidated by her presence, the disaffected Diet of Hungary; she harangued the Magnates in the Latin tongue, and brought her very enemies to swear on their sabres to die for her.   This is an indication of the prodigies that would be wrought by feminine emulation in a social order which would permit free scope to her faculties.

" And you, the oppressing sex,— would you not go beyond the faults imputed to women if you, like them, had been moulded by a servile education to believe yourselves automatons created to obey prejudices and to cringe before the master whom chance had given you? Have we not seen your pretensions to superiority confounded by Catharine, who trampled under foot the masculine sex?   In creating titled favorites, she trailed man in the dust, and proved that it is possible for him in full liberty to abase himself beneath woman, whose degradation is forced, and consequently, excusable. It would be necessary, to confound the tyranny of man that, for the space of a century, a third sex should exist, which should be both male and female, and stronger than man.   This new sex would prove by dint of blows that men as well as women were made for its pleasures; then we should hear men protest against the tyranny of the hermaphrodite sex, and confess that force ought not

9

to be the sole law of right.   Now why are these privileges, this independence, which they would reclaim from this third sex, refused by them to women.

"In singling out those women who have had power to soar, from the virago, like Maria Thresea, to those of a gentler type, like the Ninons and the Sévignés, I am authorized in saying that woman, in a state of liberty, will surpass man in all functions of the mind and body which are not the attributes of physical strength.

"Man seems already to foresee this; he becomes indignant and alarmed when women give the lie to the prejudice that accuses them of inferiority. *Masculine jealousy has especially broken out against women authors; philosophy has kept them out of academic honors, and has sent them back ignominiously to the household.*" . . (p. 148.)

"What is their existence to-day (that of women)? They exist in privations alone, even in the trades, in which man has encroached on everything, *even to the minutest occupations of the needle and the pen, while women are seen employed in the toilsome labors of the field. Is it not scandalous to see athletes thirty years old squatted before a desk, or carrying a cup of coffee with muscular arms,* as if there were not women and children enough to attend to the minor details of the counting-room and the household.

"What then are the means of subsistence for women destitute of fortune? The distaff, or else their charms if they have any. *Yes, prostitution more or less glossed over is their only resource,* which philosophy again contests to them; this is the abject fate to which they are reduced by this civilization, this conjugal slavery which they have not even thought of attacking." (p. 150.)

Fourier bitterly reproaches women authors for having neglected to seek the means whereby to put an end to such a state of affairs, and adds with great reason :

" Their indolence in this respect is one of the causes that have accrued from the contempt of man. *The slave is never more comtemptible than by a blind submission which persuades the oppressor that his victim was born for slavery.* (p. 150)."

Fourier is right, but . . . to elevate others is to risk being lost one's self in the crowd ; and every one is not capable of this degree of abnegation.

To combat for the right of the weak when men have admitted you to their ranks, is to prepare for yourself a rough way and a heavy cross.

In the first place, you are exposed to the hatred and raillery of men, then half-cultured women corroded by jealousy, invent a thousand calumnies for your destruction ; they feign to be scandalized that a woman dare protest against the inferiority and use of her sex ; they enter into league with the masters, clamor louder than they and satirize you without mercy.

Now all women are not made to shrug their shoulders in the face of this cohort of morbid minds . . . they love peace too well, they lack courage, and *they do not care enough for justice ;* is it not so, ladies ?

Let us return to Fourier. It is known that he admits several social periods. According to him, the pivot of each of them hinges on love and the degree of liberty of woman.

" As a general rule," he says, " *social progress and changes of the period will be wrought in proportion to the progress of women towards liberty, and the decay of the social order will be wrought in proportion to the decline of the liberty of women.*"

In another place, he adds in speaking of philosophers:

"If they treat of morals, they forget to recognize and to claim the rights of the weaker sex, *the oppression of which destroys the basis of justice.*"

He says again, elsewhere:

"Now, God recognizes as liberty only that which is extended to both sexes, and not to one alone; so he has prescribed that all the germs of social evils, as the savage state, barbarism, civilization, should have no other pivot than the enthrallment of women; and that all the germs of social good, as the sixth, seventh and eighth period, should have no other pivot, no other compass, than the progressive affranchisement of the weaker sex."

Fourier is reproached with having desired the emancipation of woman in love; nothing is more true. But to impute this to him as immorality, men must censure their own morals. Now, these gentlemen considering themselves as wholly *pure*, though themselves representing the *butterfly* in love, infidelity and the simultaneous possession of several women being only a pastime to them, I do not really see what they can blame in Fourier.

Either what they do is right, and therefore cannot be wrong in woman;

Or what they do is wrong; then why do they do it?

Fourier believed in the unity of the moral law and in the equality of the sexes; he believed in the lawfulness of the morals of these gentlemen, *minus perfidy and hypocrisy;* this is the reason that he claims emancipation in love for woman: he is logical.

Besides, he repeats continually that the ethics that he depicts would cause disorder in the civilized period;

and that they can only be established progressively in subsequent periods. Many among the Phalansterians reject Fourier's ethics with respect to love as well as his Theodicy, and I myself have heard several discourses in which the orator condemned, not only falsity in conjugal relations, but also looseness of morals.

Fourier and the Saint Simonian orthodoxy have both been guilty of the same error with regard to the emancipation of woman ; but, men, I repeat, must be very audacious to impute it to them as a crime, since they indulge themselves in worse ; as to women, sustained and loved by these reformers, let them imitate the pious conduct of Shem and Japhet ; one owes respect to his father, whatever may be the idea or the wine with which he is drunken.

Now that we have cited the master, let us enumerate the principal points of the Fourierist doctrine, touching the liberty of woman and the equality of the sexes :

1. Man and woman are composed of the same physical, moral and intellectual elements ; there is, therefore, between the sexes, identity of nature.

2. The proportion of these elements differs in the two sexes, and constitutes the difference that exists between them.

3. This difference is so equalized that the value shall be equal. Where man is the stronger, he takes precedence of woman ; where woman is stronger, she takes precedence of man.

4. Man belongs to the *major mode :* he has the ascendency over woman in intellect, in logic, in the larger manufactures, in friendship ; it belongs to him therefore to create positive science, to connect facts, to regulate commercial relations, to bind together interests, and

to organize groups and series.   To all these things, woman brings her indispensable aid, but by reason of her
aptitudes, her services are only secondary therein.

5. Woman belongs to the *minor mode;* she has the
ascendency over man in the kind of intellect that applies and adapts, in the intuition that puts man on the
track of the good to which masculine logic should attain; in the sphere of maternity in which she presides
over education, for she comprehends the means to be
employed to ameliorate the species in every respect better than man; in the sphere of love in which she has
the right and the power to civilize and refine the relations of the sexes; and to stimulate man to conquest of
the intellect, to the amelioration of the physical conditions of the globe, of industry, of art, of social relations, etc.

Woman intervenes to a certain point in the major
mode, so does man enter into the minor mode, in which
his coöperation is indispensable.

Thus, in general, in man the head predominates, in
woman, the heart; but as both have a heart and a head,
man, through his heart, becomes an aid in the minor
mode, and woman, through her head, becomes an aid in
the major mode.

6. There are men who are women both in head and
in heart; women who are men both in heart and in head;
in humanity they form the eighth of an exception.   Full
liberty and right are granted to them.

7. Each member of the Phalanstery follows his vocation, obeys his attractions, *for attractions are proportional to destinies.*   Therefore the eighth of an exception in both sexes, having an attraction towards labors
that belong more especially to the other sex, is at liberty to yield to them.

8. All major men and women have an equal vote.

9. All matters are regulated by chiefs *of both sexes*, chosen by the free vote of both sexes.

10. All offices, from the presidency of the group to that of the globe, are filled jointly by men and women, who divide between them the details of this common function.

11. The mother is the instructress of her children; they belong to her alone; the father has no rights over them unless the mother chooses to confer these on him.

Such is the summary of the Fourierist doctrine on the subject of which we treat.

If the Societary School has not reached perfect truth, it must be at least acknowledged that it has taken the right way to attain it. Whether its theory of the class-ification and the predominance of faculties in conformity with the sexes be exact or not, the error will not be productive of mischievous results in practice. Woman being free to follow her aptitudes, being half in rights and functions, could always place herself in the excep-tional eighth, without fear of encountering jealous indi-viduals, better fitted than herself to warble in the minor key, who would send her back to the duties of the household.

I remember, in this connection, a certain advocate, by no means *feminine*, professing a superb disdain of the sex to which his mother belonged, worthy in a word, to be the disciple of P. J. Proudhon; would you know what this man had retained of all his lessons in law? The art of sweeping a room properly, of polish-ing furniture, of hemming napkins and pocket handker-chiefs neatly, and of compounding sauces. Do you not think, illustrious Proudhon, that he might have been advised with more justice to *go and iron his collars*, than certain women who write good articles on Philosophy

But let us return to Fourier.

Among the Socialist Schools, that of Fourier occupies a distinguished place; it is the one most deserving of the gratitude of women through the principles that it has laid down. Be it understood, we separate in this connection the principles of Liberty and Equality from all that relates to the question of ethics, which we cannot resolve in the same manner as Fourier, *any more for woman than man*

CHAPTER VII.

SUMMARY.

Appear, all ye modern innovators, before your judge, the public. Sum up your opinions.

COMMUNIST. The two sexes differ, do not perform the same functions, but *they are equal before the law.*

For woman to be really emancipated, society must be remoulded economically, and marriage suppressed.

PHILADELPHIAN AND ICARIAN. We are of your opinion, brother, except in what concerns marriage.

ORTHODOX ST. SIMONIAN. If Christianity has despised and oppressed woman, it has been because, in its sight, she represented matter, the world, evil. We, who are come to give the true meaning of the Trinity, rehabilitate or explain what our predecessors have condemned. Woman is the equal of man, because in God, who comprises everything, matter is equal to spirit. With man, woman forms the couple which is the social individual, the functionary. As woman is very different from man, we do not take the liberty of judging her; we content ourselves with *summoning* her that she may reveal herself.

Notwithstanding we think that she can only be affranchised by being emancipated in love.

9*

PIERRE LEROUX *agitated.* Take care! It is not so much in sex that woman should be affranchised; it is only in her quality of *wife and human being.* She has sex only for him she loves; to all other men she is what they are themselves: sensation, sentiment, sense. She must be free in marriage and in the commonwealth as man himself should be.

FUSIONIST *interrupting him.* You are right, Pierre Leroux; yet neither is the previous speaker wholly wrong; woman is free and the equal of man in everything, because spirit and matter are equal in God; because the man and the woman form together the human androgynus, the derivation of the divine androgynus. It is not so, my dear sister?

MYSELF. Excuse me, brothers, from joining in your theological discussion; my wings are not strong enough to follow you into the bosom of God, in order to assure myself whether he is spirit or matter, androgynus or not, binary, trinary, quarternary, or nothing of all these. It is enough for me that you all grant that woman should be free, and the equal of man.

I permit myself only a single observation; that your notion of the couple or of the androgynus, at the bottom one and the same thing, tends fatally to the subjugation of my sex; if, by a metaphor, a fiction, we make of two beings, endowed each with a separate will, free-will and intellect, a single unity; *in social practice,* this unity is manifested by a single will, a single free-will, a single intellect, and the individuality that prevails in our society is that which is endowed with strength of arm; the other is annihilated, and the right given to the couple is in reality only the right of the stronger. The use that M. Proudhon has made of androgyny ought to cure you of this fancy; as the use which your predecessors made of the ternary ought to have preserved you from trinitary metaphysics. Be it said without offence to you, gentlemen, I have a decided antipathy to any trinities and androgynies whatsoever; I am a sworn enemy to all metaphysics, whether profane or sacred, — a constitutional vice, aggravated in me by Kant and his school.

PHALANSTERIAN. For God's sake, gentlemen, let us quit this mysticism. Man and woman are different, but the one is as necessary as the other to the great work that should be accomplished by humanity; therefore they are equal. As each individual has a right to develop himself integrally, to manifest himself completely in order to perform the parcellary task which his attractions assign to him, the liberty of one sex can no more be called in question than can that of the other. Man modulates in major, woman in minor, with an exceptional eighth; but, as in all the general functions, the combination of the two modes is necessary, it is evident that each of them ought to be double, and that woman ought everywhere to be equal with man.

M. DE GIRARDIN *somewhat abruptly*. Gentlemen, I agree with you that woman ought to be free and equal with man; only I maintain that her function is to manage, to economize, and to rear her children, while man labors and brings into the household the product of his industry.

As I wish woman to be freed from servitude and all children to be rendered legitimate, I suppress civil marriage, and institute universal dowry.

M. LEGOUVE *smiling*. You go too fast and too far, my dear sir, you will frighten everybody. At least, I

believe like you in the equality of the sexes through
the equivalence of their functions, but I take good care
not to breathe a word of it.　I content myself with
claiming for woman instruction, diminution of conjugal
servitude, and offices of charity; counting, between
ourselves, that these victories obtained, women will be
in a position through their education and proved utility,
to affranchise themselves completely.　Well! despite
my reserve and moderation, you see that some call me
effeminate, others *sans culotte*.

M. MICHELET, *rising with tears in his eyes.*　Alas,
gentlemen, you are all in the wrong road; and I am
very sorry, my beloved academician Legouvé, to see
you employ your elegant pen in leading woman in so
perilous and irrational a way.

As to you, gentlemen, who lay claim to liberty and
equality of rights for woman, you are not authorized by
her to do so; she demands no right, what should she do
with it — a being always feeble, always sick, always
wounded.　Poor creature!　What can be her rôle here
below, if not to be adored by her husband, whose duty it
is to constitute himself her instructor, her physician, her
confessor, her sick nurse, her waiting-maid; to keep her
in a hot-house, and with all these multiplied cares to earn
beside the daily bread; for woman cannot, ought not to
work; she is the love and the altar of the heart of man.

Some among you have dared utter the vile word:
Divorce.

No divorce!　The woman who has given herself
away, has received the imprint of man.　You should
not abandon her, however guilty she may be.　I thought
in the beginning that after your death she ought to
wear mourning to the tomb, beyond which, she and her

husband would be fused into the unity of love. But I have thought better of it; you may appoint a successor.

While Michelet is seating himself, wiping his eyes, the lid of a coffin is seen to rise, and Comte exclaims in a sepulchral tone:

Worthily and *admirably* spoken, illustrious professor !

What! you here ?. exclaims the assembly. Then one does not perish entirely, as you taught your disciples ?

COMTE. No, gentlemen, and I was very agreeably surprised to see myself mistaken. But it is not to instruct you about the life beyond the tomb that I return ; that would not have been worth the trouble of disturbing myself. It is to express to the great professor Michelet all the satisfaction that I feel in seeing him so richly poetise the ideal that I set up, and strew so many flowers over the *admirable* maxim of Aristotle and the *commandment* of the great St. Paul.

Yes, thrice illustrious Master, you have rightly said : woman is made for man, she should obey him, be devoted to him ; she is only a doll in private life, absolutely nothing in public life. Yes, men should labor for her ; yes, marriage is indissoluble ; all this is irreproachable.

AUGUSTE COMTISM. I regret but one thing—that you have not preserved the ejaculatory orisons of the wife to the husband, and of the husband to the wife; it would have been a good example and have made a fine effect to see them every morning kneeling face to face, with clasped hands and closed eyes. I hope that this is only forgetfulness, and that you will reëstablish this detail in your next edition. I congratulate you openly on the happy thought that you have conceived of justifying the absorption of woman by man by aid of a wound and the mysteries of impregnation; this will have a great effect on the ignorant.

Rebellious women, and the madmen *with corrupt hearts* who sustain them, say that you are a poetic and ingenuous egotist, that our beloved Proudhon is a brutal egotist; that I am an egotist by A + B. Let them say so; I approve and bless you."

The ʼapparition was preparing to lie down again in his coffin when, having a passion for encountering phantoms, I seized a corner of his winding sheet, and, notwithstanding an unequivocal sign from him of *vade retro*, I had the courage to represent humbly to the defunct high priest that the brow of M. Proudhon deserved quite as much to be blessed as that of M. Michelet. The defunct gravely crossed his fleshless fore finger and thumb over the haughty and irreverent head of the great critic, who neither bowed nor seemed infinitely flattered.

It being his turn to speak, Proudhon rose and said: " Gentlemen Communists, Philadelphians, Fusionists, Phalansterians, Saint Simonians, and you, MM. Girardin and Legouvé, as well as all of your adherents, you are all *effeminate*, men *hardened in absurdity*.

If my friend Michelet has gilded, perfumed and sugared the pill for you, I cannot imitate his address and moderation, for you know that in temperament I, P. J. Proudhon, am neither tender nor poetical. Permit me then roughly to tell you the truth concerning a question *of which you do not understand the first word.*

" The Church, St. Thomas d'Aquinas, St. Bonaventure, St. Paul, and Auguste Comte, as well as the Romans, the Greeks, Manu and Mahomet teach that woman is made for the pleasure and use of man, and that she should be subjected to him; now I have sufficiently established these great truths by affirmations without reply. It is demonstrated to-day, therefore, to all who believe in me that woman is a passive being, having the germ of nothing, who owes everything to man, and that, consequently, she belongs to him as the work to the workman. . Lest my solution might appear somewhat harsh to you, or to savor too much of antiquity of the Middle Ages, I have borrowed of the modern innovators their farce of Androgyny; I have made the couple the organ of Justice; in this couple, woman, transformed by man, becomes a triple deity, a domestic idol, subject in everything to her priest. I shut her up in the household, and permit her to have only the superintendence of festivals and spectacles, the education of children and maidens, etc.

"Is it not evident, gentlemen, that woman, because she is weaker than we, is, *by justice*, condemned to obey us, and that *her liberty consists in experiencing. no amorous emotion, even for her husband*? Is it not evident, in consequence, that you, who do not think as I, are *effeminate*, *absurd* men, and that the women who are no more willing to be slaves than we were in '89 are *insurgents, impure women whom sin has rendered mad?*"

The majority of the assembly laugh; De Girardin shrugs his shoulders; Legouvé bites his lip in order not to laugh; Michelet appears troubled at this sally which may spoil everything. As, in uttering the word *insurgent*, the orator glances at me with marked design, I cannot help saying "yes, I deserve the name of *insurgent* like our fathers of '89. As to you, if you do not amend, I fear greatly that I shall see you die duly confessed and blessed with extreme unction . . . . and you will have well deserved it!"

Now, gentlemen, let us ascertain the vote of your honorable assembly.

Four schools, — the Communists, the St. Simonians, the Fusionians and the Phalansterians, — with one publicist, M. de Girardin, who makes as much noise by himself alone as a whole school, are for the liberty of woman and the equality of the sexes.

MM. Comte, Proudhon and Michelet are against the liberty of women and the equality oi the sexes.

M. Legouvé and his innumerable adherents wish liberty for woman, and desire that she should labor to become equal to man through equivalence of functions.

Which means that the great majority of those *who think* are, in different degrees, for our emancipation.

Now that my readers are acquainted with your several opinions, gentlemen, it belongs to me, a woman, to speak myself in behalf of my right, without leaning on anything but Justice and Reason.

PART II.

OBJECTIONS TO THE EMANCIPATION OF WOMAN NATURE
AND FUNCTIONS OF WOMAN. LOVE. MARRIAGE.
LEGAL REFORMS. SUMMARY.

I.

What arguments do the adversaries of the emancipation of women use to refute the equality of the rights of the sexes?

Some, theosophists of the old school, claim that one half of humanity is condemned by God himself to submit to the other half, because, they say, the first woman sinned.

Not wishing to depart from the firm ground of justice, reason and proved facts, we will not argue with this class of adversaries.

Others, who claim to be imbued with the modern spirit, and pretend to be disciples of the doctrines of liberty, condemn woman to inferiority and obedience because, they say, she is weaker physically and intellectually than man;

Because she performs functions of an inferior order;

Because she produces less than man in an industrial point of view;

Because her peculiar temperament prevents her from performing certain functions;

Because she is only fit for in-door life; because her vocation is to be mother and housewife, to devote herself entirely to her husband and children;

Because man protects and supports her;

Because man is her proxy, and exercises rights both for her and himself;

Because woman has no more time than capacity to exercise certain rights.

The rights of woman are in her beauty and our love, add some, gallantly.

Woman does not claim her rights; many women themselves are scandalized by the demands made by a few of their sex, continue other men.

And they spare the courageous women who plead the cause of right, and the men who sustain them neither calumnies, nor mockery, nor insult, hoping to intimidate the former and disgust the latter.

Vain hope! the time in which we could be intimidated has gone by. If it is justifiable to fear the opinion of those whom we deem juster and more intelligent than ourselves, it would be folly to be disturbed by those whose irrationality and injustice we feel able to demonstrate.

This double demonstration we are about to attempt, taking up one by one the arguments of these gentlemen.

1. Woman cannot have the same rights as man, because she is inferior to him in intellectual faculties, you say. From this proposition, we have a right to conclude that you consider the *human faculties as the basis of right;*

That, the law proclaiming equality of right for your sex, you are all equal in qualities, all alike strong and alike intelligent.

That, lastly, no woman is as strong and as intelligent as you; I cannot say, as the least among you, since, if right is founded on qualities, as it is equal, your qualities must be equal.

Now gentlemen, what becomes of these pretensions in the presence of *facts* that show you all unequal in strength and in intellect? What becomes of these pretensions in the presence of *facts* that show us a host of women stronger than many men; a host of women more intelligent than the great mass of men?

Being unequal in strength and in intellect, and notwithstanding declared equal in right, it is evident therefore that you have not founded right on qualities.

And if you have not taken these qualities into account when your right has been in question, why then do you talk so loudly of them when the question is that of the right of woman.

If the faculties were the basis of right, as the faculties are unequal, the right would be unequal; and, to be just, it would be necessary to accord right to those who made good their claims to the necessary faculties and to exclude the rest; by this standard many women would be chosen and an infinite number of men excluded. See where we end when we have not the intellectual energy to take principles into consideration! You have but one means of evicting us of equality; namely, to prove that we do not belong to the same species as you.

2. Woman, you add, cannot have the same rights as man because, as mother and housewife, she performs only functions of an inferior order.

From this second proposition, we have a right to conclude that *functions are the basis of right;*

That your functions are equivalent, since your right is equal !

That the functions of woman are not equivalent to those of man.

You have to prove then, gentlemen, that the functions *individually* performed by each of you are equivalent; that, for example, Cuvier, Geoffroy St. Hilaire, Arago, Fulton, Jacquard, and other inventors and scholars have not done more, are not doing more for humanity and civilization than an equal number of manufacturers of pins' heads.

You have to prove next that the labors of maternity, those of the household to which the workman owes his life, his health, his strength, the possibility of accomplishing his task—that these functions without which there would be no humanity, are not equivalent; that is, as useful to the social body as those of the manufacturer of jewels or of toys.

You have to prove lastly that the functions of the female teacher, merchant, book keeper, clerk, dressmaker, milliner, cook, waiting-maid, etc., are not equivalent to those of the male teacher, merchant, accountant, clerk, cook, tailor, hatter, footman, etc;

I grant that it is embarrassing to your triumphant argument to encounter the thousands of *facts* which show us the *real* woman performing numerous functions in competition with you ;

So it is, and these facts must be taken into account. But gentlemen, I have you in a dilemma ! if functions are the basis of right, as right is equal, functions are equivalent ; in which case those performed by woman are not inferior, since none are so.   The functions which she performs are therefore equivalent to yours, and, by this equivalence, she again becomes equal.

Or else functions are not the basis of right; did you not take them into account when the establishment of your right was in question; why then do you speak of functions when the question is the right of woman?

Extricate yourself from this as you can; I shall not help you.

II.

3. Woman produces less than man industrially, you say. Admitting this to be true, do you count as nothing the great maternal function — the risks that woman runs in accomplishing it;

Do you count as nothing the labors of the household, the cares that are lavished upon you, and to which you owe cleanliness and health?

If the quantity of the product be the origin of the equality of right, why have those who produce little, those who produce nothing, and all of you who produce unequally, equal right?

Why are all those women who produce, while their husbands and sons enjoy and dissipate, destitute of the rights which the latter possess?

You do not admit the question of product into that of right when man is in question, why then do you admit it when woman is in question?

You see that this is inconsiderate, irrational, unjust.

4. Woman cannot be the equal of man, because her peculiar temperament interdicts to her certain functions.

Well, then a legislator can, without being unreasonable, decree that all men who are unfitted by temperament for the profession of arms, for instance, are excluded from equality of right!

Temperament, the source of right?

If a woman had written anything so absurd, she would have been cried down from one end of the world to the other.

Why, gentlemen, do you not exclude from equality all men who are weak, all those who are incapable of performing the functions that you *prejudge* woman incapable of performing?

When you are in question, you admit indeed that the right to perform every function supposes neither the faculty nor the inclination to make use of it; why do you not reason in the same manner when the question concerns us? What would you think of women if, having your rights while you were in subjection, they should keep you in an inferior position because you could not accomplish the great functions of gestation and lactation.

Man, they would say, being unable to be mother and nurse, shall not have the right of being instructed like us; of having, like us, civil dignity. His coarser temperament renders him incapable of being a witness to a certificate of birth or death; it is evident that his clumsiness excludes him judicially from diplomatic functions; we cannot therefore recognize his right to solicit them, etc.

Ah! gentlemen, you reason in the same manner in excluding woman from equality under the pretext that, in general, she is of a temperament weaker than your own; that is, you reason absurdly.

5. Woman cannot be the equal of man in right because he protects and maintains her.

If it is because you protect and maintain us, that we ought not to have our right, restore it then to unmarried women who are of age, and to widows whom you neither protect nor maintain.

Restore their right then to the wives who have no need of your protection, since the law protects them, even against you; to the wives whom you do not maintain, since they bring you ̂either a dowry, or a profession, or services which you would be obliged to recom-· pense if any other rendered them to you.

And if to be maintained by another, suffices to deprive an individual of his right, take it away from the host of men who are maintained by the incomes or the labor of their wives.

6. Man, in the exercise of certain rights, is the proxy of woman.

Gentleman, a proxy is chosen freely, and is not imposed on an individual; I do not accept you as proxies: I am intelligent enough to transact my business myself, and I pray you to restore to me, as well as to all the women who think as I do, an authority which you use unworthily. If married women, to have peace, are willing to continue you as their authority, it is their business; but none of you can legitimately retain that of widows and unmarried women who have attained majority.

7. Woman has not the same rights as man, because she has no more time than capacity to exercise them.

Has woman less time and capacity than your working men, pinned twelve hours a day to their petty and stultifying tasks? Affirm it if you dare!

Does it need less time and capacity to make a deposition in a criminal suit, as woman does, than to witness a civil act or a notarial contract, a right that woman has not.

Does it need less time and capacity to be the guardian of sons and to administer their fortune, as woman does, than to be the guardian of a stranger or of a nephew, and administer their property, a right that woman has not.

Does it need less time and capacity to superintend a manufactory, a commercial establishment, workmen, as do so many women, than to be at the head of an office, or of a public administration, and to superintend its officials, a right that woman has not?

Does it need less time and capacity to devote one's self to instruction in a large boarding school, as do so many women, than in the chair of a professorship, as man alone has the right to do?

Woman proves, *by her works*, that she lacks capacity and time no more than you. Facts stifle affirmations for which you should blush. Fie! I am glad that I am not a man, lest I might say like things and be led to pretend that an instructress, a literary woman, a woman artist, an experienced female merchant has not the capacity of a porter or a rag-picker because she has not a beard on her chin.

8. The rights of woman are in her beauty and in the love of man.

Rights, based on beauty, and on that fragile thing styled man's love! What are these worth, I ask you, gentlemen?

Then woman shall have rights if she is beautiful, and as long as she shall continue so; if she is beloved, and as long as she shall continue so? Old, ugly and forsaken, she must be thrown into the car of the condemned to be transported to the guillotine?

If a woman should say such things, what a universal hue and cry would be raised?

Yet men pretend that they are rational! We congratulate woman on having too much common sense ever to be so in this wise.

After all these arguments, none of which will bear analysis, comes at last the triumphant objection : women do not claim their rights, many among them are even scandalized by the demand made by a few in the name of all. Do not women demand them, gentlemen ?

What are a host of American women doing at the present time ?

What have a number of English women done already ?

What did Jean Deroin, Pauline Roland and many others, do here in 1848 ?

What am I doing to day, in the name of a legion of women of whom I am the interpreter ?

All women do not make reclamations, no ; but do you not know that every demand of right is made at first singly ?

That slaves accustomed to their chains, do not feel them until their instigators to revolt show them the bruises on their flesh ?

A few only demand their rights, you say; but is it in accordance with principle or with numbers that you judge of the justice of a cause?

Did you wait until *all* the male population demanded their right of universal suffrage in order to decree it to them ?

Did you wait for the revendication of *all* the slaves of your colonies before emancipating them ?

Yes, it is true, gentlemen, that many women are opposed to the emancipation of their sex. What does this prove ? That there are human beings abased enough to have lost all sentiment of dignity ; but not that right is not right.

Among. tne blacks, there are many whc hate, de-
nounce, and deliver up to the scourge and to death
those among them who are meditating how to break
their chains ; which is right, which has the sentiment
of human dignity, the latter or the former ?

We demand our place at your side, gentlemen, because identity of species gives us the right to occupy it.

We demand our right, because the inferiority in-
which we are kept is one of the most active causes of
the decay of morals.

We demand our right, because we are persuaded
that woman has to set her stamp on Science, Philosophy, Justice and Politics.

We demand our right, lastly, because we are convinced that the general questions, the lack of solution
of which threatens our modern civilization with ruin,
can only be resolved by the co-operation of woman delivered from her fetters and left free in her genius.

Is it not a great proof of our insanity, our *impurity*,
gentlemen, that we feel this ardent desire to check the
corruption of morals, and to labor for the triumph of
Justice, the coming of the reign of Duty and Reason,
the establishment of an order of things in which humanity, worthier and happier, shall pursue its glorious destinies without the accompaniment of cannon or the
shedding of blood ?

Is it not because the advocates of emancipation are
*impure women whom sin has rendered mad, beings in-
capable of comprehending Justice and conscientious
works ?*

III.

Gentlemen, we will conclude.

Though that were true which I deny ; that woman

is inferior to you; though that were true which *facts* prove false; that she can perform none of the functions which you perform, that she is fit only for maternity and the household, she would be none the less your equal in right, because right is based neither on superiority of faculties nor on that of the functions which proceed from them, but on identity of species.

A human being, like you, having, like you, intellect, will, free will and various aptitudes, woman has the right, like you, to be free and autonomous, to develop her faculties freely, to exercise her activity freely; to mark out her path, to reduce her to subjection, as you do, is therefore a violation of Human Right in the person of woman — an odious abuse of force.

From the stand point of facts, this violation of right takes the form of grievous inconsistency; for we find many women far superior to the majority of men; whence it follows that right is granted to those who ought not to have it, according to your doctrine, and refused to those who ought to possess it, according to the same doctrine, since they make good their claim to the qualities requisite.

We find that you accord right to qualities and functions, *because the individual is a man*, and that you cease to recognize it in the same case, *because the individual is a woman.*

Yet you boast of your lofty reason, — yet you boast of posessing the sense of justice !

Take care, gentlemen ! Our rights have the same foundation as yours: in denying the former, you deny the latter in principle.

A word more to you, pretended disciples of the doctrines of '89, and we have done. Do you know why

so many women took part with our Revolution, armed
the men, and rocked their children to the song of the
Marseillaise! It was because they thought they saw
under the Declaration of the rights of men and citizens,
the declaration of the rights of women and female citizens.

When the Assembly took it upon itself to undeceive
them, by lacking logic with respect to them, and closing
their meetings, they abandoned the Revolution, and
you know what ensued.

Do you know why, in 1848, so many women, especially among the people, declared themselves for the Revolution? It was because they hoped that this Revolution would be more consistent with respect to them
than the former had been.

When, in their senseless arrogance and lack of intelligence, the representatives not only forbid them to
assemble, but *drove* them from the assemblies of men,
the women abandoned the Revolution by detaching
their husbands and sons from it, and you know what
ensued.

Do you comprehend at last?

I tell you truly; all your struggles are in vain, if
woman does not go with you.

An order of things may be established by a *coup de
main,* but it is only maintained by the adhesion of majorities; and these majorities, gentlemen, are formed by
us women, through the influence that we possess over
men, through the education that we give them with our
milk.

We have it in our power to inspire them from their
cradles with love, hatred or indifference for certain principles; in this is our strength; and you are blind not

to comprehend that if man is on one side and woman on the other, humanity is condemned to weave Penelope's web.

Gentlemen, woman is ripe for civil liberty, and we declare to you that we shall henceforth regard whoever shall rise against our lawful claim as an enemy of progress and of the Revolution ; while we shall rank among the friends of progress and of the Revolution, those who declare themselves in favor of our civil emancipation, SHOULD THEY BE YOUR ADVERSARIES ?

If you refuse to listen to our lawful demands, we shall accuse you before posterity of the crime with which you reproach the holders of slaves.

We shall accuse you before posterity of having denied the faculties of woman, because you feared her competition.

We shall accuse you before posterity of having refused her justice, because you wished to make her your servant and plaything. We shall accuse you before posterity of being enemies of right and progress.

And our accusation will remain standing and living before future generations who, more enlightened, more just, more moral than you, will turn away their eyes with disdain and contempt from the tomb of their fathers.

I.

I think that we have sufficiently though summarily proved to all honest inquiries that social right is identical for both sexes since they are identical in species. The question of right being placed beyond discussion, we can now ask what use woman shall make of her right; in other terms, what functions she is qualified to perform in accordance with her whole nature.

Let us first mark the profound difference that exists between right and function, then define and divide the latter.

Right is the condition *sine qua non* of the development and manifestations of the human being: it is absolute, general for the whole species, because the individuals who compose it should be able lawfully to develop and manifest themselves.

Function is the use of the faculties of the individual with a view to a purpose useful to himself and to others ; function is therefore a production of utility and, in conclusion, the manifestation of the aptitudes predominating in each of us, whether naturally, or in consequence of education and habit.

Society, having needs of every kind, has functions of

every nature and various scope; these functions may be classified as follows:

1. Scientific and philosophic functions;
2. Industrial functions;
3. Artistic functions;
4. Educational functions;
5. Medical functions;
6. Functions for the preservation of safety;
7. Judicial functions;
8. Functions of exchange and circulation;
9. Administrative and governmental functions;
10. Legislative functions;
11. Functions of solidarity or of social benevolence and of institutions for the prevention of crime.

This classification, which would be very imperfect and insufficient, were this a treatise on social organization, being all that is needed for the use that we have to make of it, we shall adhere to it in this place.

Men, and women after them, have deemed proper hitherto to class man and woman separately; to define each type, and to deduce from this ideal the functions suited to each sex. Neither have chosen to see that numerous facts contradict their classification.

What! exclaims the classifiers, do you deny that the sexes differ? Do you deny that, if they differ, they should have different functions?

If our classification does not seem good to you, criticise it, we ask nothing more; but replace it by a better one.

To criticise your classification, ladies and gentlemen, is what I intend to do; but if the elements are wanting to establish a better, can you, ought you even to require me to present you one.

Do you think me a man, that you exact of me abuse
of the *à priora*, and a startling arbitrary course of reasoning. " Proudhon is right," murmur these gentlemen ;
" woman is incapable of abstract reasoning, of generalizing, of *knowing herself*". . .

Really, gentlemen, do you think that it is through incapacity that I am unwilling to present to you a classification
of the sexes, a theory of the nature of woman ? . . .
Let us hasten then to prove the contrary: instead of
one theory, we will give you *four*. Man and woman
form a series only with respect to the reproduction of
the species : all the other characteristics by which it has
been attempted to make a distinction between them are
only generalities contradicted by a multitude of facts ;
now, as a generality is not a law, nothing can be therefore concluded from these, nothing absolute deduced from
them in a functional point of view.

On the other hand, the greatest radical difference of
zoological species lies in the nervous system, especially
in the greater or lesser bulk and complexity of the en-
cephalus ; now, Anatomy admits, after numerous experiments, that, in proportion to the whole size of the
body, the brain of woman equals in volume that of man ;
that the composition of both is the same, and Phrenology adds that the organs of the brain are the same in
both sexes.

Lastly, it is a biological principle that organs are developed by exercise and atrophied by continued repose ;
now, man and woman do not exercise their encephalic
organs in the same manner; educational training, manners, prejudice, enforced habits tend to develop in the
masculine what becomes atrophied in the feminine head ;
whence it follows that the differences empirically estab-

l:shed are by no means the result of Nature, but of the accidental causes by which they have been produced.

Conclusion: the two sexes therefore, when reared alike become developed alike, and are fit for the same functions, except those which concern the reproduction of the species.

Here, gentlemen, is a theory complete in all its parts, tenable in an anatomo-biologic point of view, and which I challenge you to prove false, for I shall find replies to all your objections.

II.

We admit the principle that the sexes form series in physical, moral, intellectual, consequently functional respects.

We believe that they should become subordinate to each other in proportion to their relative excellence; and we take the destiny of the species as the touchstone of their respective value.

If we compare the sexes with each other, we prove in a general way, that man is merely woman on a coarser scale; we prove in the second place that he is far more animal than woman, since his muscular system is more fully developed and since he respires lower; so that he is most evidently a medium between woman and the higher species of apes.

Woman alone contains and develops the human germ; she is the creator and preserver of the race.

It is not quite certain that the co-operation of man is necessary for the work of reproduction; *this is the means chosen by Nature*, but human science will succeed, we hope, in delivering woman from this insupportable subjection

Analogy authorises us to believe that woman, the sole depositary of the human germ, is equally the sole depositary of all the moral and intellectual germs, whence it follows that she is the inspirer of all knowledge, all discoveries, all justice, the mother of all virtue. Our analogous deductions are confirmed by facts; woman employs her intellect in the concrete; she is an acute observer; man is only fit to construct paradoxes and to lose himself in the abyss of metaphysics; science has only emerged from the limbo of *à priora* without confirmation, since the advent into this domain of the form of the feminine mind; we shall affirm, therefore, that true scholars are feminized minds.

In moral respects, man and woman differ greatly; the former is harsh, rough, without delicacy, devoid of sensibility and modesty; his habitual relations with the other sex modify him only with great difficulty; woman is naturally gentle, loving, feeling, equitable, modest; to her, man owes justice and his other virtues, when he has any; whence it follows that it is really to woman alone that social progress is due; hence it is that every step made towards civilization is marked by an advance of woman towards liberty.

If we consider each of the sexes in their relation to human destiny, we are forced to admit that, if there was reason for the predominance of man in the necessity of hewing out this destiny, the pre-eminence of woman is ensured in the future reign of right and peace.

It was necessary to struggle and fight in order to establish justice and to subject nature to humanity; this belonged of right to man, who represents muscular force, the spirit of conflict; but as we already foresee in the approaching future, the coming of peace, the substitution of pacific labor and negotiations for war, it is clear that woman will take rightfully the direction of human affairs, to which she will be called by her faculties, found better adapted to the end henceforth to be pursued.

Woman should be the last to develop and manifest herself socially, for the same reason that the human species is the last creation of our globe ; the perfect being always appears after those that have served to pave the way.

ʹAs it is demonstrated, on the other hand, that, in the scale of the various organisms, the organ that is superadded to the others to constitute a change of species, governs those which the individual derives from inferior species, so woman, fully developed in a social body organized for peace and pacific labor, will be the new organ that will govern the social body.

Does this signify that woman should oppress man ? By no means ; she would thus be ungrateful for the services rendered her, and would trespass against her gentle nature ; but she will teach him to comprehend that *his glory is to obey*, to become subordinate to the other sex, because he is less perfect, and because his qualities are no longer necessary to the general good.

You laugh, gentlemen, at this second theory ; you think it absurd. . . . So it is ; for it is the counterpart of the thetic woman of Proudhon.   Let us proceed then to the third theory.

III.

Every classification of the human species is a pure subjective creation ; that is, one which exists only in the form given to the perception by the intellect ; the very conception of humanity with the enumeration of the characteristics which are reputed to distinguish it from the other species, is stamped with subjectivity.

The truth is that not a single human being resembles his neighbor ; that there are as many different men and women as there are men and women composing the species.

Classifications, in all things, are illusions of the mind, for nature hates identity and never repeats herself : there are not two grains of sand, not two drops of water, not two leaves alike ; and most probably the sun, since the commencement of its existence, has not appeared twice identically the same at its rising.   Yet despite the evidence of these truths, despite the conviction which we have attained of the illusion of the senses, of the weakness of our intellect, which can know nothing of the inmost nature of beings ; which can only seize upon a few fleeting traces of their personal characteristics ; yet despite all these things we dare establish series, attribute to them characteristics which are speedily contradicted by facts, and torture and do violence to the only beings that really exist ; namely, individuals, in the name of that other thing which exists only in our sick brain : kind, class !

The bitter fruits that have been produced by our mania for classification ought to cure us of this.   Has not this malady, impelling theocratists and legislators to divide humanity into castes and classes, caused most of the calamities of our species ? Have we not, thanks to these execrable divisions, a hideous past, the echoes of which bring back to our shrinking ears naught but sobs, cries of anger, rebellion, malediction and vengeance, and sinister clanking of weapons and chains?

Have we not also to thank them that, on the pages of our history, all stained with blood and tears and exhaling an odor of the charnel house, we read nought but tyranny, brutishness and demoralization?

Have we not further to thank them that king and subject, master and serf, white and black, man and woman become demoralized by oppression, injustice and cruelty on one hand; and intrigue, baseness, and vengeance on the other?

Are not wrong and wretchedness found everywhere, because inequality, the offspring of insane classifications, is found everywhere?

Ah! who shall deliver us from our infatuation!

Let us class animals, vegetables, minerals if we will! our errors do not influence and cannot disturb them; but let us respect the human species which will escape all classification, however reasonable the process may be, because every human being is changeable, progressive, and differs far more from his fellows than the most intelligent animal from the rest of his species.

Let us leave each one then to make his own autonomic law and to manifest himself in conformity with his nature, and take care only that right shall be equal for all; that the strong shall not oppress the weak; that each function shall be entrusted to the one individual that is proved the best qualified to perform it; this is all that we can do, all that we should do, if we seek to show ourselves wise and just.

Harmony exists in nature, because each being in it follows peaceably the laws that govern his individuality; it will be the same in humanity, when universal reason shall comprehend that human order is pre-established in the co-operation of individual faculties left free in their manifestations; and that to establish a factitious, wholly imaginary order; that is, true disorder, is to retard the coming of order, peace and happiness.

Let us refrain then from all classification of faculties and functions according to the sexes: besides being false, they will lead us to cruelty; for we shall oppress those, whether men or women, who are neither yielding enough to submit to it nor hypocritical enough to appear to do so; and we shall do this without profit to human destiny, but, on the contrary, to its detriment.

Here, gentlemen, is a *nominalistic* theory which I challenge you to overthrow by sufficient reasons: for, as in the first, I shall have answers to all your objections.

We now come to our last theory, which is yours in the major and minor terms, but the opposite in the conclusions.

IV.

All the different parts of the same organism are modified by each other, and in this manner the functions become mutually modified.

Now, man and woman differ from each other in important organs.

Each of the sexes must therefore differ from the other not only through the organs that distinguish them, but through the modifications produced by the presence of these organs.

This, gentleman, is my first syllogism: I know that we shall not contest this point — it is classical Biology.

Let us investigate anatomically the organic differences to which sexuality subjects man and woman.

Nervous System. The so called nerves of feeling are more fully developed in woman than in man, those of motion are less developed in the former than in the latter; the cerebellum is more fully developed in the head of man than in that of woman; in the latter, the antero-posterior diameter of the brain preponderates over the bi-lateral, which is greater in proportion in the masculine sex: it is also observed that the organs of observation, circumspection, subtleness and philoprogenitiveness are more prominent in the head of woman than in that of man, in which the reasoning organs, with those of combativeness and destructiveness predominate.

Locomotive System. Man is larger than woman, he has more compact bones, and larger and better developed muscles, his thorax is the reverse of that of woman, in which, the greatest breadth is between the shoulders, while, with him, it is at the base; the pelvis is larger and broader in the female than the male sex.

Epidermic and cellular systems. Man has a more hairy skin than woman; what is called fat is less abundant in the masculine than in the feminine organism; in general, the skin of man is rougher, and his form less round; woman has longer and more silky hair. *Splanchnic organs.* The cerebral mass is the same in proportion in both sexes, as well as the organs of the brain, with the exception of the predominances which we have pointed out; the respiratory systems differ somewhat; woman breaths higher than man; in the latter, the circulation is more active and energetic.

To these physical differences correspond intellectual and moral differences.

Woman, having the nerves of feeling more fully developed, is more impressionable and more mobile than man.

Being weaker and as persistent, she obtains by address and stratagem what she cannot obtain by force; her weakness gives her timidity, circumspection, the necessity of feeling herself protected.

The kinds of labor that require strength are repugnant to her.

Her maternal destiny renders her an enemy of destruction, of war; and her more delicate organization makes her dread and shun contention. This same maternal destination impresses a peculiar stamp on her intellect; she loves the concrete, and is always inclined to transform thought into facts, to incarnate it, to give it a fixed form; her reasoning is intuition or quick perception of a general relation, of a truth that man elucidates only with great dificulty, by the aid of stilted logic.

Woman is a better observer than man, and carries induction farther than he; she is consequently more penetrating, and is a much better judge of the moral and intellectual value of those about her.

She has, more than man, sentiment of the beautiful, delicacy of heart, love of good, respect for modesty, veneration for everything superior.

More provident than he, she has more order and economy, and looks after administrative details with a carefulness which is often carried to puerility.

Woman is adroit, sedulous; she excels in works of taste, and possesses strong artistic tendencies.

Gentler, more tender, more patient than man, she loves everything that is weak, protects everything that suffers; every. sorrow, every calamity brings a tear to her eye and draws a sigh from her breast.

This is woman, such as you paint her, gentlemen.

You then add:

The vocation of woman therefore is love, maternity, the household, sedentary occupations.

She is too weak for occupations that demand strength, and for those of war.

She is too impressionable and too feeling, too good, too gentle to be legislator, judge or juror.

Her taste for household details, a retired life, and the grave functions of maternity indicate clearly that she is not made for public employments. She is too variable to cultivate science with profit; too feeble and too much occupied beside to pursue protracted experiments.

Her kind of rationality renders her unsuited to the elaboration of theories; and she is too fond of the concrete and of details to become seriously interested in general ideas; which excludes her from all high professional functions and from those requiring serious study.

Her place is therefore · at the fireside to make man better, to sustain him, to care for him, to procure him the joys of paternity, and to fill the place of a good housewife.

Such are your conclusions: here are mine, admitting as a hypothesis, what I affirm with you of woman.

V.

1. Woman carrying into Philosophy and Science her subtleness of observation, her love of the concrete, will correct the exaggerated tendency of man for abstract

reasoning, and demonstrate the falsity of theories constructed, *à priori*, on a few facts alone. Then only will ontology disappear, then will it be recognized that a hypothesis is merely an interrogation point ; that truth is always intelligible in its nature, however unknown it may be ; we shall generalize nothing but known facts, we shall carefully avoid erecting simple generalities into laws, and we shall thus have veritable philosophy, and true human science, because they will bear the imprint of both sexes.·

2. Woman carrying her peculiar faculties into the arts and manufactures, will increasingly introduce therein art, perfection in details. Cultivated in the direction of her aptitudes, she will find ingenious methods of application of scientific discoveries.

3. Patient, gentle, good, more moral than man, she is the born educator of childhood, the moralizer of the grown man ; the majority of the educational functions revert to her of right, and she has her assigned place in special instruction.

4. By her quick intuition and her acuteness of observation, woman alone can discover the therapeutics of nervous affections ; her dexterity will render her valuable in all delicate surgical operations. On her should devolve the care of treating the diseases of women and children, because she alone is capable of fully comprehending them ; she has her especial place in hospitals, not only for the cure of disease, but also for the execution and surveillance of the details of management and the care of the patients.

6. The presence of woman in judicial functions, as juror and arbiter, will be a guarantee of veritable human justice to all ; that is, of equity.

Woman alone through her gentleness, her mercy, her sympathetic disposition, and her subtleness and observation, can comprehend that society has its share of culpability in every fault committed; for it should be organized to prevent wrong rather than to punish it. This point of view, especially feminine, will transform the penitentiary system and raise up numerous institutions. Then only will the world comprehend that the punishment inflicted on the guilty should be a means of reparation and regeneration; society will no longer slay its prisoners as if weak and fearful: it will amend the assassin instead of imitating him; it will force the thief to work to make restitution of what he has stolen; it will no longer believe that it has the right by imprisoning a criminal to deprive him of his reason, to drive him to despair, to suicide by solitary confinement; to deprive him completely of marriage; to couple him with those more corrupt than himself. Conscious of its own share of culpability, society will repair in penitentiaries the fault of its carelessness: it will be firm, yet kind and moralizing: it will give in them the education which it ought to have given outside, and will prepare work houses for the liberated convicts in order that the contempt and horror often shown toward them by men worse than they may not drive them to a second offence.

7. Woman, carrying into the social household her spirit of order and economy, her love of details and abhorence of waste and foolish expense, will reform government: she will simplify everything; will suppress sinecures and the accumulation of offices, and will produce much from little instead of, like man, producing little from much: the purse of the tax-payers will not complain of the change.

8. Under the direct influence of woman as legislator, we shall have a reconstruction of all laws ; first and before everything, we shall have preventive measures, a compulsory education ; then the form of legal proceedings will be simplified, the civil code recast, and all laws concerning illegitimate children and the inequality of the sexes banished from it ; the laws concerning morals will be more severe, and the penal code more rational and equitable.

By her administrative reforms born of the economical instinct of woman, taxes will be diminished ; her abhorrence of blood and war will greatly reduce the fearful impost of blood-shed.   Having a deliberative voice, and knowing, by her griefs and love the value of a man, it will be only from sheer necessity that she will consent to vote bevies of citizens for the shambles called wars : she will do this only when her country is menaced or when it is necessary to protect oppressed nationalities ; in all other cases, she will employ the system of conciliation.

9. Woman, being much more economical and a better analyst than man, when thoroughly instructed, will soon perceive that nations, like individuals, differ ir aptitudes, and that the end of these differences is unior and fraternity through exchange of products : she will therefore deter her country from cultivating certain branches of the acts and manufactures in which other nations excel and which they can produce to better advantage ; she will cure it of the foolish pretension of being sufficient unto itself, and will prevent it from sacrificing the interest of the mass of consumers to that of a few producers : thus the barriers and custom duties that separate the different organs of humanity will fall by

degrees; there will be treaties of free trade, and all
will be gainers by the cheapness of products, and the
suppression of the expenses of maintaining a too often
annoying department of customs.

The qualities and faculties of woman not only make
her an educator, but assure her preponderance in all
functions arising from social solidarity ; she alone knows
how to console, to encourage, to moralize with gentleness,
to comfort with delicacy ; she has the genius of charity ;
to her therefore should revert the superintendence and
direction of hospitals and prisons for women, the management of charitable institutions, the care of abandoned
children, etc.   She should create institutions to furnish
employment to workmen out of work, and to save liberated convicts from indolence and relapse into crime.

Thus, gentleman, without departing from the data of
your theory, you.behold woman placed everywhere by
the side of man, except in the hard labor from which
you yourselves will soon be released by machinery, and
in the military institutions which, in all probability, will
some day disappear.

Hitherto institutions, laws, sciences, philosophy have
chiefly borne the masculine imprint ; all of these things
are only half human ; in order that they may become
wholly so, woman must be associated in them ostensi-
bly and lawfully, consequently, she must be cultivated
like you ; culture will not make her like you, do not
fear it ; the rose and the carnation growing in the
same soil, under the same sky, in the same sunshine,
with the cares of the same gardener, remain rose and
carnation : they are more beautiful in proportion as
they are better cultivated, and as the elements which
they absorb are more abundant : if man and woman

differ, a similar education will only make them differ still more, because each will employ it in the development of that which is peculiar to himself.

For the interest of all things and people it is necessary that woman should enter all the avocations of life, that she should have her function in all the functions : *after* the general interest of humanity, comes that of the family ; it cannot go *before* it.

Since woman now is generally mother and housewife while performing at the same time a host of other functions, she will become none the less so in taking upon herself a few more ; besides, the time of life at which an individual enters certain important functions is that at which woman has finished her maternal task. A few women acting as public functionaries will not hinder the great majority of their companions from remaining in private life, any more than a few men in the same position hinder the mass of men from continuing there.

VI.

You admit a classification at last, you say, and still more you grant that there are masculine and feminine functions. You are mistaken, gentlemen : you accused me of being incapable of giving you a complete theory, I have given you the outlines of four — outlines which it would be easy for me to extend and perfect. But I do not admit a single one of these theories as a whole.

Are you eclectic, then ?

The gods forbid ! I have as much repugnance to eclecticism, as to *mystic trinitarianism* and *androgyny*.

I do not admit the theory of the identity of the sexes, because I believe with Biology that an essential organic difference modifies the entire being; that therefore woman must differ from man.

I do not admit the theory of the superiority of either sex, because it is absurd; humanity is man-woman or woman-man; we do not know what one sex would be if it were not incessantly modified by its relations with the other, and we know them only as thus modified: What we know to a certainty is that they form together the existing condition of humanity; that they are equally necessary and equally useful to each other and to society.

I do not admit my third theory because it is ultra nominalism; if it is really true that all the individuals of both sexes differ among themselves in a far more remarkable manner than those of the other species, it is none the less true that a classification, founded upon a con stant anatomical characteristic, is legitimate, and that the principle of classification lies in the nature of things, for if things appear to us classified, it is because they are so; the laws of the mind are the same as those of Nature so far as knowledge is concerned; we must admit this, unless we are sceptics or idealists, and I am neither the one nor the other; neither am I a realist in the philosophic acceptation of the word, for I do not believe that the species is something apart from the individuals in which it is manifested; it is in them and through them; this repeats the affirmation that there are individuals identical in one or several respects, although different in all others.

Lastly, I do not admit the fourth theory, although it may be true in principle, because the numerous facts that contradict the distinguishing characteristics, do not permit me to believe that these characteristics are laws established by sexuality.

In fact, there are brains of men in heads of women, and *vice versa*.

Men mobile and impressionable; women firm and insensible.

Women large, strong and muscular, lifting a man like a feather; men small, frail, and of extreme delicacy of constitution.

Women with a stentorian voice and abrupt manners; men with a soft voice and graceful manners.

Women with short, harsh hair, bearded, with rough skin and angular figures; men with long, silky hair without beard, round and portly.

Women with an energetic circulation of blood; men in whose veins it courses feebly and slowly.

Women frank, inconsiderate and daring; men strategic, dissembling and timid.

Women violent, loving strife, war and contention, and wont to storm on every occasion; men gentle, patient, dreading strife, and exceedingly timid.

Women loving abstract reasoning, generalizing and synthetizing much, and without intuition of any sort; men intuitive, acute observers, good analysts, incapable of generalizing. . . I know many such.

Women insensible to works of art, and without the sentiment of the beautiful; men full of enthusiasm for both.

Women immoral, immodest, respecting nothing or no one; men moral, chaste and reverential.

Women extravagant and disorderly; men economical and parsimonious to avarice.

Women thoroughly selfish, rigid, disposed to take advantage of the weakness, kindness, folly or misery of others; men full of generosity, mansuetude, and self-sacrifice.

What follows from these undeniable facts? that the law of sexual differences is not manifested through the several characteristics which have been laid down.

That these characteristics may be only the result of education, of the difference of prejudices, of that of occupations, etc.

That, as these generalities may be the fruit of the difference of training and surroundings, nothing can be legitimately deduced from them as to the functions of woman; would it not be absurd, in fact, to pretend that a woman who is organized for philosophy and the sciences *can not*, ought not to occupy herself with them because she is a woman, while a man, who is incapable of them but foolish and vain enough to be ignorant of his incapacity, can and ought to engage in them because he is a man?

Functions belong to those who prove their aptitude for them, and not to an abstraction called sex, for, definitively, every function is individual in its aggregate or in its elements.

VII.

We have explained why we reject the theories that we have sketched; we will now explain why we neither give nor wish to give a classification of the sexes.

We do not give a classification, because we neither have nor can have one; the elements for its establishment are lacking. A biological deduction permits us to affirm that such a one exists; but it is impossible to disengage its law in the present surroundings; the veritable feminine stamp will be known only after one or two centuries of like education and equal rights: then there will be no need of a classification, for the function will fall naturally to the proper functionary under a system of equality in which the social elements classify themselves.

My belief and my hopes concerning the future, I shall not confess ; for I may be in error, since I have no facts to control my intuitions, and everything that is purely Utopian has always a dangerous side.   Besides have I not said that, had I formed a classification, I should not give it ?   Why not ?   Because, a detestable use would be made of·it, as usual, if it were adopted.

Hitherto, have not men availed themselves of classifications based upon characteristics afterwards recognized as purely imaginary to oppress, distort and calumniate those banished to the inferior ranks ?

History is at hand to give us this salutary lesson. Where is now to-day the *ville-pedaille*, the villains and base-tenants, fit only to drain ditches and to be stripped to the skin ?   Inventing, governing, making laws for, and gradually transforming our globe, devastated by the *superior and only capable* species, into a smiling and peaceful domain.

Upon all classificasion of the human species, whether in castes, in classes, or in sexes, are based three wrongs.

The first is to make it a crime in the individual degraded into the lower series, that he does not resemble the conventional type that has been formed of this series, while the so called superior being is not required to resemble his type ; thus a weak, cowardly, unintelligent man, a *man milliner* or an *embroiderer*, is none the less a man, while a virago, a firm and courageous woman, a great queen, a woman philosopher, are not women, but men whom none love and who are given over as a prey to wild beasts, jealous, effeminate men, to devour.

The second wrong is to take advantage of the conventional type to deform the being classed in the inferior series in order to kill his energies and to hinder his progress. Then, to attain this end, education, social surroundings are organized, prejudices are invented ; and so successfully is this done in general that the oppressed, ignorant of himself, believes himself really of an inferior nature, resigns himself to his chains, and is even indignant at the rebellion of those of his series who are too energetic and individual not to react against the part to which social imbecility has condemned them.

The third wrong is to take advantage of the state of debasement to which the oppressed has been reduced, to calumniate him and deny his rights ; men exclaim, Look ! See the serf ! see the slave ! see the negro ! see the workingman ! see woman ! What rights would you grant these inferior and feeble natures ? *They are incapable of knowing and ruling themselves :* we must therefore think for them, wish for them, and govern them.

Ah no, gentlemen, these are not men and women ; they are the deplorable results of your selfishness, of your frightful spirit of domination, of your imbecility. . . . If there were infernal gods, I should devote you to them relentlessly with all my heart. Instead of calumniating your fellows that you may preserve your privileges, give them instruction and liberty ; then only will you have the right to pass judgment on their nature : for we can only know the nature of a human being when it has become freely developed in equality.

I think that I have justified my repugnance to give a classification of the sexes, both by the impossibility of actually establishing a reasonable one, and by the very legitimate fear of the bad use that would be made of it.

But it will be objected, and not without reason, that a classification is necessary for social practice.

I consent to it with all my heart, since I have reserved my positions, and proved the worthlessness of existing classifications.

As it is my principle that the function should fall to the functionary who proves his capacity, I say that at present, through the difference of education, man and woman have distinct functions; and that we must give to the latter the place that in general she deserves.

I add that it is a violation of the natural right of woman to form her with a view to certain functions to which she is destined; she should in all respects enjoy the rights common to all; it cannot rightfully be said to her any more than to man, " your sex cannot do that, cannot pretend to that ; " if it does it and pretends to it, it is because the sex can do it and pretend to it; if it could not, it would not do it; the first right is liberty, the first duty, the culture of one's aptitudes, the development of his reason and his power of usefulness: if a god should affirm the contrary, not conscience, but the god would speak falsely.

Let woman take the place therefore that is suited to her present development, but let her never cease to remember that this place is not a fixed point, and that she should continually strive to mount upwards until, her peculiar nature revealing itself through equality of education, instruction, right and duty, she takes her rightful place by the side of man and on a level with him.

Let her laugh at all the utopian follies elaborated concerning her nature, her functions determined for eternity, and remember that she is not what nature, but what subjection, prejudice, ignorance has made her; let her escape from all her chains, and no longer permit herself to be intimidated and debased.

Thus, gentlemen, all my ideas on the nature and functions of woman may be summed up in these few propositions:

I believe, because a physiological deduction authorizes me to do so, that general humanity common to both sexes is stamped by sexuality.

In *fact*, I know not, and you know no better than I, what are the true characteristics arising from the distinction of the sexes, and I believe that they can be revealed only by liberty in equality, parity of instruction and of education.

In social practice, functions should belong to those who can perform them: woman therefore should perform those functions for which she shows herself qualified, and society should become so organized that this may be possible.

What are these functions relative to her degree of present development? I will tell you directly.

I.

You tell the child that lies, " it is wrong to deceive; you would not wish others to deceive you."

You tell the child that pilfers, " it is wrong to steal; you would not wish others to steal from you.

You tell the child that takes advantage of his strength and knowledge to torment his younger companion; " you would not wish others to do these things to you; you are wicked and cowardly."

These are good lessons. Why then, when the child has become a young man, do you say: *Young men must sow their wild oats?*

To sow their wild oats is to deceive young girls, to destroy their future, to practice adultery, to keep mistresses, to visit brothels.

Yet mothers, women thus consent to the profanation of their sex!

Those who forbade their child to steal a toy, permit him to steal the honor and repose of human beings!

Those who shamed their son for falsehood, permit him to deceive poor young girls!

Those who made it a crime in their son to oppress those weaker than themselves, permit him to be oppressive and perfidious toward women!

Then they complain later that their sons treat them ill; that they dishonor and ruin themselves;

That they desire the death of their parents, in order to enrich the usurers from whom they have borrowed money to maintain their mistresses in luxury.

They complain that they destroy their health, and give their mothers puny grandchildren, for whose existence they are in continual anxiety.

Ah! ladies, you have only what you deserve; bear the weight of a joint responsibility which you cannot escape.   You authorized your sons to sow their wild oats; endure the consequences.

But a mother cannot be the confident of her son, it is said.

Why not, madam, if you have brought him up in such a way as to have no dishonorable confidence to make to you.

He would have none to make, if you had accustomed him to conquer himself, to respect every woman as though she were his mother, every young girl as though she were his sister; to treat others as he would think it right to be treated by them; if you had fully inculcated on him the that there is but one system of morality, which both sexes are equally bound to obey; if you had caused him to honor, love and practice labor; if you had told him that we live to improve ourselves, to practise justice and kindness, and to render back to humanity what it does for us in protecting us, enlightening us, rendering us moral, surrounding us with security and comfort; that in fine our glory lies in subjecting ourselves to the great law of Duty.

If you had reared him in this manner, madam, on surprising in your son the first signs of the ardent at-

traction that man feels toward the other sex, far from
abandoning the education of this instinct to the chances
of inexperience, you would do for it what you did for
the others ; you would teach the young man to subject it
to a wise discipline.

Instead of repeating the stupidly atrocious phrase ;
young men must sow their wild oats, you would have
taken your son's hand affectionately in your own, and,
looking in his face, would have said : " My child, Nature
decrees that a woman should henceforth attract you
more strongly than I, and should maintain or destroy
what I have so laboriously built up : I do not murmur
at this ; it must be so.   But my affection and duty require me to enlighten you in this grave juncture.   Tell
me, if a young man, to satisfy the instinct which is now
awakening in you, should corrupt your sister, should
sacrifice her life, what would you think of him ? what
would you do ?

The young man, accustomed from " childhood to practise Justice, would not fail to reply : I should think him
depraved and cowardly.   Would he not be punished ? "

" No, my son, the seducer is not punished by the law."

" Well ! I would kill him, for my right of justice re-
verts to me when the law makes no provision."

" Right, my child.   Then you will be neither depraved
nor cowardly with respect to any young girl ; you will
not deserve the sentence which you have pronounced ;
namely, death.   You will respect all young girls and
women as you would wish your sister, your daughter to
be respected.

" Another question : what would you think of a man
who should persuade me to betray your father ; who
should rob him of my heart and cares ; who should draw

me aside from the grave duties of maternity? What would you think of the man who should act thus with respect to your own companion?"

"I would judge him like the former and would treat him no better."

Right again. Then you will respect all married women as you would wish your mother and your wife to be respected; and if you should meet any one towards whom you should feel attracted, or who should be disloyal enough to seek to attract you, you will shun her: for flight is the sole remedy for passion.

"A multitude of women, innocent at first, have been turned aside from the right path by men who do not think as you do. They now avenge themselves upon your sex for the evil it has done them. They corrupt and ruin men who, in their company, lose all sense of morality, who learn to laugh at what you believe and venerate, and undermine and destroy their health. Do you feel the deplorable courage to expose yourself to such risks?"

The young man, practised from childhood to subject his inclinations to reason and justice, would reply: "No, mother, I will not do what I would not wish my companion to do; I will neither degrade myself morally, nor destroy my health, nor contribute my share towards perpetuating a state of things which degrades the sex to which belongs my mother, my sister, my wife and my daughters, should I be so happy as to possess them.

"I acknowledge frankly that I foresee a violent struggle with myself, but, thanks to the moral training to which you have accustomed me, thanks to the ideal of destiny which you have given me, which I have accepted in the plenitude of my reason, and which my duty

marks out for me, I do not despair of subduing myself."
— " This victory will be less difficult to obtain, if you
employ yourself usefully and seriously; for you will
thus attract your vitality to the superior regions of the
brain. You will do wisely to add to this, much physical exercise ; to abstain from too substantial a diet, and
especially from stimulating drinks ! you know the reaction of the physical upon the moral system. Carefully
avoid licentious reading and improper conversation ; give
a place in your mind to the virgin who will be united
to you ; think and act as if in her presence ; it will
guard you and keep you pure. This sweet ideal will
strengthen you against temptation, and contribute greatly to render you insensible towards those women who
should have no place in your heart.

"Love, my child, is a thing most serious in its results ;
for the beings whom it unites become modified by each
other ; it leaves its traces, however short may be its duration.

" Its end is Marriage, one of the ends of which is the
continuity of the species. Now, you know the effects
of solidarity of blood; it is most important therefore
that you should choose for your companion a woman
whose character, morals and principles are in unison with
your own ; not only for your happiness, but for the *organization* of your children, the harmony of their nature and conduct.

" If passion does not leave you sufficiently free in your
judgment, come to me : I will see for you, and if I say :
my son, this woman will debase you, will cause you to
commit faults ; be sure that your children will have
evil propensities ; she is not adapted to rear them according to your ideal, which she will never accept, be-

cause she is vain and selfish ; if I tell you this, I know, my son, that whatever may be your suffering, you will renounce a woman whom you would cease to love after a few months' union, and will prefer a transient sadness to a life of unhappiness."

II.

The mother who has just shown her son why love should be subjected to Reason and Justice, and has pointed out to him what he should do to subdue its animal phase, perceives also the awakening of this instinct in her daughter. She wins her attention and gains her confidence by revealing to her what is passing within her heart, telling her that, at her age, she felt the same.

" Hitherto," continues she, " you have been but a child ; your career as a woman is now commencing. You desire the affection of a man, and your heart is moved at the sweet thought of becoming a mother. Do not blush, my daughter ; it is lawful, on condition that your desires are made subject to Reason and the law of Duty.

" Many snares will be spread before your steps ; for men of all ages address to a young girl innumerable flattering speeches, and surround her with homage which renders her vain and coquettish if she has the weakness to suffer herself to be intoxicated thereby. Persuade yourself fully that all this adoration is not addressed to you individually, but to your youth, to the brightness of your eyes, to the freshness of your complexion, and that, were you far better than you are and far superior in intellect, these men would be ceremoniously and frigidly polite, were you thirty years older. This thought present in your mind will make you smile at their frivolous and common-place jargon, and will

preserve you from many weaknesses, such as rivalry of
dress, petty jealousies, and the ridiculous blunder of
playing the young girl at fifty.

" As you can espouse but one man, it is sufficient to
be loved by one in the manner that you wish.   A woman who comports herself voluntarily so as to captivate
the hearts of many men, and leaves each to believe
that she prefers him above all, is an unworthy coquette,
who sins against Justice and Kindness : against Justice,
inasmuch as she demands a sentiment for which she can
make no return ; as she acts towards others as she
would think it unjust that others should act towards her ;
against Kindness, inasmuch as she risks causing suffering to sincere hearts and sacrificing their repose to a
pleasurable impulse of vanity : such a woman, my
child, is contemptible ; she is a dangerous enemy of her
sex ; first, because she gives a bad opinion of it ; next,
because she is an enemy to the repose of other women ;
I know that you are too ingenuous, too true and too
worthy to fear that you will fall into such errors.

" You have acknowledged to me that your young imagination had pictured to itself a man.   Far from ban-
ishing this ideal, let it be always present to your mind,
much less in its physical aspect than in that of intellect,
morality and industry.   This image will do more to
keep you safe than all my counsels, than all the surveillance that I might, but never would exercise over you,
because this would be unworthy of us both.

" Do not forget however that an ideal is absolute ; that
the reality is always defective ; do not therefore seek in
the man to whom you shall give your heart, a realization of the ideal, but the qualities and faculties which,
with your aid, will permit him to approximate to what

you wish to see him. You yourself are the ideal of a man, not such as you are, but such as he will aid you to become.

" I dwell upon this point, my daughter, because nothing is more dangerous than to insist on finding the ideal in the reality ; this makes us over difficult and lacking in indulgence ; and, if we have a lively imagination and little reason, renders us unhappy and involves us in innumerable errors.

You know and feel that the end of love is Marriage ; now one of your duties as lover and spouse is the improvement of the one to whom you shall be united. You will stand with him in two different relations ! first as his betrothed, afterwards as his wife. Your modifying power will, in the first case, be exercised in a direct proportion to his desire to please and to be worthy of you ; in the second, in proportion to his confidence, esteem and affection for you. In the first case, he will *wish* to modify himself ; in the second, he will do so without knowing it."

" What, mother, will he not always love me the same ? "

" Love, my child, undergoes transformations which we should expect and to which we should submit ; in the beginning it is a fever of the soul ; but fever is a condition which cannot last without destroying life. Your husband, while loving you perhaps more deeply, will love you less ardently than before Marriage. Your love will become transformed, why shall not his be the same ?

" You cannot imagine how much trouble results from the ignorance of women on this point, and from the vain pursuit of the ideal in love. Many women, believing that their husband loves them no longer because

he loves them in a different manner, become detached
from him, suffer, and betray their duties; others, dream-
ing of perfection in the loved one, fancy that they have
found it, and becoming disabused after the fever has
past, quit him, accusing him of having deceived them;
they love others with the same illusion, followed by the
same disenchantment, until age creeps on without cur-
ing them of the chimera. Lastly, there are others who,
comprehending only the first period of love, cease to
love the man who has passed beyond it, and pursue another love which will bring them the same fever; these,
as you comprehend, have not the slightest idea of woman's grave duties in Love.

"What I have just said of women is equally true of
men. You will avoid these dangers, my daughter, you
who have been accustomed from childhood to submit to
reason; who know that all reality is imperfect, that
habit weakens sentiment, you will therefore take the
man who suits you, as he is, designing to improve him
and to render him happy, knowing in advance that his
love will change without becoming extinguished, if you
succeed in gaining his affection, confidence and esteem,
so that he will find in you good counsel, peace, assistance and security. You are too pure, my daughter, to
foresee all the snares that will be spread for you. It
belongs to me therefore to arm your youthful prudence:
You will perhaps encounter men married or betrothed
who, according to the common expression, *will pay
court to you*, and will utter innumerable sophisms to
justify their conduct."

"Their sophisms would fall to the ground before the
simple answer: Sir, as I should be driven to despair if
another woman should rob me of him whom I loved,

as I should despise and hate her, all your compliments
cannot persuade me that it is right for me to do what I
would not that others should do to me. If you return
to the subject, I shall inform the person interested.

"Right, my child: but if a young man who was free
should speak of love, and urge you to write to him in
secret?"

"Might he not have good reason for acting in this
manner?"

"None, my child. You must know that men are exceedingly corrupt; that many among them eschew marriage, flit from one woman to another, take advantage
of our credulity, and make use of the most impassioned
language to lead us in the way of shame and perdition.
Now, my child, know besides that we bear the weight of
men's faults as well as of our own; the verbal and
written promises of a man bind him to nothing. If,
suffering yourself to be led astray, you should become
a mother, the child would remain your charge; and
you could no longer hope for marriage; I say nothing
of our grief and shame, nor of the terrible risks to
which you would expose your brother, who might perish in punishing the vile seducer whom the law does
not touch. If a man seeks you therefore unknown to
us, be sure that it is because his intentions are evil; that
he considers you as a toy which he purposes to break when
it ceases to amuse him. Now, my daughter, you know
that woman is created to be the worthy companion of
man; that she is not born to be sacrificed to him as an
object of pleasure. Instead therefore of suffering yourself to be seduced, profit by the influence over men
which is given you by your beauty and grace, to recall
them to their duties: in this manner, you may be the

means of saving many women; you will give a favorable opinion of your sex, and will prepare a good example for your daughter by setting one to your companions, many of whom will follow it in order to share in the esteem that will surround you; always remember that our acts not only injure ourselves, but we have a joint responsibility with others, and consequently no one can be lost or saved alone.

" One word more, my child. In your uncertainties, do not hesitate to confide your troubles to me; do not say, My mother is too reasonable to understand me in this. Was it not by becoming a child again in order to comprehend you, that I fulfilled my sacred task of instructor? be persuaded that it will not be more difficult for me to become a young girl again in order to comprehend, while remaining a tender and experienced mother to advise you.

" You are free: I am not you censor, but your elder sister, who loves you with devotion and desires your happiness before all things. As a recompense for my love and my long-continued cares, I only ask to be your best friend; that is, the one in whose presence you will think and speak aloud. Is this asking too much of you, who are my joy and crown."

This is the way, ladies, in which the woman who has attained majority, strives to educate the world in Love.

III.

The young girl and young man enter into society. The prudent mother knows that it is gently insinuated to her son that she is a *prude*, a *dotard* who knows nothing of the passions; who does not suspect that *every-*

thing in nature is good, and should be respected; and who has read the history of our species to so little purpose that she has not perceived that humanity has love in all forms: the *polygamic* and *polyandric,* and even . . . . the *ambiguous.*

She knows also, that he is told that the satisfaction of the animal instinct is necessary to the *health* of man, and that brothels are places of public utility.

She knows, lastly, that young and giddy girls, with lax principles, make dangerous confidences to her daughter.

It is time, in opposition to these lax doctrines and pernicious examples, to give to her children the philosophy of Love. According to her method, she suffers is to elucidate itself.

My son, says she, what is the end of the attraction of mineral molecules towards each other?

SON. The *production* of a body having a determined form.

MOTHER. What is the end of the attraction of the plant for heat, light, air, the elements which it absorbs?

SON. The *production* of its own body, the development of its organs, and of its properties, its preservation.

MOTHER. And do you know, my daughter, what is the end of the attraction of the pistil and stamens of the flower.

DAUGHTER. The *production* of a being resembling its parents.

MOTHER. Why do we as well as the animals experience an inclination or attraction for certain kinds of food?

SON. It is evidently in order to incite to action the organs which procure to the organism the elements adapted to *produce* blood.

MOTHER. Why do both sexes of the same species experience an attraction towards each other ?

DAUGHTER. For the *production* of young to perpetuate the species.

MOTHER. Why do the females, and often males among animals experience an inclination or attraction to take care of the young ?

DAUGHTER. In order to preserve them and to educate them as far as is in their power, that they may be able to provide for themselves.

MOTHER. Are you quite sure, my children, that the end of these attractions is not the attraction itself, the procurement of a pleasure ?

SON. The pleasure seems to me only the means of impelling the being to fufil a necessary or useful function. Thus the end of our scientific, artistic and industrial inclinations or attractions is not the pleasure which we take in their satisfaction, but the *production* of science, art and industry.

DUGHTER. That is, the increase and progress of our intellect through the knowledge of the laws of Nature, in order to modify this nature with a view to our wants and pleasures.

MOTHER. To what inclination or attraction is Society due ?

SON. To our attraction for our fellow beings.

DAUGHTER. This attraction is the father of Justice and of Goodness : it *produces* them.

MOTHER. Will you generalize the character of this inclination or attraction in accordance with what we have just said ?

SON. The end of all attraction or inclination is the *production*, *progress* and *preservation* of beings.

MOTHER. Are all instincts good which are merely inclinations or attractions?

SON. For animals, which are subject to fatality, they are; because they tend directly to their end, without ever appearing to deviate from it. In our species, they are good in principle, if we regard their end; but they may become evil through the deviation to which our liberty subjects them.

MOTHER. By what token can we know that our instinct has a right tendency?

DAUGHTER. By comparing its use with its end; by assuring ourselves that this use is not prejudicial to the practice of justice, that it does not detract from the right of any of our faculties; that is, that it disturbs neither our individual harmony nor that of others; for it is on these conditions alone that it can coöperate in the realization of the social ideal.

MOTHER. Very well. Now apply this general doctrine to human love, my children.

SON. Since love is one of the forms of attraction, and since the general end of attraction is the production, progress and preservation of beings and species, it is evident that human love should possess these characteristics. Its principal function appears to me to be the reproduction of the species.

DAUGHTER. It seems to me, brother, that this is not enough; since true husbands and wives do not cease to love each other after this end has been fulfilled, and since persons may love without having children.

MOTHER. You are right, my daughter; our faculties being more numerous and more fully developed than those of the animals, our love cannot be incomplete like theirs; it cannot be of the same nature in our pro-

gressive species as in those species fatal and unpro-
gressive of themselves. In us, each faculty, properly
employed, aids in the improvement of all the rest,
wrongly employed, it interrupts our harmony and
lowers us ; it is the same with our love. Or rather this
passion is the one that most of all causes us to grow or
to decline.

You know, my children, that humanity advances only
by forming itself an ideal and endeavoring to realize it.
Every passion has its ideal, which is modified by that
of the whole. In the beginning, man, in the animal
state, made the end of love the pleasure resulting from
the satisfaction of a wholly physical want : he cared
nothing for the most evident aim — progeny. A little
later, man less gross, loved woman for her beauty and
fruitfulness ; this was the patriarchal age of love. Later
still, the Northern races wrought a change in this instinct ; love became decomposed, as it were ; the lover
possessed the love of the soul ; the woman was loved
not only for her beauty, but as the inspirer of lofty
deeds ; the husband was the possessor of the body alone
and the children were the fruit of marriage ; this was
the chivalrous age of love. Since pacific labor has been
organized and has gained a place in public opinion, love
has entered a new phase ; many among the moderns
consider it as the iniative of labor. Some regard the
attraction of pleasure as playing the chief part in industrial production, and leave full liberty to the attraction,
however inconsistent it may be ; others preserve the
couple, and transform woman into the moving power
of action ; the love that she inspires excites the efforts
of the worker.

The progress hitherto made by humanity is thererefore that love has now for its end the perpetuation of the species, the modification of man by woman, and the production of labor.

In a higher ideal of Justice, the sexes being equal in rights, love will have a higher end; the spouses will unite on account of conformity of principles, union of hearts, wedding of intellects, common labor: love will join them to double their strength, to modify them by each other, from the friction of their hearts will be struck out sentiments which neither would have had alone; from the union of their intellects will be born thoughts which neither would have had alone; from the aid that they will lend each other in their common labor will proceed works that neither would have accomplished alone, as from the union of their whole being, will be born new generations more perfect than the preceeding because they will be the product of the greatest possible harmony.   It will be only when woman shall take her lawful place that humanity will see love in all its splendor, and that this passion, subversive to-day in inequality and incoherence, will become what it should be; one of the great instruments of Progress.

We, my children, who are too rational to mistake the means by which Nature impels us to accomplish her designs for the designs themselves, will take care not to fancy that the end of love is pleasure; on the other hand, we have too much respect for equality to imagine that it is for the benefit of one sex alone. - We will remain faithful to the ideal of our lofty destinies, in defining love as the reciprocal attraction of man and woman with the end of perpetuating the species, of improving the partners mutually with respect to intellect and feeling, and of advancing science, art and industry by the labor of the pair.

IV.

Sophists have told you, my son, that all our inclinations are in Nature; that they are good and should be respected.

You asked them doubtless whether the inclinations to theft, to assassination, to violation, to anthropophagy, which are in Nature, are good, and why, instead of respecting them, society punishes their manifestation.

You demonstrated to them, I hope, that there is nothing commendable in the exaggeration or the perversion of instincts.

You demonstrated to them, I hope, that Nature is brutal fatality against which we are bound to struggle both within and without ourselves; that our Justice and virtue are composed only of conquests made over it in us, as all that constitutes our physical well-being is only the result of conquests made over it outside of us.

These sophists have told you that love comes and goes without our knowing how or wherefore; and that we can no more command it to spring up than to endure.

This is true, my son, of the brutal desires of the flesh, which is the passion of animals alone, and is extinguished by possession.

This is also true of that complex passion which has its seat in the imagination and the senses, and ends with the illusion that is always of short duration.

But it is not true of genuine love; this sees both the faults and the virtues of the loved one; but softens the first and exalts the last, and hopes by degrees to put an end to that which wounds it.

This sentiment. which takes possession of the heart,

is patient; it bears lest it become effaced, it surrounds itself with precautions in order to remain constant; if it becomes extinct, it is not unconsciously: for we suffer cruel tortures before resolving to cease to love.

You have been told that love is irrepressible; are we then beings of fatality? This sophism renders man cowardly and depraves him; for what is the use of struggling against what we know to be unconquerable, and why not sacrifice to it the best of our tendencies? Examine the conduct of the partisans of such a doctrine.

The human ideal requires that they shall not do to others what they would not think it just that others should do to them; yet they seduce maidens, make them mothers, and abandon them without caring about the children born of these unions; without caring whether the young mother commits suicide, dies of grief, or becomes depraved; without caring whether the parents go down to the grave.

Like deadly reptiles, they glide to the domestic fireside of others, rob their friend of the affection of his wife, and force him to labor for the children of adultery.

The woman who believes in irrepressible love breaks her pledges to her husband; lives a life of deceit; brings trouble and sorrow into the houses of other women, whose lives are blighted by her.

It is in this way that those who practice this sophistry fulfil their duty to be just, not to afflict their fellows, to labor for the happiness and improvement of those about them, to preserve the weak from oppression and wrong. To this pretended irrepressibility of love, they sacrifice Justice, goodness, the happiness, repose and honor of others; lead them into the path of dissipation; bring dissolution into the family and society; in a word, offer up as a sacrifice to animal instinct, moral sense and reason.

You have also been told that every species of love is found in Nature; the polyamic and polygandric, as well as that of the constant pair.

Yes, my child, every species of love is found in Nature, as is every species of vice and every species of virtue. But you know that it is not enough that a thing exists within us to prove it to be good; it must be in conformity with the ideal of our destiny, with our harmony: it is wrong in the opposite case.

Love, such as we have defined it, needs duration and equality; duration, because we do not become modified in a few months; because we do not accomplish great works in a few months; because we do not rear children in a few months; duration is so truly an aspiration of love, that it imagines that eternity will hardly suffice for it. It must have equality; division is hateful to it; it will therefore have a unit for a unit, both male and female. Now polygamy and polyandria are the negation of equality, of dignity in love.

Let us consider the effects of these two deviations of instinct.

Oriental polygamy renders human beings profoundly unequal, transforms women into cattle, mutilates thousands of men to guard the harems, depraves the possessor of women by despotism and cruelty, concentrates all his vitality upon a single instinct at the expense of intellect, reason and activity; whence it follows that he is lost to science, art, industry, society according to right: that he submits without repugnance to despotism, and passively extends his neck to the halter. There, no influence is wielded by woman, who is subjected to designed enervation, who is depraved in as hideous a manner as the eunuch, her keeper. Thus, inequality in love and in right, abandonment-of art, science and industry, intellectual and physical enervation, debasement of the moral sense — such are vices inherent to the polygamy of the East. You see that this is far from the ideal of our destinies.

In our West, polygamy *de facto* produces the cattle of the brothel, legions of courtesans who ruin families. As many of these women are diseased, they infect those who associate with them with fearful maladies which undermine their constitutions, and thus pave the way for puny offspring, consequently, for weak minds and feeble intellects. I appeal for proof to the conscription ; never were so many exemptions seen as now on account of under size, although the standard has been lowered, never were so many exemptions seen as now for constitutional imperfections and acquired disease.

To vitiate the generation in its germ is not the only crime of our polygamy ; it enervates those who practice it, for nothing leads to excess, consequently to enervation, so much as the change of relations. On the other hand, our polygamists become transformed into machines of sensation ; then intellect grows weak ; they become stupid and selfish. Look at the pitiable young men of the present time, emaciated by their vices and by those of their sires ; scoffers, faithless, jesting at the most sacred things, despising, not only the corrupt women, their worthy companions, but also the whole sex to which their mothers belong ; look at them ; so gross as to sicken the observer, nothing longer commands their respect ; they thrust aside gray haired women from the sidewalk into the gutter; they are impertinent to old men; they put young girls to the blush with their cynical speeches; polygamy has rendered them ignoble, and has destroyed our native urbanity as well as all dignity.

They will tell you that women are but little better than they. But this result becomes inevitable in a country in which women are not kept in seclusion. Polyandria becomes the necessary companion of polygamy; for since men consider themselves at liberty to have more than one woman, why should women consider themselves forbidden to have more than one man?

Finally, my son, the results of irrepressible love, Polygamy and Polyandria in our Western country are:

The seduction and corruption of women;

Adultery, debasement of character; the moral and intellectual enfeebling of both sexes;

The enervation and degeneracy of the race;

Falsehood, deceit, cruelty, injustice of every kind, the use of woman by man for her beauty, that of man by woman for his money or position;

The dissolution and ruin of the family;

Several thousand illegitimate children annually, without counting abortions;

Such is the value of these theories put in practice.

Is this in conformity with our ideal of human love? Is it in conformity with our ideal of human destiny, which requires that we shall progress and cause others to progress in good; that we shall practice Justice and Goodness;

A word more, and we have done.

When Rome had ceased to believe in chastity, in the sacredness of oaths; when she wallowed in polygamic and polyandric customs; when she took pleasure for her end, tyranny appeared. Nothing was more natural: man binds captive those only who have first suffered themselves to be bound under the yoke of bestial instinct: he who knows how to govern himself does not yield obedience to man; he bows only before the law when it is the expression of Reason.

Remember, my son, that we are powerful only through chastity; only thus can we produce great works in science, art and industry; only thus can we practice Justice, be worthy of liberty. Outside of chastity, there is nothing but degradation, injustice, impotence, slavery; and every nation that forsakes it falls from the arms of despotism into the grave.

Do not suffer yourself therefore to be moved by modern sophisms, have always before your thoughts your obligations as a moral and a free being, your duties as a member of humanity; subject all that is within you to Reason, to Justice, to the sentiment of your dignity, and live like a man, not like a brute.

READER. We are about to speak of Marriage from the stand point of the modern ideal — how do you define it?

AUTHOR. Love, sanctioned by Society.

READER. Do you consider Marriage as indissoluble?

AUTHOR. Before the law, I do not; but at the moment of their union, the spouses should have full confidence that the bond will never be dissolved.

I believe that Marriage becomes indissoluble by the will alone of the spouses; that it can be so only in this manner.

READER. What part do you assign to Society in Marriage?

AUTHOR. You shall fix it yourself after recalling our principles.

If man and woman are free beings at any period of their life, they cannot *legally and validly* lose their liberty.

If man and woman are beings socially equal in any of their relations, the one cannot *legally*, *validly* be subordinated to the other.

If the continual end of the human being is to become

perfected through liberty, and to seek happiness, no law can legitimately, *validly* turn him aside from its pursuit.

If the end of society should be to render individuals *equal* it cannot, under penalty of forfeiting its mission, constitute inequality of persons and of rights.

If Society cannot without iniquity enter the domain of individual liberty, it cannot *lawfully*, *validly* prescribe duties that pertain only to the jurisdiction of the conscience, and annul moral liberty.

Now draw your conclusions.

READER. From these principles, it follows that man and woman should remain free and equal in Marriage ; that Society has no right to intervene in their association except to render them equal ; that it has no right to prescribe to them duties which proceed only from love, nor consequently to punish their violation, that it cannot in principle grant or refuse divorce, because it belongs to the husband and wife alone to know whether it is useful for their happiness and progress to be separated from each other.

AUTHOR. Your conclusions are right, but if Society has no right over the body or the soul of the husband and wife in their capacity of spouses, if it cannot without abuse of power interfere in any of their intimate relations, it is its right and duty to intervene in Marriage as regards interests and children.

READER. In fact, in the union of the sexes, there is not merely an association of two free and equal persons, but also a partnership of capital and labor ; then, from the marriage, children are born for whose education, occupation and subsistence it is necessary to provide.

AUTHOR. Now, the general protection of material

interests and of the rising generation devolves of right
upon Society.   In the sight of the law, the husband
and wife ought to be regarded only as partners, engag-
ing to employ a certain share of capital, together with
their labor, for a definite purpose.   Society takes note
only of a contract of interests, the execution of which
it guarantees like that of any other contract, and the
breach of which it makes public, should it take place by
the wish of the parties interested.   On the other hand,
the education of the rising generation is a question of
life and death to Society.   The children being free with
respect to development, and liable to be useful or injurious to their fellow citizens according to the training
which they have received, society has a right to watch
over them, to secure their material support, their moral
future, to fix the age of marriage, to entrust the children to the more deserving parent in case of separation,
and if both are unworthy, to take them away entirely.

READER. Do you not go a little too far ; on the one
hand, do not children belong to their parents, on the
other, may not Society err with respect to the choice of
the principles to be instilled in them ?

AUTHOR. Children do not belong to their parents because they are not THINGS : to those who obstinately
persist in believing them *property*, we say that Society
has the right of dispossession for the public good.   Then
the social right over children is limited so far as principles are concerned to those of morality.   Society has
no right over religious beliefs which belong to the domain of spiritual jurisdiction.   The power that should
take away children from their parents because they
were not of a certain religious faith would be guilty of
despotism, and would merit universal execration.   If

you say that Society has no right to impose a dogma upon children, you speak truly; but I cannot conceive how you can entertain the thought of forbidding it the right to teach them, even against the will of their parents, enlightening science, purifying morality. Is it not the duty of society to secure the progress of its members, and can any one have a right to keep a human being in ignorance and evil?

READER. You are right, and I condemn myself. Let us return to Marriage. I see with pleasure that you differ in opinion from a number of modern innovators who deny the lawfulness of social interference in the union of the sexes.

AUTHOR. If the union were without protection, who would suffer by it? Not men, but rather women and children.

No one can compel a man to live with a woman whom he has ceased to love; but he must be constrained to fulfill his duties with respect to the children born of this union, and to keep his business engagements: in wronging his companion and escaping from the burdens of paternity, he takes advantage of his liberty to the detriment of others: Society has a right to prevent this.

READER. So you do not grant to Society the right of binding souls or bodies; but that of guaranteeing the contract of Marriage, and the obligations of the spouses towards their future children; of forcing them, in case of separation, to fulfill this last obligation?

AUTHOR. Yes; thus in case of the rupture of the marriage tie, society has only to state publicly the responsibilities of the spouses, the number of children, and the name of the parent on whom their guardianship de-

volves, either by mutual consent or by social authority.
And in confining itself to this part, Society would do
more to prevent the separation of married couples than
by all that it has hitherto foolishly invented for the purpose. The parties would be free to marry again ; but
what woman would be willing to unite herself to a man
who was burdened with several children, or who had
treated his first companion unkindly ? What man would
consent to wed a woman in the same position ?

Do you not think that the difficulty that would be experienced in contracting a new marriage would be a
curb on the inconstancy and bad conduct that lead to a
rupture ?

READER. I believe indeed that marriage, as you understand it, would have more chances of duration than
ours : first, because it is our nature to cling most closely
to that which we may lose. I have often asked myself
why many men remain faithful to their mistresses and
treat them kindly, while they are disrespectful and unfaithful to their wives ; I have asked myself also why
many couples who had long lived happily together
when voluntarily united, were unhappy and often driven
to a legal separation when they had finally married ;
and the only reason that I have been able to find is that
we set the most value on that which we know may
escape us. Man has more respect for a woman who
is not his legal property, his inferior, than for her who
is thus transformed by the law. Notwithstanding, it
must be acknowledged that your ideas appear eccen-
tric.

AUTHOR. Yet they are nothing more than an application of our laws ; indeed, do they not decree that
covenants can have *things* only, not *persons* for their ob-

ject. That Society *does not recognize vows*, and that proceedings cannot be instituted against their violation ?

Now the existing law of marriage *alienates* one of the partners in favor of the other ; the wife *belongs* to the husband ; she is in his *power*. What is such a contract, if not the violation of the principle which affirms that no covenant can be made involving persons ? can it be more lawful to alienate one's person by a contract of slavery ?

Some say that we are at liberty to dispose of our freedom as we choosè, even though it be to renounce it. Indeed, we may do this, as we may commit suicide, but to make use of our liberty to renounce it or to commit suicide is much less to use aright than to violate the laws of moral or physical nature ; these are acts of insanity which we should pity, but which we are not at liberty to erect into a law.

Why does Society refuse to recognize vows and to punish their violation, if not because it admits that it is forbidden to penetrate into the jurisdiction of the conscience ? if not because it does not admit that an individual may alienate his moral and intellectual being any more than his body, and devote himself to immobility when it is his duty, on the contrary, to go forward ?

I ask then if this same Society is not inconsistent in exacting perpetual vows from the husband and wife, in exacting from the wife a vow of obedience, a tacit vow to deliver up her person to the desires of the husband ?

Is not the moral liberty of the spouses as worthy of respect as that of nuns, priests and monks ?

Have married persons more right in Nature and Reason, to alienate their moral and intellectual being, their liberty and their person than the celibates of the Church ?

Another inconsistency of the law is that it declares Marriage an association; the contract of Marriage is therefore a contract of partnership. Now I ask whether, in a single contract of this kind, it is enjoined by law on one of the partners to *obey*, to be subjected to a *perpetual minority*, to be *absorbed*?

I doubt not that the law would declare such a contract between independent partners void; why then does it legalize such a monstrosity in the partnership of husband and wife? It is a relic of barbarism, as you will see if you reflect on it.

READER. I hope that, through reason and necessity, the law will be reformed sooner or later: but a reformation which will not take place is that of the forms of religious marriage, which prescribe to the spouses the same oaths as the code, and like it, subject the wife to the husband.

AUTHOR. Well, what matters it to us, since, thanks to liberty, the religious marriage is merely a benediction with which we can dispense. Those who have a disposition to go to the Church, the Temple, or the Synagogue should have full liberty to receive the blessing of their respective priests! this does not concern Society. What we need is that, if afterward their vows should not seem to them binding, social authority should not make them obligatory; they have a right to be absurd, but society has no right to impose absurdity on them. Its duty is, on the contrary, to enlighten them, and to render them free.

IV.

READER. Those who subordinate woman in marriage rest on the assertion that unity of direction, consequently a ruling power, is needed in the family ; now, your theory evidently destroys this ruling power.

AUTHOR. What is the ruling power ? Practically, it is manifested through the function of government. Formerly, it was based upon two principles, now recognized as radically false : *Divine right* and *inequality*. It was the *right* of those who exercised it to call themselves kings, autocrats, priests, men ; it was the *duty* therefore of the people, the church, woman to obey the elect of God, their superiors by the grace of right delegated from on high.

But in modern opinion, the ruling power is nothing more than a function delegated by the parties interested in order to execute their will.

It is not our business to inquire here whether this modern interpretation has become incarnated in facts ; whether the old principle is not still struggling with the new ; whether the holders of political and familial authority are not still making insane pretentions to divine right ; we have only to show what the notion of the ruling power has become in the present state of thought and feeling.

What will be the ruling power in marriage, in accordance with modern opinion, if not the delegation by one spouse to the other of the management of business and of the family — a delegation of function ; no longer a right ?

And if man and woman are socially equal in principle, if the aptitudes, upon which all functions are based, are not dependent on sex, by what right does society interfere to give the authority either to the husband or the wife ?

If there is need of a ruling power in the household,

are not the parties themselves best capable of bestowing it on the one who can best and most usefully exercise it?

But among partners, is there really room for a ruling power? No, there is room only for division of labor, mutual understanding with respect to common interests. To consult each other, to come to an agreement, to divide the tasks, to remain master each of his own department; this is what the spouses should do, and what they do in general.

The law has so little part in our customs that to-day things happen in this wise: many rich women translate two articles of the Code as follows; *the husband shall obey his wife, and shall follow her wherever she sees fit to dwell or sojourn.* And the husbands obey, because it would not do to offend a wife with a large dowry; because it would make a scandal to thwart their wife; because they need her, being unable, without dishonoring themselves, to keep a mistress.

Husbands in the great centres of population escape obedience through love outside of marriage; they lay no restrictions on their part; Madame is free.

Among the working classes of the citizens and the people, it is practically admitted that neither shall command, and that the husband shall do nothing without consulting his wife and obtaining her consent.

In all classes, if any husband is simple enough to take his pretended right in earnest, he is cited as a bad man, an intolerable despot whom his wife may hate and deceive with a safe conscience; and it is a curious fact that the greater part of the legal separations are for no other cause at the bottom than the exercise of the rights and prerogatives conceded to the husbands by law.

I ask you now, what is the use of maintaining against reason and custom, an authority which does not exist, or which is transferred to the spouse condemned to subjection.

READER. On this point, I am wholly of your opinion; not a single woman of modern times takes the rights of her husband in earnest. But your theory not only attacks his authority; it is also wages war against the indissolubility of marriage, which it is affirmed, is necessary to the dignity of this tie; to the happiness and future of the children, to the morality of the family.

AUTHOR. I claim, on the contrary, that my theory secures, as far as is humanly possible, the perpetuity and purity of marriage. At present, when the knot is tied, the spouses, no longer fearing to lose each other, find in the absence of this fear the germ of a mutual coolness; they may quarrel, be discourteous or unfaithful to each other; there will be scandal, a legal separation perhaps, but they are riveted together; they can never become strangers. Contrast with this picture a household in which the bond is dissoluble; all is changed; the despotic or brutal husband represses his evil propensities, because he knows that his companion, whom after all he loves, would quit him and transfer to another the attentions she lavishes on him; and that no honest woman would be willing to take her place.

The husband disposed to be unfaithful would continue in the path of duty, because his abandonment and offences would alienate his wife, blast his reputation, and prevent him from forming an honorable alliance.

The worn out profligate would no longer espouse the dowry of a young girl, because he would know that, promptly disenchanted, the young wife, instead of having recourse to adultery, would break the ill assorted union.

The woman who should take advantage of her dowry, of the necessity of her husband to remain faithful, to tyrannise over him, would fear a divorce which would throw the blame on her and condemn her to a life of solitude.

A shrewish wife would no longer dare to inflict suffering on her husband, or a coquette to deceive or torment him; who would marry them after a separation?

Do you not see that free marriages are happier and more lasting than any others?

Have you not yourself admitted that to separate the parties in these unions, it often suffices to join them legally?

I know myself of a voluntary union that was very happy during *twenty-two* years, and was dissolved by separation at the end of three years of legal marriage; I have known of many others of a shorter duration which legality contributed to dissolve instead of rendering eternal.

You would hardly believe how many married couples reformed in their treatment of each other in 1848, when they feared that the law of divorce might be accepted. If the simple expedient of divorce has power to produce good results, what may not be expected from a rational law.

We need only to reflect in order to comprehend that voluntary dissolubility, without social intervention, would render unions better assorted, for it would be for one's interest, for his own reputation, to enter into them only with the moral conviction of being able to preserve them; then only would no excuse be found for infidelity ; loyalty would make part of the relations of the spouses. The law of perpetuity has perverted everything, corrupted everything ; on the side of the woman, it favors, yes, necessitates stratagem ; on the side of the man, it favors brutality and despotism ; it provokes on both sides adultery, poisoning and assassination ; and leads to those separations which are daily increasing in number, and which, by giving the lie to the indissolubility of marriage, place the partners in a painful and perilous situation, and bring in their train a host of irregularities.

In fact, if the spouses are separated while young, concubinage is their refuge. The man in this false position finds many to excuse him ; but the woman is forced to conceal herself, to tremble at the thought of a pregnancy and to make it disappear. Legal separation leads the spouses not only to concubinage, to mutual hatred, but causes the birth of thousands of children whose future is compromised, destroyed by the fact of their illegitimacy. Let the spouses be free in accordance with their right, and all will fall into its proper order, for all will be done openly and truly.

READER. But the future of the children ?

AUTHOR. The morality of the children is better insured under the system of liberty than under that of indissolubility, for they will not be witnesses for years of the bitter contention and licentiousness which now render them deceitful and vicious, and inspire them with contempt or hatred for one of the authors of their being, sometimes of both, when they do not take them for models ; if life in common becomes impossible to the parents, which will be more rare under the law of liberty, the children will not be subjected to the power of

those who violate the law of received morality; they
may see these parents contract a new alliance *as now*,
but this alliance will be honored by all.

From these unions children may be born *as now*, but
these children, instead of being cast into the hospital,
will share with the first the affection and inheritance
of their father or mother. The so-styled legitimate
children will lose in fortune, it is true; but they will
gain in good examples; many children who are now in
the category of the illegitimate will be ranked among the
former, and will be no longer condemned by desertion
to die young, or else to grovel in ignorance, vice and
misery; to see their brow branded with the fault of their
parents as of their own by a host of imbeciles and men
without heart, who have no other guarantee for what
they call their legitimacy than the presumption accorded
them by the law.

III.

READER. It will be long yet, perhaps, before collective Reason comprehends liberty in the union of the
sexes as you do, and men will ascribe to themselves the
right not only of binding the interests, but the souls
and bodies of the spouses.

AUTHOR. As far as we can foresee, Society must
neccessarily pass through two stages to realize our opinion; it must first grant divorce *for a declared cause;*
later it will grant divorce decreed in private on the petition of one or both of the spouses. We will not take
up this last form of the rupture of the conjugal tie, but
that which is nearest us — divorce for a declared cause.

What are the reasons which you would consider valid
for a petition for divorce?

READER. First, those which now give rise to separation from bed and board : adultery of the wife, cruelty, grave abuses, condemnation of one of the spouses to punishment affecting the liberty or person, the fraudulent management of the property by the husband; next, infidelity of the husband, qualified adultery, incompatibility of temper, notable vices, such as drunkenness, gaming, etc.

AUTHOR. Very well; these causes suffice.

READER. During the proceedings for divorce, the wife should be as free as the husband. The child that should be born to her after more than ten months' separation should be reputed natural, even though the divorce had not been pronounced; and should bear her name and inherit from her like one of her legitimate children.

AUTHOR. Who should take custody of the children and the property during the proceedings ?

READER. The court should decide who should have the care of the children, in accordance with the causes for the petition for divorce and the testimony of the parents, friends and neighbors.

AUTHOR. But if the spouses ask to be divorced only on account of incompatibility of temper, and are both honorable ?

READER. They should be requested to agree mutually either to share the children, or to entrust them to one of the two, or to give the younger children to the mother, leaving the sons over fifteen to the father. The court, besides, should appoint from the family of the mother, a guardian to watch over the conduct of the father towards the children left in his care; and from the family of the father, a similar guardian to the mother and the children remaining with her. This guardianship, which should be strictly moral, should continue till the children had attained majority.

AUTHOR. And in case the parents should be alike unworthy ?

READER. In such a case, which would seldom happen, the judge, in behalf of society, should deprive them of the custody of the children, and entrust it to a member of the family of one of the parents, appointing a guardian to watch over his conduct and protect the interests of his ward from the family of the other.

AUTHOR. Very well ; I see with pleasure that you are cured of the erroneous belief that the children *belong* to the parents, and that you comprehend the high function of society as the protector of minors.

During the suit for divorce, who shall have the control of the property ?

READER, If the contract has been made under the system of separation of property, and for paraphernalia, there is no need of putting the question ; each one will manage his own.

But I am somewhat puzzled how to answer you in case of communion of goods, or in case the capital is embarked in a common business, carried on solely by one of the parties. The present law does not seem to me sufficiently to protect the interests of the wife in case of separation.

AUTHOR. Without entangling ourselves in a host of individual cases which modify or contradict each other, let us provide that in case of communion of goods, the administration of the property shall be taken from the spouse holding it if the petition for divorce be based on his bad management, his dissipated habits, or his condemnation to a penalty affecting his liberty or person ;

that in all other cases, he shall make an inventory of the property and the condition of the business; and a person shall be appointed from the family of the spouse excluded from the management to watch over the conduct of the spouse to whom it is entrusted, who shall be bound to pay alimony to the other until the divorce shall be decreed.

READER. And if there is no fortune?

AUTHOR. Until the spouses become strangers, they owe assistance to each other: the court should therefore require the spouse that earns the more to aid the other.

READER. How long a time should elapse between the admission of the petition and the judgment of divorce?

AUTHOR. A year, in order that the parties may have time for reflection.

READER. The divorce being granted, and the ex-partners restored to liberty, would you permit them to marry others?

AUTHOR. Most assuredly; else what signifies our arguments against separation?

READER. What! the adulterous and brutal spouse, he who has inflicted suffering on his partner, who has been wholly in the wrong, should enjoy like the other the privilege of marrying again? I confess that this shocks me.

AUTHOR. Because you are not sufficiently imbued with the doctrines of liberty and the sentiment of right. Marriage is the natural right of every adult; society has no right therefore to prohibit it or to make it a privilege; on the other hand, in every divorce, there is wrong or the lack of something on either side with respect to the other; the man or woman who commits adultery may be a model of fidelity to a partner better suited to his or her temperament and disposition; he who has been brutal and violent may be wholly different with a wife possessing a different character; in short, we repeat, to prohibit marriage is to permit libertinism, and it is not the interest of society to pervert itself. Both partners therefore should have a right to marry, but the law should take care that all should be informed of the burdens resting upon them by reason of their first marriage, and know that they are divorced. Consequently, society has a right to publish the bill of divorce, and to require that the parties divorced should provide for the necessities of their minor children, and that the bill of divorce, joined to the one setting forth this obligation, should accompany the publication of the bans of a new marriage; in this, there is neither injustice nor abuse of power; for each one will submit to the consequence of what he has done in perfect freedom.

READER. And would you not fix the number of times that a divorced person might re-marry?

AUTHOR. Why fix it? do you fix the number of times that a widow or widower may marry again?

READER. But a libertine, a bad man might marry ten times, and thus render ten women unhappy.

AUTHOR. What are you talking of! do you seriously believe that there would be a woman insane enough to marry a man *nine times* divorced, a man obliged to accompany the publication of his bans with nine bills of divorce, with nine judgements compelling him to pay so much yearly for the support of seven, eight or nine children. Do you seriously believe that a woman would consent to become the companion of such a man!

This man might indeed marry twice — but three times! do you think that it would be possible?

READER. You are right, and on reflection, the measures which you advocate appear perhaps severe.

AUTHOR. I know it; but our aim is not to favor divorces nor subsequent unions; but, on the contrary, to prevent the former as far as possible by the difficulties of forming the latter. Now for this it is not necessary to restrict the liberty of the individual, but to render him responsible for his acts, and to rivet the chain that he has forged for himself in such a manner that he can neither cast it aside nor lay the burden of it on others unless they are duly warned of it and consent thereto.

IV.

READER. Ought society to permit unions disproportioned in age? Is it not to expose a woman to adultery, to marry her at seventeen or eighteen to a man of thirty, forty or even fifty years of age? What harmony of sentiments and views can exist at that time between the spouses? The wife sees in her husband a sort of father, whom notwithstanding she can neither love nor respect like a father, and she remains a minor all her life.

AUTHOR. These unions are very prejudicial to woman and the race, and they would be for the most part averted, if the law should fix the marriageable age at twenty-four or twenty-five for both sexes. At seventeen, we marry to be called Madame, and to wear a bridal dress and a wreath of orange flowers; we certainly should not do this at twenty-five.

If the flower is not called on to form its fruit until

it is fully matured, neither should man and woman:
now, in our climate the organization of neither is complete until twenty-four or twenty-five.

Woman gives more to the great work of reproduction and wears out faster in it; to render her liable to
become a mother prematurely is therefore to expose her
to greater sufferings.

In the first place, she is forced to share between herself and her offspring the elements necessary to her own
nutrition, which weakens both her and the child.

Her development is checked, her constitution is
changed, she becomes predisposed to uterine affections,
and runs the risk of becoming an invalid at the age
when she ought to enjoy robust health.

The enervation of the body brings with it that of
the mind: the woman becomes nervous, irritable, and
often capricious; she cannot nurse her children; she
will not be capable of rearing them properly, she will
make dolls of them, and will favor the development of
faults which afterwards becoming vices, will afflict the
family and society.

This woman, a mother before her time, not only will
never become the thoughtful companion and counsellor
of her husband who, being much older than she, will
amuse himself with her as with a child, but will be his
ward for her whole life, and will have recourse to artifice to have her own way. Thus to weaken woman in
every respect, to shorten her life, to put her under guardianship, to prepare the way for puny and badly reared
offspring, — such are the most obvious results of her
precocious marriage.

To hold women in voluntary subjection and to organize the harem among us, we need only take advantage

of the permission of the law authorising their marriage at the age of fifteen.

That woman may not be in subjection; that she may be able to become a mother without detriment to her health and under circumstances favorable to the good organization of her children; that she may be a worthy and earnest wife, prepared to fulfill all her duties, she must not be married, I repeat, before twenty-four or twenty-five; and she must not marry a man older than herself.

READER. But it is claimed that the husband ought to be ten years older than the wife, because the latter grows old faster, and because it is necessary that the husband should have had experience in life in order to appreciate his wife and to render her happy.

AUTHOR. Errors and prejudices all. Woman grows old sooner than man only through premature marriage and maternity; a well preserved man and woman are alike old at the same age. But the woman consents to grow old while the man is much less willing to do so, since he does not blush when gray haired, to marry a young girl, and to set up the ridiculous pretention of being loved by her for love. Men must be broken of the habit of believing themselves perpetually at the age of pleasing; of imagining that they are quite as agreeable to our eyes when they are old and ugly as if they were Adonises. They must be told unceasingly that what is unbecoming in us is equally so in them; and that an old woman would be no more ridiculous in seeking the love of a young man, than an old man in pretending to that of a young girl.

The husband and wife should be nearly of the same age; first, to treat each other more easily as equals;

13

next, because there will be more harmony in their feelings and views, as well as in their temperaments, all
things very necessary to the organization of children.

It is necessary besides, in order that the woman may
not be tempted to infidelity; you know how many troubles arise from unions disproportioned in age.

The husband must have *seen life*, it is said; this is
the opinion of those who permit their sons to *sow their
wild oats;* who believe that man is at liberty to wallow
in the mire of dens of infamy, and that there are two
kinds of morality. We do not belong to this class.
You would not give your daughter to a man who had
seen life, because he would be *blasé*, because he would
pervert her or expose her, through the disenchantment
that would follow, to seek in another what she did not
find in her husband.

What we have said as regards your daughter applies
also to your son; he must not marry a woman younger
than himself; for you would no more desire a disadvan-
tageous position for your daughter-in-law than for your
daughter; both are dear to you and worthy of respect
before the solidarity of sex.

READER. I shall educate my son to comprehend that
the form of marriage prescribed by the Code is merely
a relic of barbarism, that his wife owes obedience only
to Duty, that she is a free being and his equal; and
that he has no rights over her person but those which
she herself accords to him. I shall tell him that love is
a tender plant which must be tended carefully to keep it
alive; that it is blighted by unceremoniousness and
slovenliness; that he should therefore be as careful of
his personal appearance after marriage as he was to be
pleasing to the eyes of his betrothed. I shall say to

him : ask nothing except from the love of your wife ; remember that more than one husband has excited repulsion by the brutality of the wedding night. Marriage, my son, is a grave and holy thing; purity is its choicest jewel; know that many men have owed the adultery of their wife to the deplorable pains that they have taken to deprave her imagination. Far from using your influence over her who will be the half of yourself in order to render her docile to your wishes, and to make her your echo, develop reason and character in her ; in elevating her, you will become better, and will prepare for yourself a counsel and stay. I have married you under the system of separation of goods in order that your wife may be protected against you, should you depart from your principles; and should you ever grieve me by straying from them, your wife will became doubly my daughter. I shall be her companion and consoler, and shall close my arms and my doors on you.

AUTHOR. Right, and you will do well to add: interest your wife in your occupation ; take care that she is always busy, for labor is the preserver of chastity.

READER. To my daughter I will say : the social order in which we live requires, my child, that you shall superintend your house ; the state of Society is still far distant in which our sex will be relieved from this function. Do not forget that the prosperity of the family depends on the spirit of order and economy of the wife. What your fortune or special business exempts you from executing, superintend and direct. Extravagance of dress and furniture now surpasses all bounds. Luxury is not wrong in itself, but in the existing state of things, it is a great relative evil, for we have not yet re-

solved the problem of increasing and varying products
without at the same time increasing the wretchedness
and debasement of their producers. Be simple therefore: this does not exclude elegance, but only those
piles of silks and laces which trail in the dust of the
streets, those diamonds and precious stones which make
the fortune of the few at the expense of the morality of
the many, and which are only dead capital, the libera-
tion of which would be productive of great good. Do
not suffer yourself to be ensnared by the sophism that
honest women must adorn themselves to hinder men
from passing their time with courtesans. Would you
not be ashamed to compete in dress with women whom
you do not esteem, and would the man who could be
retained by such means be worth the trouble?

I have instructed you in your legal position as wife,
mother and property holder; I marry you under the
system of separation of goods in order to spare your
husband the temptation of regarding himself as your
master; in order that he may be obliged to take your
advice and to look upon you as his partner. Despite
these precautions, you will be a minor, since the law
thus decrees. But our law is not Reason: never forget that you are a human being; that is, a being endowed like your husband with intellect, sentiments, free
will, and inclination; that you owe submission only to
Reason and your conscience; that if it is your duty to
make sacrifices to the peace in little things, and to tolerate the faults of your husband as he should tolerate
yours, it is none the less your duty resolutely to resist a
brutal — *I will have it so.*

You will be a mother, I hope; nurse your children
yourself, rear them in the principles of Right and Duty

which I have instilled into your intellect and heart, in order to make of them, not only just, good, chaste men and women, but laborers in the great work of Progress.

You understand the great destiny of our species; you understand your rights and duties; I need not therefore repeat to you that woman is no more made for man than man for woman; that consequently woman cannot, without failing in her duty, become lost and absorbed in man; for with him, she should love her children, her country, humanity; she owes more to her children than she does to him; and if forced to choose between family interests and generous sentiments of a higher order, woman should no more hesitate than should man to sacrifice the former to justice.

AUTHOR. It will be said that you instruct your daughter in a very manly way.

READER. Since in our days men play the mandolin, is it not necessary that women should speak seriously? Since men, in the name of their naive selfishness, claim the right to confiscate woman to their use, to extol to her the charms of the gyneceum, to suppress her rights, and to preach to her the sweets of absorption, must not women re-act against these soporific doctrines, and recall their daughters to the sentiment of dignity and individuality.

AUTHOR. I endorse you with all my heart!

Now that we are nearly agreed on all points, we have only to sum up what we have said, and to give an outline of the principal reforms necessary to be wrought in order that woman my be placed in a position more in conformity with Right and Justice.

I.

AUTHOR. Identity of right being based on identity of species, and woman being of the same species as man, what ought she to be before civil dignity, in the employment of her activity and in marriage?

READER. The equal of man.

AUTHOR. How will she become the equal of man in civil dignity?

READER. When she shall hold a place on the jury and by the side of all civil functionaries; shall be a member of boards of trade and mercantile associations; and shall be a witness in all cases in which the testimony of man is required.

AUTHOR. Why ought the testimony of woman to be admitted in all cases in which that of man is required?

READER. Because woman is as credible as man; because she is, like him, a civil personage.

AUTHOR. Why ought woman to have a place on the jury?

READER. Because the Code declaring her the equal of man as regards culpability, misdemeanor, crime and punishment, she is thus declared capable like him of comprehending wrong in others;

Because the jury being a guarantee for the male culprit, the female culprit should have a similar guarantee ;

Because if the *male* criminal is better comprehended by men, the *female* criminal will be better comprehended by women ;

Because society in its aggregate being offended by the crime, it is necessary that this society, composed of two sexes, should be represented by both to judge and to condemn it.   Because, lastly, where the moral sense is concerned, the feminine element is the more necessary inasmuch as men. claim that our sex is in general more moral and more merciful than their own.

AUTHOR. Why ought woman to hold a place among civil functionaries ?

READER. Because society, represented by these functionaries, is composed of two sexes ;

Because even now in a number of public functions, there is a department more especially belonging to woman ;

Because, in the ceremony of the marriage celebration for instance, if woman does not appear as magistrate, not only is society insufficiently represented, but the wife may regard herself as delivered up to the power of a man by all the men of the country.

AUTHOR. Why ought woman to have her place in boards of trade and mercantile associations ?

READER. Because she shares equally in industrial production ;

Because she shares equally in commerce ;

Because she understands business transactions and contracts as well if not better than man ;

Because, in all questions of interests, she should be her own representative.

AUTHOR. When will woman become the equal of man in the employment of her activity and of her other faculties ?

READER. When she shall have colleges, academies and schools for special instruction, and when all vocations shall be accessible to her.

AUTHOR. Why ought women to receive the same national education as men ?

READER. Because they exercise a vast influence over the ideas, sentiments and conduct of men, and because it is for the interest of society that this influence should be salutary ;

Because it is for the interest of all to enlarge the views and elevate the sentiments of women, in order that they may use their natural ascendency for the advancement of progress, of truth, of good, of moral beauty ;

Because woman has a right, like man, to cultivate her intellect, and to acquire the knowledge bestowed by the state ;

Because, lastly, as she pays her part of the expenses of national education, it is robbery to prohibit her from participating in it.

AUTHOR. Why ought woman to be admitted to academies and professional schools?

READER. Because Society, not having a right to deny the existence of any aptitude among its members, has consequently no right to prevent those who claim to possess them from cultivating them, nor to lock up from them the treasures of science and practice which are at its disposal.

Because there are women who are born chemists, physicians, mathematicians, etc., and because these women have a right to find in social institutions the same resources as man for the cultivation of their aptitudes ;

Because there are professions practised by women who need the instruction that is interdicted them.

AUTHOR. Why ought every field of occupation to be accessible to woman?

READER. Because woman is a free being, whose vocation no one has a right to contest or to restrict;

Because she, no more than man, will enter vocations forbidden her by temperament, lack of aptitude or want of time; and it is therefore quite as unnecessary to interdict them to her as to those men who are unfit to enter them.

AUTHOR. Do you not even interdict to her those vocations in which strength is needed, or which are attended with danger?

READER. Women are not forbidden to be carpenters or tilers, yet they do not become such, because their nature opposes it; it is precisely because nature does oppose it, that I think society unreasonable in meddling with the nature. There is no need to prohibit what is impossible; and if what has been declared impossible is done, it is because it is possible: now society has no right to prohibit what is possible to any of its members; this appears even absurd where vocation is in question.

AUTHOR. Let each one follow his private occupation at his own risk and peril, then; but are there not certain public functions which are not suitable for women?

READER. No one knows this, since they are not open for her admission; and, were it so, the prohibition would be useless: competition would show the falsity of ill-founded pretentions.

AUTHOR. When will woman become the equal of man in marriage?

READER. When the person of the wife is not pledged

18*

in marriage; when the engagements are reciprocal, and when the wife is not treated as a minor and absorbed in the husband.   And this should be so:

Because it is not allowable to alienate one's personality, such an alienation, being *immoral* and *void* of itself;

Because the wife being a distinct individual, cannot be actually absorbed by the husband, and a law is absurd when it rests on a fiction and supposes an impossibility;

Because, in fine, woman, being the equal of man before Society, cannot, under any pretext, lose this equality by reason of a closer association with him.

AUTHOR. There are two questions in marriage, aside from that of the person — property and children.   Do you not think that the married woman ought, like the unmarried woman who has attained majority, to be mistress of her property, to be free to exercise any profession that suits her, and to be at liberty to sell, to buy, to give, to receive, and to institute suits at law?

READER. The married man having all these rights, it is evident that the married woman ought to have them under the law of equality.   Are you not of the same opinion?

AUTHOR. In all partnerships, we pledge a portion of our liberty on certain points agreed upon.   Now the husband and wife are partners; they cannot therefore be as perfectly free with respect to each other as though they were strangers; but it is necessary, we repeat, that their position should be the same and their pledges mutual.   If the wife can neither sell, nor alienate, nor give, nor receive, nor appear in court without the consent of the husband, it is not allowable for the husband to do these things without the consent of the wife; if the wife is not permitted to practise a profession without the consent of the husband, the husband is not at liberty to do so without the consent of the wife ; if the wife cannot pledge the common property without authority from the husband, the husband cannot pledge it without the consent of the wife. I go further ; I would not willingly permit the wife, before the age of twenty-five, to give her husband authority to alienate anything belonging to one of the two; the husband has too much influence over her for her to be really free before this age.

READER. But what if one of the parties through caprice or evil motives is unwilling that the other should do something that is proper and advantageous ?

AUTHOR. Arbiters are frequently chosen in the differences that arise between partners in business ; society, represented by the judicial power, is the general arbiter between the husband and wife ; still we think that it would be well to establish between them a perpetual arbiter, holding the first degree of jurisdiction : this might be the family council, organized differently from the present. Before this confidential tribunal, better fitted than any other to understand the case, the husband and wife should carry, not only the differences arising between them concerning questions of interests, but those relating to the education, profession and marriage of the children. This tribunal should give the first judgment, and much scandal would be avoided by its decisions, from which besides one could always appeal to the social court.

I need not add that the right of the father and the mother over the children is absolutely equal, and that, if the right of either could be contested, it would not be that of the mother, who alone can say, I *know*, I am *certain* that these children are mine.

READER. In fact, it is odious that the plenitude of right should be found on the side of the mere legal presumption, the act of faith, uncertainty.

Regarding marriage as a partnership of equals, do you not think that it would be well to mark this equality and the distinction of personalities in the name borne by the spouses and their children ?

AUTHOR. Certainly, on the day of marriage each of the spouses should join his partner's name to his own ; this is done already in certain cantons of Switzerland, and even in France, among a few individuals.

The children should bear the double name of their parents until marriage, when the daughters should keep the mother's name, and the sons the father's ; or else, if we wish to bring into the question the system of liberty, it might be decreed that, on attaining majority, the child himself should choose which of the two names he would bear and transmit.

II.

READDR. Now, let us take up the political right.

AUTHOR. A nation is an association of free and equal individuals, co-operating, by their labor and contributions, to the maintenance of the common work ; they have an incontestible right to do whatever is necessary to protect their persons, their rights and their property from injury. Man has political rights because he is free and the equal of his co-partners ; according to others, because he is a producer and a tax-payer ; now, woman being, through identity of species, free and the equal of man ; being in point of fact, a producer and a tax-payer ; and having the same general instincts as man, it is evident that she has the same political rights as he. Such are the principles, let us proceed to the application.

We have said elsewhere, that it is not enough that a thing should be true in an absolute sense ; it is necessary under penalty of transforming good into evil, to take into account the surroundings into which we seek to introduce it ; this men too often forget, the *practical* truth in our question is that it is profitable to recognize political rights *only to the extent to which it is demanded*, because those who do not demand it are intellectually incapable of making use of it, and because if they should exercise it, in a majority of cases, it would be against their own interests ; Prudence exacts that we should be sure that the possessor of a right is really emancipated, and that he will not be the blind tool of a man or a party.

Now, in the existing state of affairs, women not only do not demand their political rights, but laugh at those who address them on the subject ; they pride themselves on being thought unfit for that which regards general interests ; they recognize themselves therefore as incapable.

On the other hand, they are minors civilly, slaves of prejudice, deprived of general education, submissive for the most part to the influence of their husbands, lovers or confessors, clinging as a majority to the ways of the past. If therefore they should enter without prepararation into political life, they would either duplicate men or cause humanity to retrograde.

You comprehend now why many women who are more capable than an infinite number of men of coöperating in great political acts, choose rather to renounce them than to compromise the cause of progress by the extension of political right to all women.

READER. Personally, I am of your opinion ; but it is necessary to foresee and to refute the objections that may be made to you by very intelligent women ; these women will say, Reflect, the negation of right is iniquitous, for it is the negation of equality and of human nature. It is as false as dangerous to lay down the principle of the recognition of right only to the extent in which it is claimed ; for it is notorious that slaves are not the ones in general to demand their own rights ; your affirmation therefore condemns the emancipation of slaves and serfs, and universal suffrage.

The objection that you raise against the right on account of the incapacity of women and the low use which they would make of it, might apply quite as well to men who are scarcely more fully emancipated than they ; who are often the duplicate of their wife or confessor, or who have no other opinion than that of their electoral committee.

In right, as in everything else, an apprenticeship is necessary : woman will make use of it at first badly, then better, then well ; for we learn to play on an instrument much more quickly by using it than by learning its theory.

The exercise of right gives elevation and dignity, elevates the individual in his own esteem, and causes him to study questions which he would have neglected had he not been obliged to examine them in order to concur in and resolve them. Do you wish women to take to heart matters of general interest ? Then give them political right.

These objections, may be raised against you.

AUTHOR. They were raised against me in 1848 by a number of eminent women, and by many men devoted to the triumph of the new principles.

I answered them then and I answer them again to day: We should speedily agree, if our modern society were not the scene of conflict between two diametrically opposite principles.

The question is not to decide whether political right belongs to woman, whether she would develop it, enlarge it, etc., but rather whether she would use it to ensure the triumph of the principle that says to humanity, Advance! or of that which gives as the word of command, Retreat!

What is the end of political right? Evidently, to accomplish a great duty in the direction of progress. Well, is it not dangerous to accord it to those who would employ it against this end?

What! you struggle for right, in order to obtain the triumph of a holy cause, yet feel no hesitation in according it to those who would certainly make use of right to kill right!

Your reproach me for acting like the Jesuits, who value justice much less than expediency. Well, gentlemen, if you had had half their ability, you would have been successful long ago. Like true savages, you would think yourselves dishonored by possessing prudence and practical sense, by offering yourselves to battle otherwise than with naked bodies; this may be very fine, very courageous — but as to being sensible, that is another thing.

I am not guilty of the crime of denying right, since I do not deny it; I only desire that it shall not be demanded since this would be suicidal, I do not lay down the principle that *every kind* of right should be recognized only to the extent in which it is claimed, since I speak to you of political rights alone; there are rights which make their own demand, such as those of living, of development, of enjoyment, of the fruit of one's labor, and it is shameful for society not to recognize them to their full extent. But we awaken later to the sentiment of civil right, and still later to that of political right; take the logical advance of humanity into account therefore and do not remain in the absolute.

I know that my objection on the score of the incapacity of women is quite as applicable to that of men; but is it a reason, because you have admitted the right of the ignorant masses of men who had not demanded it, to show yourselves equally unwise with respect to women who are in the same position? I will correct myself, gentlemen, of what you term my *aristocratic* spirit, when I see your political freedmen comprehending the tendencies of civilization, and making use of their right to drive the abettors of the past to despair by promoting the triumph of liberty and equality. Until then, permit me to keep my opinion.

And I have kept my opinion, which is this: the exercise of political right is a means of reform and progress, only if those who enjoy it believe in progress and are anxious for reforms: in the opposite case, the popular vote can be nothing but the expression of prejudices, errors and passions — instead of learning to exercise it through the use of it, as it is urged, they employ it simply to cut their own fingers.

READER. May it not be objected that, in accordance with your theory of right, all being equal, no one can arrogate to himself the function of distributing rights?

AUTHOR. Theory is the ideal towards which practice should tend; if we had not this ideal, we could not know by what principle to guide ourselves; but in social *reality*, there are individuals who have attained majority, and others who, being minors, are destined to attain it.

If I should assert that those who have attained majority can rightfully accord or refuse right to the minors, I should depart essentially from my principles; it is by the *law*, which is the expression of the conscience of those most advanced, while waiting till it shall be the conscience of all, that political majority is decreed and that its conditions are established. The right is virtual in each of us; no one therefore has the right to give it, to take it away, or to contest it; it is recognized when we are in a condition to exercise and to demand it; and we prove that we are in a condition to exercise it when we satisfy the conditions fixed by the law.

READER. What should be these conditions for the enjoyment of political right, in your opinion?

AUTHOR. Twenty-five years of age; and a certificate attesting that the individual knows how to read, write and reckon, that he possesses an elementary knowledge of the history and geography of his country; together with a correct theory with respect to Right and Duty, and the destiny of humanity upon earth. The knowledge of a small volume would be sufficient, as you see, to enable every man and woman, twenty-five years of age and healthy in mind, to enjoy political rights, after having been subjected to an initiation by the enjoyment of civil rights. But, I ask you, what could those do with political right who confound liberty with license, who scarcely know the meaning of the words

Right and Duty, and who are even incapable of writing their own vote! Men have their rights, let them keep them! a right once admitted cannot be taken away: let them render themselves fit to exercise them. As to women, let them first emancipate themselves civilly and become educated: their turn will come.

READER. It is very important that men should comprehend that you do not deny, but merely postpone the political rights of our sex.

AUTHOR. Be easy; they will comprehend it rightly; they will not mistake counsel dictated by prudence for an acknowledgement of inferiority and a resignation of functions.

III.

READER. Will you now state the legal reforms which we should demand successively.

AUTHOR. So far as civil life is concerned, we should ask:

That a woman who is a foreigner may be able to become naturalized in a country otherwise than by marriage.

That woman shall not lose her nationality by the same sacrament.

That woman be admitted to sign, as a witness, all certificates of social condition, with all others that have been hitherto interdicted to her.

You know that already, in derogation of the law, midwives sign certificates of birth of unacknowledged natural children, and that, in certain notarial documents, drawn up by justices of the peace, to attest to a fact in the absence of written evidence, the testimony of women is admitted.

We demand that tradeswomen and merchant women shall form a part of the boards of trade; that in every criminal trial, women shall be placed on the jury: that to women shall be entrusted the management and super-intendence of hospitals, prisons for women, and charitable associations.

That in every district, a woman shall be appointed to superintend girls' schools, infant asylums, and nurses.

You know that women are already filling public employments in derogation of the law, since the teaching and inspection of girls' schools, and other asylums, are entrusted to them, and since women keep post-offices, stamp offices, etc.

READER. This regards civil Right in general; what reforms shall we demand concerning married women?

AUTHOR. That the conjugal abode shall be that which is inhabited by the husband and wife *together*, no longer by the man alone.

That the articles shall be suppressed which command the wife to obey her husband, and to follow him wherever he sees fit to reside.

That the prohibition to sell, mortgage, receive, give, appear in law, etc., without the consent of the husband or court, shall be extended to the husband as far as to the wife.

That marriage under the system of separation of goods shall become the public law.

READER. What reforms do you demand with respect to the family council and guardianship?

AUTHOR. We demand that the family council shall be composed of twenty persons; ten men and ten women, parents, relatives and friends, chosen by the spouses.

That the powers of this council, presided over by the justice of the peace, shall be so determined that it shall give the first judgment in differences arising between the spouses as to children, property, guardianship, etc.

We demand that every woman may be qualified to be appointed guardian or to watch over the conduct of the guardian towards the ward.

That the guardianship of the spouse interdicted shall be always confessed by the family council.

That the wife like the husband, may name a definitive guardian and a council of guardianship for her surviving spouse.

That the spouses may name during their lifetime, the father, a male inspecting guardian from his family, the mother, a female inspecting guardian from hers, that in case of pre-decease, the children may be always under the influence of both sexes.

That this superior guardianship, in the absence of any expressed desire, belongs of right to a member of the family of the defunct, who must be of the same sex.

That in case of a second marriage, if the child is maltreated or unhappy, the inspecting guardian, whether male or female, can have it adjudged to him by the family council, without excluding the appeal of the guardian to the courts.

That in case of the death of the father or mother, the guardianship belongs of right to the nearest ancestor, and the inspecting guardianship to the nearest ancestor of the other line.

If there be competition between the two lines, the family councils shall choose the guardian from one family and the inspecting guardian from the other, and of opposite sex.

That the duties of guardianship and inspecting guardianship shall comprehend, not only the material, but also the moral and intellectual interests of the wards.

That the father who is guardian, shall lose the right of guardianship over the children if he re-marries without first having had it continued to him by the family council.

That lastly, the State shall so organize a board of guardianship for abandoned children that the boys shall be under the superintendence of the men and the girls under that of the women; this board will form a great family council.

READER. I like your system better than that of the law, not only because woman is the equal of man therein, but because wards will be better protected by it; I have known men to cause their wives, over-excited by their ill treatment, to be placed under interdict, in order to remain masters of their property; on the other hand, you know how many children are wronged or made unhappy by the second marriage of their father. A stepmother has full power to inflict suffering on the little unfortunates.

But you have said nothing of the authority of parents over their children.

AUTHOR. The authority of the parents over the children is the same; the expression, paternal authority, is incomplete; the true phrase would be *parental* authority. On this head, we demand that if there be dissension between the father and mother with regard to the children, the family council shall decide in the first instance.

That neither the father nor the mother shall have power to shut up the child unless *both are agreed*.

That the father or the mother acting as guardian shall not have power to have recourse to this measure except with the concurrence of the inspecting guardian, or, in case of difference, with the approbation of the family council, always reserving the right of appeal to the court.

That the marriageable age shall be fixed at twenty-five for both sexes.

READER. Shall we demand the suppression of separation from bed and board?

AUTHOR. No; but we must demand that *divorce shall be established.*

That divorce may be obtained for the adultery of one of the parties, cruelty, grave abuses, condemnation to punishment affecting the liberty or person, notorious vices, incompatibility of temper, mutual consent.

That, during the suit for separation or for divorce, the guardianship of the children shall be given to the most deserving parent; and that, if both are alike unworthy, a guardian and inspecting guardian of different sexes shall be appointed.

That, if both are deserving, they shall settle it amicably between themselves before the family council.

That parties married under the dotal system or under that of the separation of goods, shall have control of their own property.

That if the petition for divorce be on account of the bad management of the common property, the administration shall be taken away from the husband and entrusted to the wife.

That if the petition be on account of the condemnation of one of the parties to punishment affecting the liberty or person, the other shall remain administrator.

That, in all other cases, an inventory shall be made and the spouse best fitted to the task be appointed guardian under the surveillance of one or two members of the family of the other spouse, with the obligation of furnishing estovers to the other.

That the decree granting the divorce or separation shall bear the number, name and age of the children born of the marriage, together with the annual sum that each party is bound to furnish for their maintenance and education.

That this decree shall state to whose custody the children are entrusted, whether by natural consent or by familial or judicial authority.

That it shall be placarded publicly in the courts, and inserted in the leading journals of the vicinity.

That this instrument shall accompany the publication of the bans of a subsequent marriage, under pain of heavy penalties.

READER. These measures are severe; if it would be easy to become divorced, it would not be easy to marry afterwards.

AUTHOR. I do not deny it; but it is better to prevent divorce by the difficulty of marrying afterwards, than by placing restrictions upon it; in the first case, tho difficulty comes from the fetters which the individual has forged for himself; he makes his own destiny; in the second, individual liberty is infringed upon by social authority, which is an abuse of power.

READER. Let us enter upon the legal reforms concerning morals.

AUTHOR. We demand that every promise of marriage which is not fulfilled shall be punished with a fine and damages.

That every man whom an unmarried mother can prove by witnesses or letters, to be the father of her child, shall be subject to the burdens of paternity.

That the investigation of paternity shall be authorized like that of maternity.

That the seduction of an unmarried woman under twenty-five shall be severely punished.

That no unmarried woman can be registered among the public women before twenty-five years old, and that she shall be put into the house of correction if she abandons herself to prostitution before this age.

That every abandoned woman who receives a man under twenty-five years of age shall be punished with fine and imprisonment, and that the penalty shall be terrible if she is diseased.

READER. It will be said that paternity cannot be proved.

AUTHOR. I do not deny that it may be possible that the father attributed to the natural child will not be the true one ; but it will be necessary to establish by proofs that he has rendered himself liable to be reputed such : it is the probability of paternity in marriage extended to paternity out of marriage. So much the worse for men who suffer themselves to be caught ! it is shameful to attach impunity to the most disorderly and subversive of selfish desires ; women must no longer bear alone the burden of natural children, and no longer be tempted to abandon them.

READER. But what if it be proved that a married man has rendered himself liable to become a father outside his household.

AUTHOR. This should be first a case of divorce ; next, of punishment for him and his accomplice. As to the child, the man should bear the charge of it in concert with the mother.

READER. These are indeed Draconian laws!

AUTHOR. Do you not see that corruption is shutting us in, body and soul; and that if we do not create a vigorous reaction against it by the severity of the laws, the reform of education, and the awakening of the ideal, our society will be, ere long, only an immense brothel?

READER. Alas! it is but too true.

AUTHOR. Let us demand then, not only a rational reform of the national education, but also that the number of lyceums shall be doubled for girls.

That all the institutions of higher instruction dependent on the state shall be open to them as to boys.

That they shall be admitted to receive the same university degrees, and the same diplomas of capacity as men.

That every field of occupation shall be opened to them as to men;

So that, elevated in public opinion by equality, their activity shall no longer be nominally compensated; that they may live by their labor, and that want, discouragement and suicide may no longer terminate their life when they do not make choice of the sad part of elements of demoralization.

14

I.

Progressive women, to you, I address my last words, Listen in the name of the general good, in the name of your sons and your daughters.

You say: the manners of our time are corrupt; the laws concerning our sex need reform.

It is true; but do you think that to verify the evil suffices to cure it?

You say: so long as woman shall be a minor in the city, the state and marriage, she will be so in social labor; she will be forced to be supported by man; that is to debase him while humbling herself.

It is true; but do you believe that to verify these things suffices to remedy our abasement?

You say: the education that both sexes receive is deplorable in view of the destiny of humanity.

It is true; but do you believe that to affirm this suffices to improve, to transform the method of education?

Will words, complaints and protestations have power to change any of these things?

It is not to lament over them that is needed; it is to act.

It is not merely to demand justice and reform that is

needed; it is to labor ourselves for reform; it is to prove *by our works* that we are worthy to obtain justice; it is to take possession resolutely of the contested place; it is, in a word, to have intellect, courage and activity.

Upon whom then will you have a right to count, if you abandon yourselves?

Upon men? Your carelessness and silence have in part discouraged those who maintained your right; it is much if they defend you against those who, to oppress you, call to their aid every species of ignorance, every species of despotism, every selfish passion, all the paradoxes which they despise when their own sex is in question.

You are insulted, you are outraged, you are denied or you are blamed in order that you may be reduced to subjection, and it is much if your indignation is roused thereby!

When will you be ashamed of the part to which you are condemned?

When will you respond to the appeal that generous and intelligent men have made to you?

When will you cease to be masculine photographs, and resolve to complete the revolution of humanity by finally making the word of woman heard in Religion, in Justice, in Politics and in Science?

What are we to do, you say?

What are you to do, ladies? Well! what is done by women believing. Look at those who have given their soul to a dogma; they form organizations, teach, write, act on their surroundings and on the rising generation in order to secure the triumph of the faith that has the support of their conscience. Why do not you do as much as they?

Your rivals write books stamped with supernatural-ism and individualistic morality, why do you not write those that bear the stamp of rationalism, of solidary morality and of a holy faith in Progress?

Your rivals found educational institutions and train up professors in order to gain over the new generation to their dogmas and their practices, why do not you do as much for the benefit of the new ideas?

Your rivals organize industrial associations, why do not you imitate them?

Would not what is lawful to them be so to you.

Could a government which professes to revive the principles of '89, and which is the offspring of Revolutionary right, entertain the thought of fettering the direct heirs of the principles laid down by '89, while leaving those free to act who are more or less their enemies? Can any one of you admit such a possibility?

What are we to do?

You are to establish a journal to maintain your claims.

You are to appoint an encyclopedic committee to draw up a series of treatises on the principal branches of human knowledge for the enlightenment of women and the people.

You are to found a Polytechnic Institute for women.

You are to aid your sisters of the laboring classes to organize themselves in trades associations on economical principles more equitable than those of the present time.

You are to facilitate the return to virtue of the lost women who ask you for aid and counsel.

You are to labor with all your might for the reform of educational methods.

Yet, in the face of a task so complicated, you ask: what are we to do?

Ah, ye women who have attained majority, arise, if ye have heart and courage !

Arise, and let those among you who are the most intelligent, the most instructed, and who have the most time and liberty constitute an *Apostleship of women.*

Around this Apostleship, let all the women of Progress be ranged, that each one may serve the common cause according to her means.

And remember, remember above all things, that *Union is strength.*

THE END.

NEW BOOKS

And New Editions Recently Issued by

CARLETON, PUBLISHER,

NEW YORK.

418 *BROADWAY, CORNER OF LISPENARD STREET.*

Victor Hugo.

LES MISERABLES.—The only unabridged English translation of "the grandest and best Novel ever written." One large octavo vol., paper covers, $1.00,   .   or cloth $1.50

LES MISERABLES.—A superior edition of the same Novel, in five octavo vols.—"Fantine," "Cosette," "Marius," "St. Denis," and "Valjean." . .   Cloth, each vol., $1.00

THE LIFE OF VICTOR HUGO.—(Understood to be an Autobiography.) "As charming and interesting as a Novel." octavo, ...   cloth $1.50

By the Author of "Rutledge."

RUTLEDGE.—A deeply interesting novel.   12mo. cloth, $1.50

THE SUTHERLANDS.—   do.   . . do. $1.50

FRANK WARRINGTON.—   do.   . . do. $1.50

LOUIE'S LAST TERM AT ST. MARY'S.— .   . do. $1.50

A NEW NOVEL.—*In press.*

Hand-Books of Good Society.

THE HABITS OF GOOD SOCIETY; with Thoughts, Hints, and Anecdotes, concerning nice points of taste, good manners, and the art of making oneself agreeable. Reprinted from the London Edition. The best and most entertaining work of the kind ever published. . .   12mo. cloth, $1.50

THE ART OF CONVERSATION.—With directions for self-culture. A sensible and instructive work, that ought to be in the hands of every one who wishes to be either an agreeable talker or listener.   .   .   .   12mo. cloth, $1.25

Mrs. Mary J. Holmes' Works.

DARKNESS AND DAYLIGHT.—*Just published.*   12mo. cl. $1.50
'LENA RIVERS.—   . .   A Novel.   do. $1.50
TEMPEST AND SUNSHINE.—   .   do.   do. $1.50
MARIAN GREY.—   .   .   .   do.   do. $1.50
MEADOW BROOK.— .   .   .   do.   do. $1.50
ENGLISH ORPHANS.—   .   .   do.   do. $1.50
DORA DEANE.—   .   .   .   do.   do. $1.50
COUSIN MAUDE.—   .   .   .   do.   do. $1.50
HOMESTEAD ON THE HILLSIDE.—   do.   do. $1.50

Artemus Ward.

HIS BOOK.—An irresistibly funny volume of writings by the
immortal American humorist and showman; with plenty
of comic illustrations.   .   .   12mo. cloth, $1.25

Miss Muloch.

JOHN HALIFAX, Gentleman. A novel.   12mo cloth, $1.50
A LIFE FOR A LIFE.—   do.   do. $1.50

Charlotte Bronte (Currer Bell).

JANE EYRE.—A novel.   .   .   .   12mo. cloth, $1.50
SHIRLEY.—   do.   .   .   .   .   do. $1.50
VILLETTE.—   do.   .   .   .   .   do. $1.50

Edmund Kirke.

AMONG THE PINES.—A thrilling work.   12mo. cloth,
MY SOUTHERN FRIENDS.—   do.
DOWN IN TENNESSEE.—*Just published.*   do.

Cuthbert Bede.

VERDANT GREEN.—A rollicking, humorous novel of student
life in an English University; with more than 200 comic
illustrations.   .   .   .   .   12mo. cloth, $1.50

Richard B. Kimball.

WAS HE SUCCESSFUL?—   A novel.   12mo. cloth, $1.50
UNDERCURRENTS.—   do.   do. $1.50
SAINT LEGER.—   do.   do. $1.50
ROMANCE OF STUDENT LIFE.— do.   do. $1.50
IN THE TROPICS.—Edited by R. B. Kimball.   do. $1.50

Epes Sargent.

PECULIAR.—One of the most remarkable and successful novels
published in this country.   .   .   12mo. cloth, $1.50

Miss Augusta J. Evans.

BEULAH.—A novel of great power.   12mo. cloth, $1.50

A. S. Roe's Works.

A LONG LOOK AHEAD.—	A novel.	12mo. cloth,	$1.50
TO LOVE AND TO BE LOVED.—	do. . .	do.	$1.50
TIME AND TIDE.—	do. . .	do.	$1.50
'VE BEEN THINKING.—	do. . .	do.	$1.50
THE STAR AND THE CLOUD.—	do. . .	do.	$1.50
TRUE TO THE LAST.—	do. . .	do.	$1.50
HOW COULD HE HELP IT.—	do. . .	do.	$1.50
LIKE AND UNLIKE.—	do. . .	do.	$1.50
A NEW NOVEL.—*In Press.*		do.	$1.50

Walter Barrett, Clerk.

OLD MERCHANTS OF NEW YORK.—Being personal incidents, interesting sketches, bits of biography, and gossipy events in the life of nearly every leading merchant in New York City. Two series. . . 12mo. cloth, each, $1.50

T. S. Arthur's New Works.

LIGHT ON SHADOWED PATHS.—A novel.			12mo. cloth,	$1.50
OUT IN THE WORLD.—*In press.*	do.	.	do.	$1.50
NOTHING BUT GOLD.—	do.	do. .	do.	$1.50

The Orpheus C. Kerr Papers.

A COLLECTION of exquisitely satirical and humorous military criticisms. Two series. . 12mo. cloth, each, $1.25

M. Michelet's Works.

LOVE (L'AMOUR).—From the French.		12mo. cloth,	$1.25
WOMAN (LA FEMME.)—	do. . .	do.	$1.25
WOMAN MADE FREE.—French of D'Hericourt,		do.	$1.50

Novels by Ruffini.

DR. ANTONIO.—A love story of Italy. ·		12mo. cloth,	$1.50
LAVINIA; OR, THE ITALIAN ARTIST.—		do.	$1.50
VINCENZO; OR, SUNKEN ROCKS.—		8vo. cloth,	$1.50

Rev John Cumming, D.D., of London.

THE GREAT TRIBULATION.—Two series.		12mo. cloth,	$1.25
THE GREAT PREPARATION.—	do. .	do.	$1.25
THE GREAT CONSUMMATION.—	do. .	do.	$1.25
TEACH US TO PRAY.—		do.	$1.25

Ernest Renan.

THE LIFE OF JESUS.—Translated by C. E. Wilbour from the celebrated French work. . . 12mo. cloth, $1.50 ·
RELIGIOUS HISTORY AND CRITICISM.— 8vo. cloth, $2.50

Charles Reade.

THE CLOISTER AND THE HEARTH.—A magnificent new novel, by the author of ".Hard Cash," etc.   .   8vo. cloth, $1.50

The Opera.

TALES FROM THE OPERAS.—A collection of clever stories, based upon the plots of all the famous operas.   12mo. cl., $1.25

J. C. Jeaffreson.

A BOOK ABOUT DOCTORS.—An exceedingly humorous and entertaining volume of sketches, stories, and facts, about famous physicians and surgeons.   12mo. cloth, $1.50

Fred. S. Cozzens.

THE SPARROWGRASS PAPERS.—A capital humorous work, with illustrations by Darley.   .   .   12mo. cloth, $1.25

F. D. Guerrazzi.

BEATRICE CENCI.—A great historical novel.   Translated from the Italian; with a portrait of the Cenci, from Guido's famous picture in Rome.   .   .   12mo. cloth, $1.50

Private Miles O'Reilly.

HIS BOOK.—Rich with his songs, services, and speeches, and comically illustrated.   .   .   .   12mo. cloth, $1.25

The New York Central Park.

A SUPERB GIFT BOOK.—The Central Park pleasantly described, and magnificently embellished with more than 50 exquisite photographs of the principal views and objects of interest. A large quarto volume, sumptuously bound in Turkey morocco,. $25.00

Joseph Rodman Drake.

THE CULPRIT FAY.—The most charming faery poem in the English language. ' Beautifully printed. 12mo. cloth, 75 cts.

Mother Goose for Grown Folks.

HUMOROUS RHYMES for grown people; based upon the famous "Mother Goose Melodies."   .   .   12mo. cloth, $1.00

Stephen Massett.

DRIFTING ABOUT.—A comic illustrated book of the life and travels of "Jeems Pipes."   .   .   12mo. cloth, $1.25

A New Sporting Work.

THE GAME FISH OF THE NORTH.—One of the best books on fish and fishing ever published.   Entertaining as well as instructive, and full of illustrations.   .   12mo. cloth, $1 ;0

Balzac's Novels.

CÆSAR BIROTTEAU.—From the French.   12mo. cloth, $1.25
THE ALCHEMIST.—   do.   do. $1.25
EUGENIE GRANDET.—   do.   do. $1.25
PETTY ANNOYANCES OF MARRIED LIFE.—   do. $1.25

Thomas Bailey Aldrich.

BABIE BELL, AND OTHER POEMS.—Blue and gold binding, $1.00
OUT OF HIS HEAD.—A new romance.   12mo. cloth, $1.00

Richard H. Stoddard.

THE KING'S BELL.—A new poem.   .   12mo. cloth, 75 cts.
THE MORGESONS.—A novel.   By Mrs. R. H. Stoddard. $1.00

Edmund C. Stedman.

ALICE OF MONMOUTH.—A new poem.   12mo. cloth, $1.00
LYRICS AND IDYLS.—   .   .   .   .   . do.   75 cts

M. T. Walworth.

LULU.—A new novel.   .   .   .   12mo. cloth, $1.50
HOTSPUR.— do.   *in press.*   .   .   do.

Author of "Olie."

NEPENTHE.—A new novel.   .   .   12mo. cloth, $1.50
TOGETHER.—   do.   *in press.*   .   do.

Quest.

A NEW ROMANCE.—*In press.*   .   .   12mo. cloth,

Victoire.

A NEW NOVEL.—*In Press.*   .   .   12mo. cloth, $1.50

Red-Tape

AND PIGEON-HOLE GENERALS, as seen by a citizen-soldier in the
Army of the Potomac.   .   .   12mo. cloth, $1.25

Author "Green Mountain Boys."

CENTEOLA.—A new work, *in press.*   12mo. cloth, $1.50

C. French Richards.

JOHN GUILDERSTRING'S SIN.—A novel.   12mo. cloth,

J. R. Beckwith.

THE WINTHROPS.—A novel, *in press.*   12mo. cloth, $1.50

Jas. H. Hackett.

NOTES AND COMMENTS ON SHAKSPEARE.—   12mo. cloth, $1.50

Miscellaneous Works.

ALEXANDER VON HUMBOLDT.—Life and travels. 12mo. cl. $1.50
LIFE OF HUGH MILLER, the Geologist. . . do. $1.50
ADAM GUROWSKI.—Diary for 1863. . . do. $1.25
DOESTICKS.—The Elephant Club, illustrated. . do. $1.50
HUSBAND AND WIFE, or human development. do. $1.25
ROCKFORD.—A novel by Mrs. L. D. Umsted. do. $1.00
THE PRISONER OF STATE.—By D. A. Mahony. do. $1.25
THE PARTISAN LEADER.—By Beverly Tucker. . do. $1.25
SPREES AND SPLASHES.—By Henry Morford. . do. $1.00
AROUND THE PYRAMIDS.—By Gen. Aaron Ward. do. $1.50
CHINA AND THE CHINESE.—By W. L. G. Smith. do. $1.00
WANDERINGS OF A BEAUTY.—Mrs. Edwin James. do. $1.00
THE U. S. TAX LAW.—"Government Edition." do. 75 cts.
TREATISE ON DEAFNESS.—By Dr. E. B. Lighthill. do. $1.00
LYRICS OF A DAY—or newspaper poetry. . do. $1.00
GARRET VAN HORN.—A novel by J. S. Sauzade. do. $1.25
THE NATIONAL SCHOOL FOR THE SOLDIER.— do. 50 cts.
FORT LAFAYETTE.—A novel by Benjamin Wood. do. $1.00
THE YACHTMANS PRIMER.—By T. R. Warren. do. 50 cts.
GEN. NATHANIEL LYON.—Life and Writings. . do. $1.00
PHILIP THAXTER.—A novel. . . . do. $1.00
LITERARY ESSAYS.—By George Brimley. . . do. $1.50
HAYING TIME TO HOPPING.—A novel. . . do. $1.25
THE VAGABOND.—Essays by Adam Badeau. . do. $1.00
EDGAR POE AND HIS CRITICS.—By Mrs. Whitman. do. 75 cts.
TACTICS; or, Cupid in Shoulder-Straps. . do. $1 00
JOHN DOE AND RICHARD ROE.—A novel. . do. $1.25
LOLA MONTEZ—Her life and lectures. . . do. $1.50
DEBT AND GRACE.—By Rev. C. F. Hudson. . do. $1.50
HUSBAND vs. WIFE.—A comic illustrated poem. do. 50 cts.
TRANSITION.—Edited by Rev. H. S. Carpenter. do. $1.00
ROUMANIA.—By Dr. Jas. O. Noyes, illustrated. do. $1.50
VERNON GROVE.—A novel. . . . . do. $1.25
ANSWER TO HUGH MILLER.—By T. A. Davies. do. $1.25
COSMOGONY.—By Thomas A. Davies. . 8vo. cl., $1.50
NATIONAL HYMNS.—By Richard Grant White. do. $1.50
TWENTY YEARS Around the World. J. Guy Vassar. do. $3.50
SPIRIT OF HEBREW POETRY.—By Isaac Taylor. do. $2.50